Mexican Women in American Factories

Mexican Women in American Factories

Free Trade and Exploitation on the Border

BY CAROLYN TUTTLE

University of Texas Press ❤ *Austin*

Requests for permission to reproduce material from this work should be sent to:
 Permissions
 University of Texas Press
 P.O. Box 7819
 Austin, TX 78713-7819
 utpress.utexas.edu/index.php/rp-form

Library of Congress Cataloging-in-Publication Data
Tuttle, Carolyn.
 Mexican women in American factories : free trade and exploitation on the
border / by Carolyn Tuttle. — 1st ed.
  p.   cm.
 Includes bibliographical references and index.
 ISBN 978-0-292-75684-7

 1. Offshore assembly industry—Mexico. 2. Women offshore assembly industry workers—Mexico. 3. Corporations, Foreign—Mexico. 4. Manufacturing
industries—United States—Employees. 5. International business enterprises—
United States—Employees. 6. Mexican-American Border Region—Economic
conditions. 7. Mexican-American Border Region—Social conditions. I. Title.
 HD9734.M42T88 2012
 331.40972'1—dc23

                                                            2011049722

This book is dedicated to two courageous women, Juana and Polita.

Contents

Figures, Tables, and Boxes

Figures

Tables

Boxes

Abbreviations

AC	Asociaciones Civiles (Civil Associations)
ACLU	American Civil Liberties Union
AFSC	American Friends Service Committee
AFO	Alianza Fronteriza de Obreros (Border Workers' Alliance)
ANAD	Asociación Nacional de Abogados Democráticos (National Association of Democratic Lawyers)
BIP	Border Industrialization Program
CAFTA–DR	Central American Free Trade Agreement–Dominican Republic
CANAMEX	Canadian-American-Mexican Corridor
CEO	Chief Executive Officer
CETRAC	Centro de Trabajadores y Comunidades (Center for Workers and Communities)
CFO	Comité Fronterizo de Obreras (Workers' Border Committee)
CGT	Confederación General de Trabajadores (General Confederation of Labor)
CJM	Coalición por Justicia en las Maquiladoras (Coalition for Justice in the Factories)
COLEF	El Colegio de la Frontera Norte (College of the Northern Border)
COR	Confederación de Obreros Revolucionarios (Revolutionary Workers' Confederation)
CPI	Consumer Price Index
CREA	Center for Reflection, Education, and Action

CROC	Confederación Revolucionaria de Obreros y Campesinos (Revolutionary Confederation of Workers and Peasants)
CROM	Confederación Regional de Obreros Mexicanos (Regional Confederation of Mexican Workers)
CRT	Confederación Revolucionaria de Trabajadores (Workers' Revolutionary Confederation)
CT	Congreso del Trabajo (Workers' Congress)
CTC	Confederación de Trabajadores y Campesinos (Confederation of Workers and Peasants)
CTM	Confederacion de Trabajadores Mexicanos (Confederation of Mexican Workers)
DODS	Derechos Obreros y Democracia Sindical (Union of Workers' Rights and Democracy)
FAT	Frente Auténtico del Trabajo (Authentic Front of Workers)
FDI	Foreign Direct Investment
FNSI	Federación Nacional de Sindicatos Independientes (National Federation of Independent Unions)
FSTSE	Federación de Sindicatos de Trabajadores al Servicio del Estado (Federation of State Workers' Unions)
FTAA	Free Trade Agreement of the Americas
FTZ	Free Trade Zone
GATT	General Agreement on Tariffs and Trade
GSP	Generalized System of Preference
ILRF	International Labor Rights Fund
JLCA	Juntas Locales de Conciliación y Arbitraje (Local Committees of Conciliation and Arbitration)
HEPAC	Hogar de Esperanza y Paz (Place of Hope and Peace)
INFONAVIT	Instituto del Fondo Nacional de la Vivienda para los Trabajadores (National Institute of Workers' Housing)
IMSS	Instituto Mexicano del Seguro Social (Mexican Social Security Institute)
INEGI	Instituto Nacional de Estadística Geografía e Información (National Institute of Geographic Statistics and Information)
LFT	Ley Federal del Trabajo (Federal Labor Law)
LISR	Ley Federal del Impuesto sobre la Renta (Mexican Federal Income Tax Rules)
MIP	Mexican Industrialization Program

MNC	Multinational Corporation
MPI	Movimiento Proletario Internacional (International Labor Movement)
NAAEC	North American Agreement on Environmental Cooperation
NAALC	North American Agreement on Labor Cooperation
NAFTA	North American Free Trade Agreement
NAO	National Administrative Office
NGO	Nongovermental organization
PRI	Partido Revolucionario Institucional (Revolutionary Institutional Party)
PRONAF	Programa Nacional Fronterizo (National Border Program)
SEDVASR	Strategic Economic Development Vision for the Arizona Sonora Region
STPS	Secretaría del Trabajo y Previsión Social (Secretariat of Labor and and Social Welfare)
UERMW	United Electrical, Radio, and Machine Workers
UNIDO	United Nations Industrial Development Organization
USAS	United Students Against Sweatshops
U.S. GAO	U.S. General Accounting Office

Acknowledgments

I would like to express my heartfelt thanks to Juana and Polita for their never-ending support during the fieldwork on which this book is based. I am forever indebted to them for their guidance, insight, and patience (with my Spanish!) during the four months I lived on the border. I am grateful for the assistance of the five women who conducted interviews on my behalf: Elpidia, Ivonne, Juana, Mary Cruz, and Polita. Their agility and strength navigating the streets, climbing tire steps, and obtaining entrance to workers' homes made it possible to interview over six hundred women in the neighborhoods of Nogales. I am thankful to Yolanda and her children for sharing their home with me during my research. Living and learning with these Mexican women was a life-altering experience.

I would like to thank BorderLinks for allowing me to participate in their semester program during my sabbatical. Jerry Gill, Jeannette Pazos, and Chris Kjonaas connected me with individuals and resources that were crucial to my research. Their knowledge of Nogales and the maquilas was extremely useful. Susanna McKibben's knowledge of Spanish was vital. Her translations of the women's words preserved their honesty and integrity. I am eternally grateful for the energy and sense of humor that Arlene provided every day as we ventured out to interview the women. I also appreciate the emotional support the semester students—Brett, Bridget, Kate, and Tiffany—provided throughout my home stay.

I am deeply indebted to two research assistants at Lake Forest College, Mackenzie Knowling and Nelka Fernando, whose dedication and resourcefulness I relied on for data entry, data analysis, and Spanish translations. They went above and beyond the duties of a research assistant and accompanied me to Nogales in search of missing information.

Neal Connors, Halie Jespersen, David Kuriniec, Brian Lee, and Carolyn Lowry also provided assistance on various aspects of this research.

I am extremely thankful for the editing skills of Wendy Ohman, whose attention to detail and tenacity transformed my draft into a publishable manuscript. My dear friends Francia Street and Debbie Spack proofread drafts of chapters. I would like to acknowledge the helpful comments of the anonymous reviewers who read drafts of the manuscript.

My family has helped me in so many ways that I cannot list them. My son Daniel supported me throughout the process by encouraging me to live in Mexico and consistently inquiring about progress on the book. I would like to thank two special boys in my life, Jayme and Josh, for their patience and understanding when I could not join in their fun because I had to work on my book. I am especially grateful to Dorothy Margo for her love and compassion as I completed this book. Her patience during the writing and editing process prevented me from leaving the manuscript on the shelf to collect dust.

Mexican Women in American Factories

Introduction

Prior to the new millennium economists and policy makers argued that free trade between the United States and Mexico would benefit both Americans and Mexicans. These individuals believed that NAFTA would be a "win-win" proposition that offered U.S. companies new markets for their products and Mexicans the hope of living in a more developed country with the modern conveniences of wealthier nations. Workers on both sides of the border were promised an increased number of jobs paying high wages as well as an increased variety of goods at a lower price. In addition, the new factories (*maquiladoras/maquilas*) were expected to bring advanced technology and modernization to Mexico's economy. This book examines the reality of free trade and the impact of NAFTA on workers in a Mexican border town. It has been over ten years since this experiment of free trade between developed countries and a developing one was initiated. All the phases and grandfathered clauses of the numerous trade restrictions on a vast variety of goods and services have expired. Global and domestic markets have absorbed the changes and reflect their consequences. At this juncture it is important to compare the realized outcomes with the expectations raised by the trilateral agreement. Evidence collected from the people most affected by NAFTA, those living along Mexico's northern border, both support and refute the predictions of this free trade policy.

Much of the existing literature on maquiladoras was written in the 1990s when NAFTA was new, and the analyses focused on raising challenging questions or offering thought-provoking predictions. Was the expansion of the maquila industry the path to Mexico's economic development? Would the jobs created by the industry lift Mexico's poor population out of poverty? Proponents predicted that Mexico would prosper and become a first world country. They also claimed that the United States would benefit from the low-cost labor in Mexico by helping U.S. industries become globally competitive once again. Proponents argued that the early labor-intensive maquilas would be replaced with capital-intensive maquilas requiring more skilled labor earning higher wages. It was envisioned that maquila workers would see their incomes grow and their standard of living improve. Opponents feared the worse, predicting that the "maquilization" of the entire Mexican economy would occur. They believed that Mexico would not prosper because its comparative advantage, cheap labor, would be exploited by multinationals in the unavoidable "race to the bottom." They feared the maquila industry would spread from the northern border to the southern states and bring with it labor and environmental problems.

The overarching goal of my research is to explore the impact of free trade, as it is embodied in NAFTA, on the border towns in Mexico. Specifically, the primary objective is to examine the socioeconomic consequences of the maquiladora industry. To do this it was necessary to obtain authentic reliable answers to four main questions: (1) What role does the maquiladora industry have in the Mexican economy? (2) Who works in the maquilas and why? (3) What are the conditions inside these maquilas and how are the women treated? (4) Are the maquilas improving the lives of the Mexicans who live in the cities where they are built?

Chapter 1, "American Factories in Mexico," describes the theoretical benefits and costs of free trade and then turns to North America to explore the consequences of American factories outsourcing to Mexico. The winners and losers are delineated. The chapter concludes with an explanation of why Nogales, in Sonora, Mexico, was chosen as the location for this study.

Chapter 2, "The Border City of Nogales," describes how Nogales has changed over the past decade due to NAFTA. Photographs and personal interviews reveal both the visual changes and those that are hidden to the naked eye. The socioeconomic implications of the successful maquila industry for this border town are investigated, and consequences of living on the Mexican minimum wage are quantified and illustrated.

Chapter 3, "House to House: The Method of Analysis," explains the method used to create the data set that is crucial to the conclusions in chapters 5, 6, and 7. Over a period of four months in 2004, while I was living in Nogales, Sonora, I collected responses to a survey of over six hundred working women. Details of how and where the surveys were conducted are explained. These data capture the women's work and home life and include information on wages, benefits, hours, previous employment, and reproductive rights. Additional interviews were conducted over the next five years to monitor the changes taking place in the maquiladora industry by talking with female workers, union organizers, directors of nongovernmental organizations (NGOs), and longtime residents of Nogales.

Chapter 4, "The History of the Maquila Industry," discusses the maquila industry from its inception with the Border Industrialization Program to its twenty-first-century manifestation. The benefits and costs of the various options established by Mexican law to attract foreign direct investment are explored. The many advantages to companies, and particularly American multinationals, that operate maquiladoras in Mexico are examined. The possibilities of unionization in maquilas are described in order to understand workers' responses to foreign management.

The heart of the findings from this research is presented in chapters 5, 6, and 7. In Chapter 5, "Are the Maquilas Sweatshops?" careful examination and interpretation of NAFTA yields the set of international laws that were put in place to protect workers in foreign factories. In addition, the Mexican labor laws that apply to all workers employed within Mexico's borders are presented. An assessment of labor law violations by the maquilas is reviewed using the data on the work requirements and benefits of the women surveyed. In addition, the Government Administrative Office's definition of a sweatshop is applied to shed light on the type of factories multinationals operate along the border.

Chapter 6, "Liberation or Exploitation of Women Workers?" examines the treatment of the Mexican women by their employers. Existing feminist literature on the role of women in industrialization continues to debate the nature of the impact of factory jobs on women: Are they liberated from their traditional domestic role at home, or are they exploited on yet another level in the workplace? The integration thesis argues that industrialization leads to female liberation and gender equality by placing women in the formal labor market (Boserup 1970; Stoddard 1987; Wilson 1992; Wright 2006). The exploitation thesis claims the opposite, that assembly plants exploit women by deepening preexisting patriarchal relations (Cravey 1998; Fernandez-Kelly 1993a; Tiano 1994). Both quantitative and qualitative information from the surveys is analyzed to provide a personal and work profile of maquila workers. Summary statistics from the sample reveal the age, education, family size, and economic responsibilities of the women working in the American factories.

This information sheds light on the reasons women work and their motivations to continue.

The book concludes by reflecting on the reality of NAFTA as it is experienced by the Mexican workers employed by American companies. Chapter 7, "Fancy Factories and Dilapidated Dwellings," provides a summary of the visible and invisible consequences of NAFTA at the Mexico-U.S. border. The dilapidated dwellings and fancy factories stand as testimony to the fact that the results of NAFTA are very different from the early predictions. Photos, factory tours, and workers' descriptions reveal one manifestation of progress: attractive modern factories. Across the street is another manifestation of globalization: unsightly rustic shacks. Personal observation, interviews, and a household survey describe *colonias* where workers live with few social services. The chapter then explores the invisible consequences of NAFTA. The voices of the women provide evidence regarding the business practices of many American companies operating maquilas in Mexico. In particular, the chapter explores the extent of discrimination occurring in the maquilas. The survey responses of the women to questions pertaining to their reproductive rights shed light on practices initially reported by Human Rights Watch in 1996.

The chapter and the book conclude by raising concerns about responsibility and corporate accountability: Who should be held accountable for what happens inside the new factories? Are the various players in this global game ready to share the benefits of free trade and reduce the costs? It is hoped that the findings of this research will assist policy makers in both the United States and Mexico as they assess NAFTA's overall effectiveness and that it will be useful to Central American governments in pointing out why relying on the maquiladora industry for development could be a type of Faustian bargain.

CHAPTER 1

American Factories in Mexico

Consumers often do not consider where a product has been manufactured or who has assembled it. They recognize Sony and Toyota as Japanese companies; Samsung and Daewoo Electronics as Korean companies; Adidas and Volkswagen as German companies; Coppel and Elektra as Mexican companies; and Motorola, Coca-Cola, and Nike as American companies. Behind these familiar corporate names, however, are labels indicating the product was manufactured in a third world country. In fact, the majority of personal and household items American consumers buy today have not been "made in America." For example, Nike sneakers are made in Vietnam, Indonesia, and China; Wal-Mart clothes, in Bangladesh; Hershey chocolates, in Mexico; Apple iPods, in China; Disney pajamas, in Haiti; and Reebok NFL Jerseys, in El Salvador. Globalization has provided easy access to goods produced worldwide. Free trade makes it possible to produce and exchange these goods at lower prices. The economic implications of free trade have far-reaching gains for consumers. They are able to buy a wider variety of products at significantly reduced prices, thereby allowing them to enjoy a higher standard of living. It is an undeniable fact that consumers have benefited greatly from free trade.

These benefits have been touted for centuries. Classical economists first wrote about the economic advantages of increasing the efficiency and production of businesses and consequently the incomes and welfare of entire populations of countries. John Stuart Mill (1848) delineated the economic gains from trade in two categories, static and dynamic. The static gains from trade occur as expanding markets outside a country's borders make it possible to develop its comparative advantage and for businesses to exploit economies of scale. The dynamic gains are derived because trade promotes competition, which stimulates innovation and productivity growth. David Ricardo (1817) further developed the myriad benefits of comparative advantage. Rather than be independent and self-sustaining, countries could specialize in what they were relatively more efficient in producing and trade with other countries for everything else. This specialization would yield tremendous increases in the productivity, production, and the quality of the goods and services produced within each country. Historians have studied how free trade promoted economic growth and pushed European countries from societies dependent on the land to ones limited only by the inventiveness of their people (Allen 2009; Ashton 1964; Landes 1969). Economic historians have demonstrated how lessons from the past inform the present by examining the first countries to industrialize (Crafts 1977; Mokyr 2004, 2010; O'Rourke and Williamson 2000). They have identified specific "prerequisites" for industrialization and economic progress. Development economists have applied these theories to address challenges within developing countries (Bhagwati 2004; Sachs 2006, 2008; Stiglitz 2006, 2007). The goal has been to industrialize and lift the poverty-stricken populations out of the vicious cycle in which they seem to be trapped. Policy makers armed with this knowledge have devised national and international policies hoping to speed up the industrialization process.

The conventional economic model of development remained the foundation for many economic growth strategies throughout the eighteenth, nineteenth, and twentieth centuries. Although there are many opponents and skeptics, free trade remains one of the foundations of economic policy around the globe in the twenty-first century. Despite scholarly attempts to disprove the contemporary applicability of free trade, a review of recent trade policies between industrialized and developing countries provides the evidence that it is still pervasive. Beginning in 1947 with the General Agreement on Tariffs and Trade (GATT), the number of free trade agreements involving the United States has grown rapidly. According to the Office of U.S. Trade Representative (n.d.), the United States has free trade agreements with seventeen countries. Many of these are unilateral agreements with countries eager to establish ties with the richest country in the world. Others are multilateral, with countries on both ends of the negotiations less than enthusiastic about the supposed advantages of lowering their trade barriers. The lack of political support for the Free Trade Area of the Americas (FTAA) did not stop the United States from creating trade blocs with Canada and Mexico and signing the North American Free Trade Agreement (NAFTA) in 1994 and the Central American Free Trade Agreement–Dominican Republic (CAFTA–DR) in 2005. Although enthusiasm for passing both a U.S.-Panama and U.S.-Colombia free trade agreement has waned, the government's desire to expand free trade has not.

Critics have raised concerns about the effectiveness of these trade agreements as a development strategy and their consequences for the developing country's economy and population. Now that NAFTA, one of the most significant trade agreements of the twentieth century, has had time to take effect we can evaluate these criticisms and examine the actual consequences.[1] The stakes are high as the United States and its neighbor Mexico forge a new relationship. Mexico is hopeful that NAFTA and investment from the United States will lift the 47 percent of its population living below the poverty line out of misery. The United States hopes that NAFTA will create more skilled jobs and higher corporate profits for Americans and at the same time decrease immigration from Mexico. The relative success of this relationship will have serious implications for the economies and populations of El Salvador, Honduras, Nicaragua, Costa Rica, Guatemala, and the Dominican Republic as CAFTA–DR begins to be fully implemented. This makes what is happening to Mexico and the Mexican people extremely important to political officials of these respective governments and to the policy makers who advise them.

From an economic perspective, globalization has sharpened the competition for producers, pitting the advanced technology of the developed world against the cheap labor of the developing world. Companies, large and small, domestic and multinational, compete for consumer dollars by searching for cost-reducing methods of producing and delivering their products. One viable solution has been to move assembly operations from developed to developing countries, where labor is relatively cheap and the costs of trade are minimal. Free trade agreements such as GATT, NAFTA, and CAFTA–DR have reduced the costs of trade by eliminating tariffs and custom duties and import and export quotas in certain regions. Consequently, multinationals can move the manufacturing of a product outside of the United States while still maintaining control over the quality of the product and the profits generated. Mobile manufacturing, as it is often called, has permanently altered the flow of production and dramatically changed the relationship between the companies that sell the product and the workers who make it.

Multinational corporations call their international production facilities "offshore sourcing" or "outsourcing" and argue that the jobs they have created are helping the third world industrialize. Proponents of free trade claim that foreign factories increase employment both directly and indirectly. By moving operations to foreign soil, often referred to as foreign direct investment, companies create jobs directly by hiring foreign workers. These low-skilled, labor-intensive jobs ostensibly offer poor people who have been unemployed or underemployed for years a chance to pull themselves and their families out of poverty. As the manufacturing plants become established and begin to use local suppliers for raw materials, companies create new jobs indirectly by helping local businesses expand. In the long run, the owners of these local companies create jobs, ranging from unskilled to highly skilled depending on the type of intermediate goods produced. These jobs usually pay above the minimum wage and offer long-term stability and security. As a consequence, smaller and medium-sized domestic companies offer jobs that will remain within their borders and become more and more integrated into the production processes of larger multinational companies.

This new business model of the "discarded factory" has been extremely profitable for the multinational corporations but not necessarily for the destination country. Companies lease or buy land and build modern factories on foreign soil. Technology is transported into the factories, creating assembly lines with machines imported from the United States. The inputs for production are usually also imported from suppliers in the United States. Workers from the surrounding community are subsequently hired and trained to perform specific tasks using U.S. machines and materials. The workers are as productive as their American counterparts but are paid considerably less. They are paid less because they live in a poor country that is still developing. The standard of living is much lower, and the government-established minimum wage is commensurate with other wages in the economy. This cheap labor significantly reduces the costs of producing a product. If these lower costs are passed on to the consumer, lower prices result, and households are able to purchase more goods and services. It is clear that households around the world thereby experience an increase in their standard of living, especially in the company's country of origin. Another benefit many companies expect is for the demand for their products to grow because assembly workers can now afford to purchase them. This benefit of free trade has yet to materialize: workers can barely afford food and would consider suitcases, cell phones, and iPods a luxury. If these lower costs do not result in lower prices, companies earn higher profits. This has clearly been the case for Nike, Levi Strauss, and Apple: their sneakers, jeans, and iPods are still among the most expensive products sold in the United States. Consequently, this new model of manufacturing creates an even greater disparity between the earnings of corporate executives and workers. Furthermore, if the wealthy corporate executives live in developed countries while the low-wage workers live in developing countries, economic growth and industrialization in the developing country will occur more slowly.

"Why are we still paying so much for sneakers if they are made by little slave kids?

-Flight of the Concord

Maquilas and Economic Development

As the Import Substitution Industrialization (ISI) policy was abandoned and replaced with the manufacturing for export strategy, the maquiladora industry took center stage in economic development. Several Latin American countries adopted policies aimed to promote successful maquila industries. NAFTA expanded and extended the trade liberalization in 2004 that had begun with the Border Industrialization Program (BIP) in 1965 in Mexico. CAFTA–DR copied the strategy and tools and applied them to Central America in 2005. Public officials and policy makers were convinced of the linkages between free trade agreements, a successful maquila industry, and economic growth. As the research of Jansen et al. (2007, 21) reveals, "The results of the CAFTA negotiations have been positive for the Central American maquila industry," and they have made it possible to keep U.S. apparel companies and retailers producing in Central America. The positive consequences measured in this exceptional empirical study are increases in employment and exports in El Salvador, Honduras, Guatemala, and Nicaragua. The findings make clear the pivotal role of the maquila industry in economic growth:

> In Central America, the textile and clothing sector (often referred to as *maquila*) is the most important industrial and nontraditional export sector. It has been responsible for most of the growth of manufactured exports and foreign exchange earnings, as well as for most of the employment generated, since the late 1980s. Because relatively modern technology can be adopted at relatively low investment cost, the sector has become a typical first rung on the industrialization ladder in many developing countries. (Jansen et al. 2007, 1)

As governments and policy makers look to CAFTA–DR to stimulate the industrialization of Central America, scholars must examine the impact NAFTA has had on Mexico. The evidence this research uncovers will shed light on whether promotion of the maquila industry is the best path for achieving economic growth. Mexico is an excellent case study since the maquila industry is the main driving force behind its push for economic development into a first world, industrialized country. This dependence implies that when the maquila industry is booming, the Mexican economy is expanding, and if the industry declines, the economy experiences a recession. An article in *Business Week* stated it simply, "Mexico's maquiladora sector accounts for nearly half the country's total exports, so if it thrives, Mexico thrives" (Smith 2004). As the leading sector, the maquila industry affects employment, income, and total output or gross domestic product (GDP). Humberto Núñez (2002, 439) stated what is commonly accepted by Mexican scholars, "It is well known that the maquila industry plays two roles in the Mexican manufacturing sector: it is both a major source of employment and an important producer of exports." Although NAFTA did not create the maquila industry, it did help it grow in size and prominence. The BIP of 1965 created a twenty-one-kilometer free trade zone (FTZ) along the Mexico-U.S. border to encourage foreign direct investment. The Mexican government hoped to attract successful foreign companies by promising cheap labor and few safety and environmental restrictions on production. Many American companies seized the opportunity to reduce costs and increase profits. Companies from Japan, Germany, and Korea also established operations in Mexico, and the maquila industry grew. In 1994, the year NAFTA was passed, there were already 2,085 maquilas employing 583,044 workers. Since 1994 the maquila industry has expanded rapidly and become the second largest sector of the Mexican economy (after tourism). Working in a maquila became common in border towns where upwards of half of the population was employed in maquilas. The growth in the industry over the past three decades has been smooth and continuous, except for two setbacks during recessions in the United States. The maquila industry peaked in 2000: 3,703 maquilas employed over 1.3 million workers in Mexico. Although there was a decline in the period 2001 through 2003, the industry experienced a revival from 2004 to 2007 and reached a new peak of 5,138 maquilas employing nearly two million people. The industry declined more recently due to the U.S. financial crisis but has begun to recover. Official statistics reveal that the maquila industry has successfully established itself as a global leader in the electronics, computer equipment, automotive goods, and apparel industries. Industry specialists are hoping to expand this list in the future as newer maquilas are able to produce highly competitive products in the aviation, aeronautical, and pharmaceutical industries. The maquilization of Mexico is proceeding rapidly with the continued support of the government.

The Mexican government wants the maquila industry to remain a permanent feature of Mexico's economy. Current President Felipe Calderón and his predecessor, Vicente Fox, have promoted the growth and prosperity of the maquila industry. In a speech at a national maquiladora convention in the city of Guadalajara, Fox agreed to sign a decree that would create new incentives for the maquiladora industry. He explained his decision by arguing that "because of how much it [the sector] means to Mexico, we're going to double efforts to support our maquiladora industry. We will be at your sides through both the good and the bad" (qtd. in Guthrie 2003, 1). In his state of the union speech on December 1, 2007, President Calderón lauded the creation of 800,000 jobs and the attraction of $18 billion in foreign investment as signs of a strong economy. He concluded proudly, "Despite the stagnation that threatens the economy of the United States, upon which we are dependent and which limits us, our growth of a little more than 3 percent this year, from December 1 of last year to now, [shows] the confidence in Mexico that permitted the creation of formal employment" (Frontera Norte-Sur [FNS] News 2007). Recently, Calderón used the opening of new maquiladoras as an opportunity to promote Mexico's favorable position in competition for manufacturing plants. He believes that international economic developments favor Mexico: "Our strategic geographic position allows us to bring inputs from the east, give them added value, manufacture them in Mexico and export them to the west coast or east coast or center of the United States or to Europe. Mexico can be and is called on being the economic link between the European Union, the American and Asian markets, not to mention the emerging markets of Latin America" (FNS News 2008). Surprisingly, China is outsourcing to Mexico, and the company Foxconn Mexico Precision Industry currently employs close to ten thousand people in five plants. Mexican newspapers picked up this unexpected outcome of a trade discussion:

> An Dali, a representative of the Mexican Office of the Chinese Council for the Promotion of International Trade, said China was interested in border export assembly plants, or maquiladoras, as a way of get-

[handwritten margin note: Pres. Calderón notó la dependencia de la econ. Mx en la econ. EEUU.]

ting around U.S. trade restrictions and utilizing the North American Free Trade Agreement as an advantage in the U.S. market. Dali specifically mentioned the television, telecommunications and textile sectors as holding particular interest for Chinese investors. (Garcia et al. 2005)

These new opportunities to establish partnerships outside of North America promise a bright future for Mexico's economy and the government in office.

American Companies Outsourcing to Mexico

The exodus of manufacturing plants from the United States to Mexico has been steady and continuous in the years since NAFTA was passed. Although many politicians and economists disagreed with Ross Perot's prediction of the negative effects of NAFTA, the "giant sucking sound" of jobs heading south to Mexico has been even louder than predicted. Dozens of American companies have expanded their production by opening new manufacturing plants in Mexico and operating maquiladoras along the border as well as in many of Mexico's southern states. A few American companies—Delphi Automotive, Moen, New Brunswick, and Hershey's, to name just a few—have taken the new business model to an extreme and have closed all their factories in the United States and moved them to Mexico. Currently, Lear Corporation, General Electric, Whirlpool, Tyco International, Motorola, Honeywell, Chamberlain, and Mattel are among the "100 Top Maquilas," Mexico's largest maquiladora employers. In 2004 four American companies employed almost 150,000 workers in Mexico—Delphi Automotive Systems was the largest, with 68,000 workers employed in fifty-four plants; Lear Corporation operated eight plants and employed 34,000 workers; General Electric operated thirty-four plants and employed 30,900 workers; and the Offshore Group employed 13,270 workers in three plants. Two years later the same four American companies employed over 100,000 workers in Mexico—Delphi Automotive Systems and Lear Corporation with the same number of plants and workers; General Electric operations declined to 30 plants and employed 20,700 Mexican workers; and The Offshore Group operated the same number of plants but increased the number of workers to 16,590. By 2008, despite the economic downturn in the United States, four American companies still employed over 100,000 workers in Mexico. Lear Corporation took the place of Delphi

Automotive as the largest maquila employer in Mexico and continued to employ 34,000 employees in eight plants; General Electric still operated thirty plants but increased the number of workers to 25,000; Johnson Controls, Inc., moved up the list and employed 24,000 in thirty plants; and Jabil Circuit, Inc., operated four plants employing 21,000 workers (Maquila Portal 2008). The products of these companies are no longer "made in the USA" but *hecho en México*.

The benefits to American companies who outsource to Mexico are numerous and significant. The Mexican government and Mexican entrepreneurs not only encourage the cross border movement but offer considerable assistance by eliminating paperwork, interpreting labor and environmental laws, and even recruiting, hiring, training, and paying workers. There are several websites directed at corporate executives considering outsourcing possibilities in Mexico. One in particular, called Made in Mexico (www.madeinmexicoinc.com) lures companies with almost every word on their home page. The heading "Discover the Cost-Saving Benefits of Mexico Manufacturing with Maquiladoras" has a clear and direct message: bring your business to Mexico and your profits will increase. The shelter company, Maquiladora Management Services, which created this website, provides an attractive list of benefits of doing business in Mexico: "Why risk the pitfalls of operating in a foreign country? Inexpensive labor, possible duty-free importation into Mexico, favorable U.S. Tariffs, reduced freight costs and turnaround time and more—competitive advantages abound with Maquiladoras" (Made in Mexico n.d.). In particular, they emphasize how "Mexico's low cost labor force" is extensively trained to be efficient and highly productive in assembling high quality products. It can hardly be surprising that many profit-maximizing companies from the United States view moving operations to Mexico as both efficient and profitable.

American companies leave the United States and locate their factories and assemble their products in Mexico. They shed their manufacturing operations entirely and pay little attention to product assembly, standardization, uniformity, and quality. The primary concern of companies shifts from the production of goods to the creation of product images. Instead of worrying about the best way to make products, their efforts, expertise, and financial resources focus on establishing brand identity, or as Naomi Klein calls it, a "corporate consciousness" (2002, 7). As a result, companies develop and create marketing, advertising, and research and development departments. As Phil Knight has said, "There is no value in making things anymore. The value is added by careful research, by innovation and by marketing" (Katz, 1994, 204). Unionized factory workers in the United States are permanently replaced by nonunionized Mexican maquila workers. Some economists argue this is the deindustrialization phase of economic development, which will create new jobs in the service sector requiring higher education and paying higher wages. Although the adjustment will be tough, especially on the manufacturing sector, the U.S. will grow to levels unimaginable. Russell Roberts, professor of economics at George Mason University, compares the current economic development with America's transformation from an agrarian economy to an industrial economy fifty years ago. He claims that "industries have been started because we have been more productive in the manufacturing areas" and the resources freed up can be used to produce other goods and provide new services (qtd. in Rhodes 2004, 16). Alan Blinder, an economic professor at Princeton University who served on the White House Council of Economic Advisers from 1993 to 1994, expresses similar sentiments in his article titled "Offshoring: The Next Industrial Revolution?":

> The third Industrial Revolution will play out similarly over the next several decades. The kind of jobs that can be moved offshore will not disappear entirely from the United States or other rich countries, but their shares of the work force will shrink dramatically. And this reduction will transform societies in many ways, most of them hard to foresee, as workers in rich countries find other things to do. But just as the first two industrial revolutions, massive offshoring will not lead to massive unemployment. In fact, the world gained tremendously from the first two industrial revolutions, and it is likely to do so from the third—so long as it makes the necessary economic and social adjustments. (2006, 3)

According to this, it is a win-win situation for the American workers and the Mexican workers.

Vanishing Jobs for American Factory Workers

Several of the first companies to adopt the "discarded factory" model were successful and profitable—Nike, Adidas, Sara Lee, and Levi Strauss. Many others have followed their lead, taking millions of jobs with them—Wal-Mart, Sears, J. C. Penney, Ann Taylor, and Liz Claiborne . . . and the list goes on. As Klein points out in her section titled

"This Is Not a Job-Flight Story," the closure of manufacturing plants in the United States is permanent (2002, 201). The jobs have moved overseas—sometimes ending up in a factory owned and operated by a multinational company but more often than not in a factory operated by a shelter company which produces finished goods for a number of multinational companies:

> Unlike factories that hop from one place to another, these factories will never rematerialize. Mid-flight, they morph into something else entirely: "orders" to be placed with a contractor, who may well turn over those orders to as many as ten subcontractors, who—particularly in the garment sector—may in turn pass a portion of the subcontracts on to a network of home workers who will complete the jobs in basements and living rooms. (Klein 2002, 201)

[handwritten margin note: Contracting = Subcontracting out each part of production = "Shelta" companies]

As jobs move south of the border, local communities are hit hard by plant closures. In many cases, union workers lose more than their jobs, they lose a way of life. Typically, family members have worked in the same plant for the same company generation after generation. Most workers know each other because the majority of the people in the town worked at the factory. Each person worked hard and earned a wage that made it possible to support a family living modestly. They were trained to work on the assembly line and their jobs were secured by contracts. Due to collective bargaining, most assembly line workers received health benefits, paid sick days, paid vacations, contributions to a retirement fund, and disability. The company, the factory, and the job were all they knew and without it they were lost. It is hardly surprising, therefore, that local media coverage of plant closings is often emotionally charged. Headlines, websites, and blogs have raised public awareness of the negative consequences of outsourcing by American companies. The *New York Times* story on the closure of the Indiana Whirlpool factory was more than just a factual account:

> Having seen her father make a solid living at the Whirlpool refrigerator factory, Natalie Ford was enthusiastic about landing a job there and was happy years later when her 20-year-old son also went to work there. But that family tradition will soon end because Whirlpool plans to close the plant Friday and move the operation to Mexico, eliminating 1,100 jobs here. Many in this city in southern Indiana are seething and sad—sad about losing what was long the city's economic centerpiece and a ticket

to the middle class for one generation after another. . . . At a time when the nation's economy is struggling to gain momentum, Whirlpool's decision is an unwelcome step backward. It continues a trend in which the nation has lost nearly six million factory jobs over the past dozen years, representing one in three manufacturing jobs. (Greenhouse 2010, 1)

Similarly, chocolate lovers were angry, shocked, and disgusted about the end of another American tradition when Hershey's Chocolate decided to move production to Mexico. "Chocolate Bytes," a website for chocolate lovers (now owned by blisstree.com), ran the news story to get people's reactions:

> In February 2007, Hershey's announced it would be cutting more than ten percent of its workforce and closing some of its U.S. plants. It expects to do away with about 1,500 jobs over the next three years from its current workforce of more than 13,000 and also plans to reduce the number of manufacturing lines it operates by almost a third. The company is building a new facility in Monterrey, Mexico, that it says will be focused on both low-value added products and on emerging markets and it is setting up a joint manufacturing venture in China with Lotte Confectionery of South Korea. Hershey's Canadian operations are almost ended. Its Dartmouth, Nova Scotia plant, Hershey's last remaining facility in Canada, will close December 2007. Other plant closures include facilities in Oakdale, California; Naugatuck, Connecticut; and Reading, Pennsylvania. (Heather 2007)

Many of the responses from chocolate lovers expressed anger and disgust over the move to Mexico. George wrote, "Sorry to see Hershey's pull out, and go to Mexico. I always thought them to be an American Company. Sorry to say, but they will not make gains doing this, but may lose the company all together. Americans will not eat chocolate made in Mexico. Good bye for good Hershey. Mexico is a contaminated country" (November 15, George 2007). And Dana wrote, "I think this is so horrible. Because of Hershey's being so money hungry both my parents are losing their jobs along with thousands of other people. Do you actually think the quality will be the same?" (Dana, August 22, 2007). Nothing seems to be sacred, not even the industry whose product became symbolic of American life—automobiles. Two of the Big Three American automobile manufacturers continue to build new assembly plants in Mexico while hundreds of thousands of laid off auto workers join the ranks of the unemployed in Michigan. Ironically, as Mexico's general director of ProMexico's Automotive Sector announced additional foreign direct investment by General Motors and Ford, the CEOs of GM, Ford, and Chrysler were asking the U.S. government for a "bailout" (Oneal 2008, 1, 4).

> Investments announced by General Motors, Volkswagen and Ford to expand their vehicle production capacity will yield fruit in 2015, Emilio Mosso, General Director of ProMexico's Automotive Sector. According to Mr. Mosso, some consulting firms have been anticipating that Mexico could assemble 5 million vehicles in 2015. "This is a conservative number, taking into consideration the investments recently announced by Ford, General Motors and Volkswagen, which will add to more than US$7 billion, so we are speaking about a considerable increase, but we must wait and see which will be Volkswagen's production levels then; it is very likely they will be manufacturing between 450 and 500 thousand units," Mosso pointed out at the end of his participation in PriceWaterhouse Coopers' Forum on Automotive Strategies and Challenges. ProMexico's estimates consider the investment of US$1.6 billion by General Motors in a new plant in San Luis Potosi, which will assemble compact vehicles for the domestic market, such as the new Chevrolet Aveo, of which 80 thousand units will be manufactured in a first stage. As far as Ford is concerned, the US$3 billion investment in Cuautitlan, Chihuahua and Guanajuato plants will provide for the assembly of up to 300 thousand units more, with the incorporation of the new Ford Fiesta. (Maquila Portal n.d.)

According to the economist Blinder, this phenomenon is spreading rapidly and will have long-lasting effects. He concluded with a warning in his article on industrialization: "We have so far barely seen the tip of the offshoring iceberg, the eventual dimensions of which may be staggering" (2006, 114).

Liberating Jobs for Mexican Maquila Workers?

According to neoclassical trade theory, promoting the maquila industry to push the economy up the ladder of development is sound. The predicted outcomes are positive and far reaching. The Mexican government is successful in creating economic growth and the expansion of output and income. Mexican entrepreneurs, business owners, and workers experience growing sales and personal income. Individuals and families stuck in poverty can work their way up and live above subsistence. The reality, however, is considerably different from the positive predictions of theory. Although trade has increased between Mexico and the U.S., the incomes and standard of living of the workers have not. For Mexico, free trade has not benefited everyone, the winners are the multinational companies and the losers are the people who work for these companies. Does this imply that the model is fundamentally flawed? No, but it does mean that the theory must be reconsidered when trade occurs between countries at very different stages of economic development. The theory of comparative advantage implicitly assumes that each country has the resources to offer consumers products of value they want to buy. In some cases, countries are endowed with valuable resources and sell these inputs to countries that need them, oil being an obvious example. In both cases, trading these resources or products for currency benefits all participants and expands a country's consumption possibilities beyond its production possibilities. If this is not the case and a country has an abundant resource or products of little value to others, the owners and producers must accept the low market price. If a country is still in its infancy of development, like Mexico, it may have little to offer industrialized countries with highly efficient and technologically advanced industries. In negotiating NAFTA, however, Mexico understood its comparative advantage to both the United States and Canada—cheap labor.

NAFTA turned one of the most protected economies of the world into a trading partner with two industrialized countries—one that is the richest country in the world. The "success" of free trade for Mexico is tied to the success of the maquiladora industry. Unavoidably, the success of the maquiladora industry depends on its ability to rely on its comparative advantage—employing cheap labor. Rather than increase investment in businesses, creating jobs, raising family income, and improving the lives of Mexican workers, maquiladoras drain the resources of Mexico leaving empty factories, temporary jobs, and falling family incomes behind. The number of economists, labor rights activists, and members of independent *sindicatos* (unions) who argue this viewpoint is growing. They claim that the maquila industry has not helped the Mexican economy grow but instead has benefited U.S. companies at the expense of Mexican workers. They believe that "the maquila industry has become a quintessential export enclave" (Núñez 2002, 439):

It assembles products using processed materials from the U.S. and therefore has never consumed more than a modest number of products manufactured in Mexico. It has few economic linkages with the domestic economy and has done little to advance the development of existing industries, much less to create any new ones. (439–440)

A publication of the American Friends Service Committee titled *The Maquiladora Reader* (1999) argues that the maquiladora industry offers a vivid example of the costs of economic policies that privilege corporate profits above all other considerations instead of bringing them into balance with the needs of workers, communities, and the environment (Kamel and Hoffman 1999, 4).

This research focuses on whether the needs of the workers and their communities are satisfied by this development strategy to promote the maquila industry. The maquiladoras create nonunionized jobs. These jobs are filled primarily by women, whose story this book tells. My focus is on the women working in the maquilas because of the historiography of the labor force participation of women during industrialization. Historically, women (and children) have been employed in large proportions of factories in leading industries during a country's industrialization process. Great Britain employed a considerable number of women in northern textile mills (Berg and Hudson 1992; Horrell and Humphries 1992, 1995; Pinchbeck and Hewitt 1973; Tuttle 1999), and America used women extensively in New England textile mills (Goldin and Sokoloff 1982; Hindman 2002). Thus it should come as no surprise that women make up a high proportion of maquila workers in Mexico: "those [women] from ages sixteen to twenty-five provide 80 to 90 percent of all maquila unskilled workers" (Stoddard 1987, 60). As Susan Tiano (1991) discovered, by the late 1960s U.S. electronic firms had moved 90 percent of their labor-intensive assembly operations to the third world. Women, ages sixteen to twenty-four, constituted 80 to 90 percent of the export processing labor force in Southeast Asia, Mexico, and other export platform nations by 1979 (Tiano 1991, 19). Kopinak, who also studied the workforces of the maquiladoras along the northern border, found that during Stage 1 the operations were labor-intensive and the maquilas similar to the factories in Great Britain. The production process was "rudimentary," using assembly line techniques, division of labor, and repetition of tasks with machinery that required operators or general workers. The labor force was composed primarily of single young females (1996, 8).[2] More recently, Jansen et al. (2007)

[handwritten margin note: why are women the main labor force in industrializ?]

found that in the clothing industry in every Central American country except Costa Rica, an estimated 80 percent of the workers are women (4). In the competitive global economy, women are hired to work in factories because they are seen as cheap, hardworking, and less rebellious.

The female Mexican maquila workers find themselves working long hours with only a few minutes to use the bathroom. They work six days per week and often have only four paid vacation days per year. They are lucky if they have contracts and receive medical benefits for themselves and their families. Many of the women stand all day and are exposed to minerals, chemicals, and fumes that permanently damage their health. In exchange for this hard labor in miserable working conditions, the workers receive minimum wage. The minimum wage, moreover, is so low that the worker's family lives in poverty. The dirt roads are littered with trash, electrical wires hang in the balance, and the smell of untreated sewage permeates the air. The makeshift wooden and cinderblock structures that maquila workers call "home" often do not have running water or any local services (natural gas, sewage treatment, or trash pickup). To make matters worse, the rapidly growing population of border towns has overburdened their fragile infrastructure and public services. Lozano concluded, "Since Mexican workers earn such miserable wages and American companies pay such minimum taxes its schools are a shambles, its hospital crumbling, its trash collection slapdash, and its sewage lines collapsed. Half of Acuña's 150,000 residents now use backyard latrines" (Dillon 2001, 2).

This hardship is particularly visible along the border where many of the maquiladoras are located. "While supporters of the maquiladoras argue that the industry transformed border towns from entertainment centers catering to visitors from the United States into booming industrial cities, critics counter that detailed analyses prove that the export sector drains and destabilized the rest of Mexico's economy" (Kamel and Hoffman 1999, 2). Whether it is Tijuana, Nogales, Ciudad Juárez, or Acuña, the impact of the maquiladoras on the workers' living conditions is the same: devastating. Javier Villarreal Lozano, a Mexican historian who directs a government-financed cultural institute in Coahuila (the state that includes Acuña) feels Acuña is a disgrace: "A hundred years ago, U.S. employers would have been ashamed of these conditions. Henry Ford's workers living in cardboard boxes? He'd never have tolerated it" (Dillon 2001, 2). Polita, who was born and raised in Nogales, remarked as we drove through the streets, "Qué feo" (How ugly). Rather than feel a sense of civic pride for her birthplace and home, she was embarrassed about the dirt, trash, and crumbling houses.

Nogales as a Case Study

Nogales is an excellent border city to study the maquila industry because it is the seventh largest maquiladora center in Mexico and its maquila industry continues to grow. In 2004 it had 77 maquiladoras, and by 2009 the number reached 94 (see tables 1.1 and 1.2). Although Tijuana and Ciudad Juárez have the largest numbers of maquilas, they were not chosen for this study because research has already been carried out there.[3] On the other hand, Altha Cravey (1998) and Kathryn Kopinak (1996) have already studied the maquila workers in Nogales, but their data are outdated and do not reflect the impact of NAFTA. Catalina Denman (2008) has completed a more recent study on maquiladora women living along the border in Nogales, but she focuses primarily on women's health, in particular, their reproductive health. Since her research explores the impact of women's working and living conditions on their health during pregnancy, there is little repetition in our work. Although Nogales does not have the largest number of maquilas among the border cities, it has more employees per plant than most others (Kopinak

Table 1.1. Major Maquiladora Cities in Mexico

City	Number of Maquila-doras in 2004	City	Number of Maquila-doras in 2004
Border Cities		*Nonborder Cities*	
Tijuana	575	Monterrey	189
Ciudad Juárez	288	Guadalajara	101
Reynosa/Río Bravo	139	Mérida	87
Mexicali	130	Chihuahua	76
Matamoros	127	Puebla/Tehuacán	78
Tecate	111	Ensenada	75
Nogales	**77**	Torreón	43
Ciudad Acuña	47	Gómez Palacio/Lerdo	38
Nuevo Laredo	41	Aguascalientes	34
Piedras Negras	31	Hermosillo	29
San Luis Río Colorado	30		
Agua Prieta	20		

Source: Christman 2004, 15; IHS Global Insight, Inc.

Table 1.2. Growth of the Maquiladora Sector in Major Border Cities

	Number of Maquiladoras	
Border Cities	2004	2009
Tijuana	575	606
Ciudad Juárez	288	338
Reynosa/Río Bravo	139	142
Mexicali	130	163
Matamoros	127	130
Tecate	111	Na
Nogales	**77**	**94**

Source: Instituto Nacional de Estadística y Geografía [INEGI] 2009, "Estadística de la industria maquiladora de exportación."

1996, 8). According to *MexicoNow*, the number of plants has increased between 2004 (167) and 2011 (254), and the level of employment has increased from 76,400 to 96,518 in the state of Sonora (2006a, 92). Thus, unlike Agua Prieta, which has turned into a border city where the trafficking of drugs and people has replaced working in the maquilas, Nogales remains a border city where the majority (70 percent) of its population derive their livelihood from the maquiladoras.

The maquila industry was at its peak in Agua Prieta in 2000, with 36 maquiladoras and 7,200 workers, whereas by 2004 it had dropped to 20 maquiladoras and 6,570 workers (Bloom 2001, 1; INEGI 2004). Even if there were more factories in Agua Prieta, interviewing maquila workers may have been more difficult. In Agua Prieta workers for the Comité Fronterizo de Obreras (CFO) have found that "maquiladora workers are afraid to organize and act. . . . [W]orkers don't yet believe that they can organize themselves to get better wages and working conditions. Other workers fear being fired while fighting for something they may not win" (Bloom 2001, 1). This atmosphere of fear and distrust would make obtaining truthful responses on sensitive survey questions more difficult.

Ciudad Juárez would be a good choice for a case study because of the large number of maquilas that are located there. The women who work in the maquilas, however, may be reluctant to be interviewed because of the many murders that have taken place over the past fifteen years.[4] Despite efforts by federal and state commissions and public condemnation by former President Fox and his wife, most of the cases remain unsolved. Nogales was the preferred location for my research because in Ciudad Juárez the data may be difficult to obtain and once obtained may not be entirely truthful. In Ciudad Juárez, women working in the maquilas are likely to feel they are putting themselves at risk if they speak publicly about the working conditions in the maquilas.

Considering the research objectives, Nogales was the first choice largely due to the Semester on the Border Program of the BorderLinks organization.[5] This program is vastly different from other study abroad programs because participants have "homestays with families in communities on the Mexican side of the border" instead of living in a dormitory or an apartment (BorderLinks n.d.). This allows participants to learn the language and the culture firsthand, by living and experiencing it, instead of relying mostly on textbooks for information. BorderLinks structures the time in Mexico so that the "primary activities are meetings, conversations, and experiences with persons holding differing perspectives and viewpoints on the wide variety of social, economic, faith and political issues at play in the border region" (BorderLinks n.d.). The Semester on the Border Program is a cross-border educational and service-oriented program that has extensive contacts with civic leaders, maquila workers, union organizers, and maquila supervisors in Nogales. This contributed to the breadth of interviews obtained while participating in the program. Access to maquilas was possible because several BorderLinks staff members had established relationships with some of the receptionists at the maquilas and set up tours at them as part of the semester experience.

According to its mission statement, the BorderLinks Semester Program "offers students a unique opportunity for academic studies, experiential learning and community living along the U.S./Mexico border in Tucson, Arizona and Nogales, Sonora. BorderLinks is committed to providing a challenging and transformative experience through a variety of interdisciplinary approaches focusing on border studies and the impact of globalization" (BorderLinks 2005). As one observer put it, "The BorderLinks experience takes concepts like globalization and intercultural communication and makes them part of students' everyday life. Nogales, Sonora, with its maquiladoras and immigration-spurred growth, allows students to deal with its social reality in its own right while gaining an appreciation of how the city's life is linked with their neighbors to the north" (Gordon 2002, 5). The information obtained in this project was more extensive and richer in detail because of the staff, friends, and network that BorderLinks has established in Nogales over the past two decades.

Along the U.S.-Mexico border the intended and unintended consequences of free trade are the reality that residents on both sides of the border confront every day. The border cities are unique because they are the only place in the world where the first world and the third world physically touch. Nogales, Sonora, is an excellent example of the impact NAFTA has had on a border town as the maquiladora industry is a permanent feature of its local economy. This book focuses on maquilas and their impact on the workers they employ and the border towns in which they are located. Photographs and personal interviews reveal both the visual changes and those hidden to the naked eye. The words of 620 women who work in the maquilas and live in colonias document the working and living conditions they endure day after day. The quantitative data offer a personal and work profile of maquila workers (age, education, family size, employment history, hours worked, wages, and benefits). The qualitative data give a glimpse into their thoughts and what they like and do not like about their jobs. The questions I seek to answer are, What are their experiences on the assembly lines? Do the American companies respect the Mexican workers' labor rights and human rights?

perspective of Two worlds meeting [handwritten marginalia]

CHAPTER 2

The Border City of Nogales

What makes the border a special place is the juxtaposition of two conflicting realities—the poverty of the country and the richness of the people. As you cross the border and your eyes scan the landscape you see wooden slabs hammered together to form the walls of small one-room homes. Up the hill, you spot bright green and orange homes made from cement blocks, with old tires creating steps leading up to the door. As you scan the hillside, more and more homemade structures become distinguishable—made out of wood, cinderblock, and cardboard. Surrounding the homes are broken-down refrigerators and stoves, trash, rusted cars without tires or engines, and pickup trucks without doors and windows. Large green metal drums full of nonpotable water sit by the outhouses, which often have three walls and a blanket for a door. Everywhere you look there is brown desert; no flowers can survive the heat and lack of rain. The roads are not paved but full of small rocks and large holes. There are no lines distinguishing traffic lanes or sidewalks. Nothing but dust and dirt covers your clothes and face each time a car or bus rushes by. As you listen to the sounds around you, you are overcome by the barking, growling, and yelping of mangy dogs that roam the streets looking for something to eat. You hear the horns of the water and gas trucks making their daily rounds to sell nonpotable water for washing clothes, food, and dishes and tanks of gas for those families lucky enough to own a stove. As you enter the city you find colorful murals on cement walls and paintings of the Virgen de Guadalupe on stores, schools, churches, homes, and rocks.

There is much more to this city than the makeshift wooden and cement structures that first come into view. Within these homes live the friendliest, most hospitable people in the world; people who are busy going about their daily lives, working long and hard without complaining about their lack of indoor plumbing, electricity, warm clothes, fresh food, or medicine. If you stay for a while or live with a family in a colonia, you will witness the daily rhythm of their lives. People waking to the crowing of roosters as the sun rises, signaling a new day. Women cooking rice, onions, and beans in lots of oil and warming tortillas over a wooden stove. Families eating refried beans and rice twice a day, once for breakfast and then again at dinner. Mothers walking their uniform-clad children to school and then walking to work, or to town, or to *la frontera* (the border) to shop for groceries. Women and children avoiding the dogs roaming the streets because they likely have rabies. Men and women caring for sick children, coughing because of the dust from the roads and the chill in the air. Families gathering together after dinner to watch *telenovelas* (soap operas) on black-and-white TV sets. Fathers, mothers, and children climbing into one bed together to rest their weary eyes and legs. Families dressing up and going to church on Sunday with all their relatives.

The Border from Both Sides

Many people argue that the border is a country unto itself, neither American nor Mexican but a blend of two cultures that creates an entirely new place. The manifestation of this mixture of two cultures, however, varies across the border region. On the one hand, each pair of border cities is a unique intersection of the social, cultural, and economic nuances of each country. On the other hand, they all share the struggle to merge the people, cultures, languages, businesses, and politics of a developed country with a developing country. Nogales is representative of most border cities where the consequences of a shared geographic boundary are being played out each day.[1] On the U.S. side Nogales is located in Arizona, fifty miles south of Tucson, and on the Mexican side it is in the state of Sonora. Sonora is bordered on the west by the Mexican state of Baja, California; on the north, by Arizona; on the east, by the Mexican state of Chihuahua; and to the south, the Mexican state of Sinaloa (map 1). At six thousand feet above sea level, Sonora is a region whose mountainous terrain is dotted by vast areas of desert. Its climate is one of extremes: temperatures can reach freezing in the winter months and climb to 100 degrees in the summer. Nogales's climate also poses challenges. Without heat for homes in the winter or swamp coolers in the summer, everyday living can be quite uncomfortable. Despite

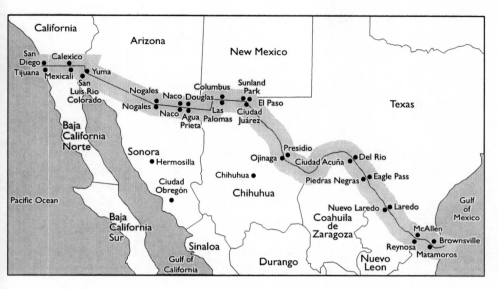

Map 1. The U.S.-Mexico Border

the fact that the cities on either side of the border share the same name, exchange between the two is restricted. An artificial divider was built by the United States in an attempt to control illegal Mexican immigration and drug trafficking. The divider, moreover, is not invisible but instead an eyesore. It creates a physical barrier between the United States and Mexico and "carries a symbolic weight that does not coincide with the realities of immigration and border crossings on the ground" (Barclay 2005, 2). There is not one wall that covers the entire 2,200 miles of the border but instead a number of walls that are erected at the major points of crossing.[2]

> The walls—which are especially obvious and numerous in the state of California but also present along segments of the Arizona, Texas and New Mexico border regions—are composed of concrete and sheet metal and are as thick as three layers deep in some parts. Some reach 15 feet in height and are surrounded by razor wire, spotlights, cameras, motion detectors and magnetic sensors, and are patrolled by armed guards with attack dogs. (Barclay 2005, 2)

It is hardly surprising that in 2000 President-elect Vicente Fox wanted the United States to tear down the formidable walls.

The fence as a artificial division

Construction on the twelve-foot-high wall began in 1994 as part of "Operation Gatekeeper" in San Diego and "Operation Enhanced Safeguard #0151" in Nogales and continued under the Illegal Immigration Reform and Immigration Responsibility Act of 1996. The additional construction of 650 miles of fence along the border has been completed as a result of the passage of the Secure Fence Act of 2006. Although the construction has been challenged by environmental agencies, the Tohono O'odham Nation, and landowners along the border, it continues today. The divider in Nogales was constructed from leftover temporary landing mats used in Operation Desert Storm and is a corrugated sheet metal made of steel roughly one to three inches thick.[3] It has been called "the line," "the wall," *la frontera*, and "the border." As Rick Ufford-Chase, founder of BorderLinks, remarked:

> When you arrive in Ambos Nogales, you'll find a rusty steel wall dividing Nogales, Arizona, from Nogales, Sonora—now two cities, though historically one. Nogales, Arizona, is a city of 30,000 people—downhill and downwind from its sister city of 400,000 to the south, Nogales, Mexico. You won't have trouble finding the wall, for it rises twelve feet high and snakes almost four miles through the canyons of downtown Ambos Nogales. (Ufford-Chase 1999, 14)

Mexicans express their feelings about the wall in graffiti, on murals, and in the placement of small wooden crosses representing the people who have died trying to make their way into the United States (see photos 1, 2, and 3). Ufford-Chase continued:

> Look around you. These homes made of packing crates, cardboard, scrap lumber, and corrugated tin are packed together so tightly on the canyon walls that you could easily reach from one to another. Most city streets are narrow, rutted dirt paths winding up the sides of the hills. The early morning air hangs thick in the canyon. Car exhaust and wood smoke (from home heating) conspire before moving slowly up the canyon and across the border. . . . This is a city of desperation. Few people have the luxury to question their participation in the global economy. They may live anywhere from five feet to five miles from the United States. But, thanks to the rigid divisions enforced by the wall, they struggle to raise their families without such basic amenities as running water, sewage systems, electricity, or weather-protected homes. Cross back now into Nogales, Arizona, and take a look around you. On the surface, the people

Photos 1 and 2. The "wall" that separates Nogales, Arizona, from Nogales, Sonora.

Photo 3. The "wall" that separates Nogales, Arizona, from Nogales, Sonora.

north of the border may appear to be the winners in the global economic adventure. But in reality, they are no more secure than their Latin American brothers and sisters. The paved roads, clean sidewalks, shiny fast food restaurants, the K-Mart and the Wal-Mart—they belie the reality. For Nogales, Arizona is also a city at risk, a city whose destiny is interwoven with Nogales, Sonora, that city just across the wall. (14–15)

The History of Nogales

Originally, the states called Arizona and Sonora were part of Mexico and home to the Apache. With the United States victorious in the Mexican-American War, "the Gadsden Purchase of 1853 severed the geographic unity of southern Arizona and Sonora and placed a border directly in the midst of Sonora's Apache frontier" (Heyman 1991, 23). The U.S. border was open from 1853 to 1929, when visas were severely restricted.[4] Nogales was founded by President Porfirio Díaz in 1880 as a customs post between the United States and Mexico (this was much later than the founding of other Spanish colonial towns such as Hermosillo, Santa

Ana, Magdalena, and Tucson). *Nogales* means "walnuts" in Spanish, and at one time the area was sparsely populated and blessed with fertile ground and walnut trees. During the Díaz presidency, Sonora experienced rapid growth in mineral mining (gold, silver, and copper) and railroads. In commerce, Sonora soon became a leader in wheat, flour milling, and cattle (Heyman 1991, 26). In the twenty-first century Sonora is a national producer of cotton, wheat, and cattle (*Columbia Encyclopedia* 2008). In 1889 it officially became a town and in 1920 a city. Currently, the city is the third largest port of entry into the United States, but its infrastructure is the weakest among the border crossings.

As a major port of entry, U.S. border policies have an impact on the border economies of both Nogales, Arizona, and Nogales, Sonora. Changes in U.S. border policy have been caused by economic as well as political factors. The primary reason for Mexican and Central American migration to the United States, however, has remained the same: economic necessity. Starving peasants flooded the borders during the dictatorship of Porfirio Díaz and the Mexican Revolution (1910–1920). Before 1929, when the U.S. economy was booming and farms, mines, railroads, and construction needed workers there was an "open border" policy. There was no restriction on immigration from Mexico to the U.S., and many "Sonorans came to work in the copper mines and railroads of Arizona" (Heyman 1991, 9). With the onset of the Great Depression in 1929, the United States began denying visas to Mexicans. With one-third of Americans out of work, bank closures leading to lost savings, and the stock market crash reducing wealth, Mexicans were seen as an additional burden on an already overburdened government. President Herbert Hoover ordered government officials to gather up all the Mexicans they could find and send them back to Mexico in trucks and railroad cars. Roughly two million Mexicans and Mexican Americans, many of them legal citizens, were deported. This massive deportation was later called the Mexican Reparation. Immigration policy during the period 1929–1942 could be dubbed that of a "restrictive controlled border."

The need for laborers resumed, however, with the U.S. entry into World War II. Mexican migrants were welcomed across the border to work in all sectors of the formal economy. Following the war, it was discovered that the Southwest needed temporary labor to work the fields, and the Bracero Program was born. This period, 1942–1965, is what Josiah Heyman calls the controlled border period.[5] In the 1980s the pesos crisis led to declining minimum wages for workers, which "created pressures that brought hundreds of thousands of migrants from the Mexican countryside to the United States" (Global Exchange 2000, 4).

In the 1960s the Mexican government began the development of the border regions, incorporating them into the national economy. In an effort to stimulate industry here the National Border Program (PRONAF), which provided funding for business investment, was established in 1961. Nogales benefited from special attention during the first years of PRONAF due to patronage by the director and received nearly 20 percent of the total PRONAF budget. In 1963 the first assembly plant, COMCO of Mexico, was built in Nogales with capital of $500,000 and eighteen workers (Barnett n.d.). Optimistic about the border's economic potential for the entire country, the government continued to concentrate on the region, and two years later the Border Industrialization Program (BIP) was established. The state government of Sonora created the Directorate of Industrial Promotion in 1961. Over the next twenty years several industrial parks were built on government-expropriated land, and assembly plants were built to industrialize through the "mechanical and electronic assembly of products, mainly for export" (Barnett n.d.).

Although certainly not one of its objectives, the North American Free Trade Agreement (NAFTA) has indirectly increased Mexican migration to the United States. When NAFTA took effect in 1994 it created three problems for Mexican workers. First, since it required the Mexican government to permit foreign ownership of communal and *ejidal* lands,[6] peasant farmers were driven off their land with a small check in hand but no prospects for work to sustain themselves. Second, the elimination of quotas and tariffs on U.S. agricultural goods pushed small corn farmers out of business as large U.S. agribusiness flooded the market with its cheaper corn. And third, the maquilas promised workers a living wage with 10 percent of the company's profits along with medical and old age benefits. Instead, workers have received the minimum wage with no profit sharing, and only some have access to the medical services of the Mexican Social Security Institute (IMSS). Consequently, once the workers have reached the border looking for these "decent jobs" in the maquiladoras, economic necessity pushes them to cross the border in search of better-paying work to support themselves and their families.

The first maquila arrived in Nogales in 1967 and was owned by Motorola. One of the advantages of operating maquilas in Nogales was that the shelter plan originated there.[7] The proximity of Nogales, Arizona, to Nogales, Sonora, is another reason maquilas have been so successful. The fact that a U.S. town is five minutes from the border makes it cheaper to obtain raw materials and intermediate goods from U.S. suppliers, to ship final goods, and to train Mexican supervisors and managers with American personnel. The close physical proximity, moreover, permits transactions to occur more quickly, which improves the delivery of "just-in-time" production processes. In the twenty-first century, more and more companies are using "just-in-time" production to keep up with the rapidly changing fads of American consumers. Instead of holding large inventories of product to meet sudden increases in demand, firms keep very small inventories and instead produce as orders are received. Companies save money because they do not get stuck with large inventories of "old" products that no one wants. This type of production, however, requires a fluid and flexible workforce. Ideally workers would have short-term contracts so that the firm can easily and cheaply hire additional workers when demand for the product is high and dismiss workers when demand is low.

Just-in-Time" production

Scholars examining the emergence of important new trade zones created by globalization have identified the Arizona-Sonora border as a transborder economic region (González 2004; Pavlakovich-Kochi 1995). They believe that both NAFTA in 1994 and the Strategic Economic Development Vision for the Arizona Sonora Region (SEDVASR) of 1995–1997 promoted the economic development of this border region. Pablo González argues that one of the most important trade "superhighways" in North America is the CANAMEX Corridor (2004, 132).[8] He attributes the success of this corridor, moreover, to the growth of the maquila industry (138–139). Nogales figures prominently in the industry's growth since the majority of its employees is concentrated in the border cities of Sonora (Nogales, Agua Prieta, and San Luis Río Colorado). González argues that considerable private and public resources have been devoted to the formal integration of the region with the creation of the Arizona-Mexico West Trade Commission in 1959, the agreement to implement SEDVASR in 1993, and the passage of NAFTA in 1994. He believes "the region expects to be well positioned to respond to the demands of the economy in the twenty-first century, and to the challenges of the 'Third Industrial Revolution' encompassing the microelectronics, robotics, and informatics industries" (142).

Business magazines and websites promoting Sonora as the optimal location for offshore operations highlight the competitive advantages of Sonora over other Mexican or Chinese locations. They argue that the state of Sonora offers "a highly sophisticated communication system, an integrated and extensive distribution system (with five airports, 22,500 miles of highway, 1,250 miles of railroad, and six ports of entry), and a complicated and strong infrastructure with 43 industrial parks in

17 different cities. They can ensure steady delivery of power with a generating capacity of 2020 MW and a 16″ natural gas pipeline extending 211 miles" (*MexicoNow* Staff Report 2005, 37). In a front-page advertisement, the Economic Development Council announced the many benefits Sonora offers: "home to the largest automotive project in North America; the Mexican hub for Aerospace manufacturing operations; high availability of skilled work force; world class infrastructure; and pro-business oriented government" (*Manufacturing in Sonora, Mexico* 2010, inside cover). The council's website, moreover, boasts:

> The people of Sonora have distinguished themselves with a reputation for excellent work ethics and employer loyalty. Sonorans take great pride in learning new skills and are immersed in the characteristics of manufacturing environments as part of their culture. Topics such as standards compliance and quality of manufacturing are second nature to the workers in this geography. The culture of Sonora supports strong family values and this translates into the workplace where integrity and sense of accomplishment translate to high productivity. (Economic Development Council for Sonora n.d.)

It is easy to imagine that the successful businesses and productive workers in Sonora will stimulate economic development. The border, where businesses have operated for almost forty years, offers living proof of the relative success of these economic strategies. The economic extremes of the town of Nogales, however, are perplexing to visitors and residents alike. Situated closest to the border are the maquiladoras, which are surrounded by paved roads and modern electrical and sewage treatment plants. Driving along the roads it is hard not to notice the beautiful palm trees, flowering bushes, and green grass that fill the landscape. Directly across the hill are several colonias, where the workers in these maquiladoras live. The sharp contrast is almost as offensive to the eyes as it is to the heart. The roads are not paved, and there are no electrical lines or underground drainpipes. Instead of order and calm, there is chaos and confusion. These opposing realities exist side-by-side in Nogales, and the maquila workers experience both of them every day.

Colonias: Where the Mexican Workers Live

The majority of Mexicans living along the U.S.-Mexico border reside in colonias, originally a term that was used to describe the spatial location of residences along the border. A colonia was the subdivision of homes that constituted a neighborhood or community. The term applied to residences whose household income represented all classes—the wealthy elite, the working class, and the poor. Currently the term has taken on a new meaning that carries a specific social stigma associated with poverty and living conditions in the "third world." As the population exploded along the border in the 1980s and 1990s, the government lost control of land allocation. The physical, social, and economic heterogeneity of a colonia was replaced with homogeneity. Houses were built on patches of land in areas that lacked sanitation infrastructure. Colonias became characterized as poor settlements with unsanitary living conditions. Their existence, some argue, can be attributed to the clash of socioeconomic systems created by free trade agreements. As Sarah Hill argues in her work on colonias in El Paso, Texas:

> Colonia residents are "fixed" to their class position by being fused to the landscape that is said to determine who they are, and their rights to political and social legitimacy. Colonias are now far more than just real estate that warehouses the country's poor. They serve in delineating, demarcating of space and subjects as the pincers of the free trade/neoliberal era grip, ever more tightly, the social imaginary of border cities. (2003, 153)

rootedness to social class via land [handwritten margin note]

These colonias, or poor settlements, exist on both sides of the U.S.-Mexico border and stretch from California to Texas. The colonias in Nogales, Sonora, like the majority of colonias along the border, vary in size and infrastructure as well as housing type.[9] There are eighty-seven colonias in Nogales; the oldest is called Bella Vista (Beautiful View), and one of the newest is called Rosarito I and II. Housing within the colonias differs in construction and appearance. Some contain primarily cardboard houses, while others are made up of rows of government-subsidized housing built by INFONAVIT (Instituto del Fondo Nacional de la Vivienda para los Trabajadores). Most of the colonias are squatter villages at different stages of development. A squatter village is formed when a number of individuals and/or families claim specific plots of vacant land and build shelter on that land. Typically individuals use material they find discarded by the side of the road or behind the maquilas: cardboard, wood, crates, shingles, and asphalt or cement blocks. For example, a cardboard house has two-by-fours holding the walls in place, and small windows are cut out of the cardboard. A cinderblock house is square, usually one story and with only one window (photos 4 and 5).

Photo 4. The colonia Bella Vista in Nogales, Sonora.

Photo 5. A maquila worker's home in the colonia La Torres.

Most houses have only one or two rooms. There is usually one large bed where the whole family sleeps that doubles as a couch during the day. Food is stored in a refrigerator, and meals are prepared on a hot plate or wood-burning stove. Inside the refrigerators of many poor families, there is likely to be a pot of leftover beans, a pot of leftover rice, hot-dogs, cheese, and a few onions, chilis, and peppers. Rarely is there fresh fruit, chicken, or beef, which is too costly for the family budget. Sheets or pieces of plastic cover the windows, allowing air to circulate. The floor is often dirt and uneven and is swept clean every day. The roof is either wood or hard plastic, kept in place by heavy bricks or a few nails. The roof and the walls usually do not meet, and the gaps let in the cold during the winter and the heat during the summer. Old clothes are often stuffed in the gaps to prevent the cold from entering. A sheet or blanket is used as a front door in some homes, while wood or metal doors are used in others. The bathroom is outside the house, in small wooden or cinderblock outhouses with no lights or running water. A bucket of water is used to flush the toilet, and there is no way to wash one's hands. Soiled toilet paper is discarded in the trash, and the waste from the out-house drains into the street.

In Nogales many people "own" their homes because of the "squatter's rule." Once squatters have occupied the land for five years they can buy it if no one has come along to claim it. This explains why people rush to build a structure on a piece of land without taking the time to consider the location, the level of infrastructure in that colonia, or access to electricity and running water. In Nogales a thirty- by forty-foot plot of land cost U.S.$2,000 in 2004. Although this is relatively cheap in dollars compared to housing prices in the United States, squatters pay the price in lack of comfort. It is important to keep in mind that this type of decentralized system makes it difficult to provide electricity, running water, and drainage to the colonias. Individuals, instead of construction companies, build homes without any consideration of water or electrical connections to a centralized feeder system.

Nogales is a thriving city in the state of Sonora because of the maquila industry. It is comparable to Tijuana, Mexicali, and Ciudad Juárez where the maquila industry is predominant, although on a smaller scale. The state capital of Sonora is Hermosillo, and the other main cities besides Nogales are Ciudad Obregón, San Luis Río Colorado, and Guaymas. Problems concerning housing and employment are settled in the state capital. Although the squatter villages lack infrastructure, the state has 20,402 miles of paved roads, 1,247 miles of railroads, and five international airports. This creates a welcoming business environment for the 254 maquiladoras that employ 96,518 people in the state (as of August 2011). Sonora had been a leader in agribusiness, but it has also become a magnet for the automotive, aerospace, and electronic industries. Table 2.1 lists the major companies located in Nogales in 2004, with the U.S. multinationals Chamberlain and Motorola together employing more than ten thousand workers. Business magazines boast of attracting the following companies: Goodrich, Ford, Precision Aerospace, Magna, Aerostar International, Harco Smith West, and Collins & Aikman (*MexicoNow* Staff Report 2005, 33). The government is agressively trying to attract new business to Sonora, and the response from multinationals has been overwhelmingly positive. As the secretary of the economy, Raymundo García de León, explained:

> We think and act as business people, not as politicians. We have new ideas involving a business vision. We want to convert the State of Sonora into a hospitable area for business people and investors. In our opinion, a government is not an employer, a government has to promote and generate an ambiance attractive and propitious to investors; an environment where the entrepreneur can obtain profitable investments. . . . [A]fter all, that is what he is looking for. (*MexicoNow* Staff Report 2005, 32)

Developers, subcontractors, and shelter companies also claim that Nogales is an ideal place to live because it is safe and secure and offers essential services. They proudly point out that the binational city has a public library, a municipal office building, a public hospital, a military headquarters, and seven churches. There is a primary school in each colonia and three institutions of higher learning. The two technology colleges and the University of Pedagogy train citizens to become engineers, computer specialists, and maquila managers. Electricity is provided by the state company, Comisión Federal de la Electricidad, whereas both purified and nonpotable water is supplied by many independent companies.

Maquiladoras: American Factories in Nogales

The modernized industrial zones in Nogales stand in sharp contrast to the primitive colonias. Nogales has two industrial zones, one near the railroad and one on the main road from Hermosillo to the border, ap-

Table 2.1. Main Companies in Sonora in 2004

Company	Employees	City	Year Established
Bose	1,200	San Luis Río C.	1989
AMP Tyco	3,500	Hermosillo	1988
Chamberlain	4,500	Nogales	1973
Daewoo	2,300	San Luis Río C.	1992
Ford Motor Co.	2,200	Hermosillo	1986
ITT Industries	525	Nogales	1992
Nu-kote	293	Nogales	1993
Leoni	500	Hermosillo	1994
Lear	530	Hermosillo	1987
Tosoh USA	450	Hermosillo	2002
Yazaki	5,000	Obregon	1996
Motorola	5,700	Nogales	2000

Source: *MexicoNow* 2005, 34, Exhibit 1.

propriately named Avenida Internacional. An industrial zone or park is an area separated from the center of the town, where local businesses operate. It is located in the Free Trade Zone (established by BIP) and includes the maquiladoras owned by multinational companies. It is self-contained and has a separate source of electricity, water, and natural gas. The entrance is clearly marked, the roads are paved, and the grounds are landscaped.

[handwritten margin note: FTZ is entirely separate from community]

The Old Industrial Park, Parque Nogales, was built in 1973, and Motorola was the first company to locate there. Many other U.S. companies—Xerox, Samsonite, and Canon, among others—followed. Some of the companies that first experimented with offshore production by locating plants in Nogales have shut down operations and moved to China in search of even cheaper labor. Other multinationals are just arriving and moving into plants vacated by departing companies. The older maquilas are small rectangular buildings constructed of cement and steel. The buildings have no windows, are one story high, and are situated very close together. The buildings are painted in neutral colors, and the small parking lots are overgrown with weeds. These older maquilas are not surrounded by high fences or barbed wire, allowing easy access (photos 6 and 7). Although the maquilas themselves were not very attractive, the jobs they brought were. Employees were paid well and treated

Photos 6 and 7. A maquiladora in the Old Industrial Park.

with respect. The men who worked in these maquilas were able to support their families.

As the maquila industry grew in Nogales, more industrial parks were developed. They varied in size but were clustered close together—Terrazas del Cid, with 9.5 hectares; San Ramón, with 13 hectares; the Industrial City of Nogales, with 23 hectares; and San Carlos, with 61.7 hectares (Barnett n.d.). The municipality of Nogales rented the land to the highest bidders, and these companies in turn rented to multinational corporations. The New Industrial Park, Nogales Nuevo, was built in 1998. These maquilas are nothing like the ones in the Old Industrial Park. The steel-and-glass buildings are two stories, with large reflective windows at the entrance (photos 8 and 9). They are widely spaced and painted with bright colors (orange, blue, red, and purple); the large parking lots have trees and bushes for shade. Three flags fly visibly as a reminder of NAFTA—the Mexican flag, the Canadian flag, and the U.S. flag. Each building is completely sealed from the public with armed guards at the entrance gate and a nine-foot fence topped with barbed wire surrounding the property. The front of each maquila is beautifully landscaped with palm trees, flowering bushes, and green grass (the only grass in all of Nogales). Many of the maquilas, such as those owned by Otis and Master Lock, have impressive retaining walls. Waterloo's maquila looks more like a Spanish mansion than a factory, with thirty-foot windows and beautiful stuccoed walls. Unfortunately, however, these beautiful maquiladoras brought mediocre jobs that paid poorly and exploited the workers. They preferred to hire women instead of men and did not pay them enough to support their families.

Companies who build factories in the New Industrial Park are making a long-term commitment to keep production in Mexico because they purchase the land and construct the buildings. Unlike companies in the Old Industrial Park that lease their plants, these companies face larger losses if they decide to leave Mexico. This implicit commitment brings hope for a better future for Nogales and its population with large employers such as Chamberlain (4,500 workers), Motorola (5,500 workers), and Walbro (1,550 workers) (see Appendix 1). Nevertheless, some companies have chosen to leave the New Industrial Park to relocate in China, where they expect their costs to be lower. Unlike other border cities, the maquila industry is growing in Nogales with cooperation from state and local governments and foreign entrepreneurs. A 116-acre industrial park south of Nogales accelerated the expansion of the maquila

Photos 8 and 9. A maquiladora in the New Industrial Park.

industry (Cravey 1998, 76). By 1998 Sonora had twenty-four industrial parks and by 2004 forty-three (*MexicoNow* Staff Report 2005, 32).

The Labor Market in Nogales: Living on the Minimum Wage

The labor market in Nogales is one that is plagued by tremendous unemployment and underemployment of men, women, and young people. For those fortunate enough to be employed, wages are low and falling. Economists generally attribute low wages to several factors: (1) a surplus of workers in the labor market; (2) low productivity of workers; (3) a high proportion of jobs in the agricultural sector; (4) a low cost of living and; (5) a low minimum wage. Along the border, wages are falling primarily due to a surplus of workers. When families migrate from southern Mexico to the border, the supply of labor at the border increases dramatically, pushing down the market wage. With new workers arriving every day willing to take jobs paying relatively little,[10] employed workers are left with no job security. Employed workers feel the pressure of this "buyers' market" and often work under a three-month contract with no guarantee of severance pay if they lose their jobs. The workers are paid in pesos, despite the fact that the products they make are sold in U.S. dollars.[11] This arrangement makes it possible for the real wage or purchasing power of the worker to fall when there is peso devaluation. This creates a serious problem for the worker whose purchasing power is eroded despite no changes in productivity. It is an advantage to the employer, however, who pays less in dollars (per peso) for the same amount of work merely because of currency devaluation.

The Mexican government can be blamed for part of the maquila workers' plight because it sets the minimum wage at an unsustainable level (table 2.2). This is no different from the situation in the United States where the minimum wage has not kept up with rising prices. As a result, the real minimum wage declined between 1990 and 2004.[12] In fact, the real minimum wage in Mexico for maquila workers has lost almost half of its purchasing power in a decade, falling from 63.98 to 36.75 pesos.[13] This puts workers in a precarious position. The longer they work and the more experienced and productive they become, the lower their standard of living. A major goal of Pola Pantoja, codirector of the Comité Fronterizo de Obreras of Agua Prieta, was to increase the minimum wage for maquiladora workers:

Table 2.2. Daily Real Wages of Maquila Workers (in pesos)

Year	Nominal Minimum Wage	CPI	Real Minimum Wage
1990	11.90	18.6	63.98
1991	12.32	22.8	54.04
1992	13.33	26.3	50.68
1993	14.27	28.9	49.38
1994	15.27	30.9	49.42
1995	20.15	41.7	48.32
1996	26.45	56.0	47.23
1997	26.45	67.6	39.13
1998	34.45	78.3	44.00
1999	34.45	91.3	37.73
2000	37.90	100.0	37.90
2001	40.35	106.4	37.92
2002	42.15	111.7	37.73
2003	43.65	116.8	37.37
2004	45.24	123.1	36.75
2005	46.80	100.0	46.80
2006	48.67	103.6	46.98
2007	50.57	107.7	46.95
2008	52.59	113.3	46.42
2009	54.80	119.3	45.93

Sources: CPI: OECD Factbook 2005. Minimum wage: Comisión Nacional de Salarios Mínimos, 1992-2010. This table uses the minimum wage for Área Geográfica "A" since Nogales, Sonora, is classified in this area.

Labor activists are pushing for an increase in Mexico's minimum wage, saying workers are struggling to survive in areas like American-owned maquiladora factories along the Mexican-Arizona border. They plan to tell President-elect Vicente Fox and a national commission that the minimum wage of 38 pesos ($3.80) a day is inadequate in the border's "dollarized" economy. They say it doesn't conform to Mexico's Constitution, which mandates compensation that provides for the basic needs and dignity of the worker and his family. (Qtd. in Ibarra 2000, 1)

All maquiladora workers are affected by the government's policy of setting a low minimum wage.[14] The wages of maquiladora workers in Nogales, however, are lower relative to other maquiladora workers working along the border (tables 2.3 and 2.4). This can be attributed to three factors: the large supply of labor, the limited demand for labor (due to productivity), and the low minimum wage set for that geographic area. According to the Sonora newspaper *El Imparcial*, Sonora workers earn less than residents of all the other states on the border. The salaries in Baja California, where Tijuana is located, are the highest at 5,041 pesos per month, then Tamaulipas (with Reynosa) at 4,676 pesos a month, and Chihuahua (with Ciudad Juárez) at 4,617 pesos a month (see table 2.3). A rough estimate of what these salaries would be in U.S. dollars can be derived by dividing the total amount in pesos by 10 to get the equivalent in U.S. dollars.[15] For example, workers in the state of Sonora earned roughly $400 a month, compared to roughly $700 a month in Mexico City.

Sonora ranks twenty-second in Mexico's thirty-two federal entities in terms of the average worker's salary. This partially explains why the maquiladora industry is growing in Nogales and why maquila workers are

Table 2.3. Average Mexican Workers' Income by State in 2004 (in pesos)

State	Average Monthly Salary
Distrito Federal	6,939
Nuevo León	5,661
Querétaro	5,550
Estado de México	5,250
Campeche	5,243
Baja California	5,041
Tamaulipas	4,676
Chihuahua	4,617
Coahuila	4,569
Sonora	**4,042**
Nayarit	3,626
Yucatán	3,568
Chiapas	3,453
Durango	3,437
Zacatecas	3,282

Source: Manjarrez and Corral 2004.

Table 2.4. Average Assembly Line Wages in Border Cities (includes obligatory fringe benefits, dollars per hour)

Border City	2000	2001	2002	2003	2004	2005[a]	2009[a]
Agua Prieta	$1.71	$1.66	$1.91	$1.89	$1.92	$1.99	$2.26
Ciudad Acuña	1.77	1.71	1.94	1.91	1.93	1.99	2.23
Ciudad Juárez	2.15	2.11	2.44	2.42	2.48	2.59	2.95
Matamoros	2.58	2.49	2.74	2.69	2.73	2.80	3.09
Mexicali	1.90	1.84	2.16	2.12	2.16	2.23	2.53
Nogales	**1.94**	**1.88**	**2.19**	**2.15**	**2.19**	**2.27**	**2.57**
Nuevo Laredo	2.52	2.44	2.58	2.78	2.84	2.94	3.32
Piedras Negras	1.96	1.92	2.27	2.25	2.30	2.39	2.74
Reynosa	2.01	1.96	2.15	2.28	2.41	2.53	2.90
Tijuana	1.91	1.86	2.15	2.12	2.17	2.26	2.57

(handwritten margin note: w/o fringe benefits, take home pay was @ 80¢/hr in 2001, nationally)

Sources: Christman 2004, 24; IHS Global Insight, Inc.
[a]Projections by IHS Global Insight, Inc.

struggling to survive. The average monthly salary of a worker in Sonora in 2004 was 4,042 pesos, compared to the national average for Mexico, 5,051 pesos per month. Moreover, salaries increased just 3.5 percent in Sonora between 2001 and 2003, compared to the national average of 4.8 percent. Table 2.4 presents hourly wages of maquila workers for every major city in Mexico. Clearly, maquila workers in Nogales have lost ground in the past five years. In 2000 the nominal wages in Nogales were in the middle of the wages paid in other cities, with Matamoros offering the highest hourly wage of $2.58 and Agua Prieta offering the lowest hourly wage of $1.71. By 2005 Nogales fell to the bottom quarter, with only three cities paying less: Agua Prieta, Ciudad Acuña, and Tijuana. Whatever the cause, the consequence is the same: considerable hardship for the maquila workers trying to provide for their families.

The usual justification for paying lower wages in Mexico than in the United States is its lower cost of living. Most Americans would argue that it is much cheaper to live in Mexico than in the United States. This often leads American consumers to conclude that the decent wages paid by the multinationals allow Mexicans to live quite comfortably. This argument does not apply to the border region. Instead, the cost of living is higher along the Mexican side of the Mexico-Arizona border than in the interior of Mexico. Although American tourists may find real bargains shopping in the *barrio* (commercial district) for handmade ceramics, cotton dresses, glassware, or wool blankets, everyday perishable items such as milk, poultry, rice, and beans are relatively expensive. There are two main reasons for the higher prices of necessities (or what economists call "normal goods") at the border: the increase in demand from the large population that has moved to the border, and the fact that the border economy has become "dollarized"—that is, increasing numbers of people use dollars instead of pesos for purchases. Maquila workers end up spending roughly 85 percent of their weekly incomes on food and a few household items. Table 2.5 lists the prices of a number of common items purchased for a family of four on a weekly basis in 2004. The items chosen for the "typical basket of goods" were selected by

Table 2.5. Market Basket of Goods in Nogales

Item	Price in Pesos
2 kg pinto beans—*frijoles*	21.70
30 eggs—*huevos*	17.20
1 kg rice—*arroz*	4.50
1 gal milk—*leche*	30.20
1 kg potatoes—*papas*	9.35
2 kg tortilla flour—*harina*	5.50
100 g instant coffee—Nescafé	20.30
1 liter cooking oil—*aceite*	8.75
1 kg lard—*manteca*	11.50
2 liters Coca-Cola	13.50
16 oz. corn flakes—*maizoro*	18.50
425 g cheese—*queso*	40.00
1 qt mayonnaise—*mayonesa*	7.00
1 kg tomatoes—*tomates*	9.69
1 kg whole chicken—*pollo entero*	15.90
8 rolls toilet paper—*papel higiénico*	32.80
44 disposable diapers—*pañales*	49.95
50 corn tortillas—*tortillas de maíz*	38.25
1 kg onion—*cebollas*	11.90
0.5 kg beef—*carne/pulpa negra*	34.75
0.5 kg pork—*paleta de puerco*	14.45
1 kg (one bag) detergent—*detergente*	15.90
TOTAL	431.59

Source: BorderLinks exercise at the main grocery store, Casa Ley, in the center of Nogales, Sonora, by spring semester students, February 10, 2004.

the BorderLinks staff and based on hundreds of home visits with maquila families living in Nogales. In 2004 it cost 431.59 pesos weekly to
buy these items, and maquila workers earned on average 480 to 500 pesos per week. This leaves only 48.41 to 68.41 pesos for everything else.
Clearly, this makes it very difficult to afford other necessities such as purified water, nonpotable water, a tank of gas, telephone, electricity, and
school supplies for the children.

Transfer us ?

Not only are the prices of daily essentials more expensive along
the border than in Mexico, but many essential food items are actually
cheaper on the U.S. side of the border. Consequently, if Mexicans have
a travel visa they will often cross the border just to buy their groceries.
Table 2.6 compares the prices of a variety of foods, toiletries, and cleaning supplies purchased by a family on a weekly basis in 2004. Figures in
the first column were obtained from Casa Ley, a grocery store in Nogales, Sonora. It was the first grocery store in Nogales and was where
most residents shopped. Figures in the second column were obtained
from an American grocery store in Nogales, Arizona, Food City. The
third column of prices was obtained from Soriana, a newer Spanish grocery store in Nogales, Sonora. As table 2.6 reveals, families spend the
most money for the same food items if they shop in Mexico at the main
grocery store, Casa Ley. The total cost of this basket of goods at Casa
Ley is 941.92 pesos, at Soriana 997.63 pesos, and at Food City $63.62
(699.82 pesos). This comparison of identical items at three different
grocery stores clearly dispels the myth that it is cheaper to live in Mexico. Families living along the border who are supported by the wages of
a maquila worker will find it very difficult to pay for the basic necessities.
The staples of many maquila workers' diet, rice and beans, cost 22.4 pesos at Casa Ley, 23.39 pesos at Soriana, and $2.27 (24.97 pesos) at
Food City. Families with young children who need to buy milk, formula,
and diapers would spend 187.30 pesos at Casa Ley, 149.35 pesos at Soriana, and $14.20 (156.20 pesos) at Food City. On a tight family budget
where every peso counts, women often shop at all three stores in order
to expand the purchasing power of their meager earnings. The reality for
workers is a relatively high cost of living and relatively low wages.

The perception by many Americans—consumers, producers, and
workers alike—that maquila workers have "decent jobs" that pay relatively well is wrong. Instead, they join the ranks of the working poor
whose wages are low and declining. On careful consideration of the
wages and cost of living of maquila workers living along the border, we
can conclude that the minimum wage is not a living wage.[16] Full-time

Table 2.6. Comparison of Food Prices on Both Sides of the Border

Food Item	Main Store, Casa Ley, MX (in pesos)	Spanish Store, Soriana, MX (in pesos)	American Store, Food City, AZ (in dollars)
Rice—1 kg	pesos 7.50	pesos 7.10	0.907 kg for $.89
Beans—1 kg	14.90	16.29	0.454 kg for .59
Milk—1 gal.	36.00	32.00	2.39
Flour—1 kg	5.30	4.95	2.27 kg for 1.49
Hotdogs—1 kg	126.50	109.50	0.454 kg for .99
Cheese—4 kg	187.60	310.95	0.454 kg for .49
Butter—400 g	11.50	15.45	0.454 kg for 1.69
Pastry—1 piece	2.90	4.70	3 for .99
Soda—2 liters	10.90	11.69	.99
Sugar—1 kg	10.90	9.49	.907 kg for .99
Bread—1 loaf	14.50	15.30	.69
Formula—900 g	72.00	69.85	366 g for 1.79
Onions—1 kg	10.55	9.45	1.5 kg for .99
Chiles—1 kg	19.90	19.95	.454 kg for 1.29
Cucumbers—1 kg	5.85	8.95	2 for .99
Lettuce—1 head	6.69	6.90	.79
Carrots—1 kg	4.90	9.45	1.00
Limes—1 kg	6.69	4.25	15 kg for .99
Apples—1 kg	15.49	12.95	.454 kg for .69
Watermelon—1 kg	4.90	3.75	1.36 kg for .99
Bananas—1 kg	9.25	8.45	1.5 kg for .99
Coffee—200 g	44.50	40.30	3.99
Oil—1 liter	10.90	9.90	1.99
Orange juice—1 gal.	22.90	16.50	.99
Eggs—1 dozen	34.90	29.90	1.37
Chicken legs—.775 kg	29.09	25.19	.454 kg for 1.37
Ground beef—.525 kg	33.76	22.74	.454 kg for 2.19
Clothes detergent—1kg	14.50	14.45	1.49
Clorox bleach—1 liter	6.90	5.99	2.5 liter for 1.19
Floor cleaner—1 liter	13.50	13.49	.99
Napkins—500	20.55	18.90	2.48
Toilet paper—4 rolls	14.50	29.90	.99
Shampoo—960 ml	15.90	9.55	.99
Bar of soap—200 g	7.95	7.05	.66
Toothpaste—201 g	18.95	14.90	2.19
Diapers—40	79.30	47.50	7.49

Source: Individual survey of prices at Casa Ley, Food City, and Soriana, February 15, 2005.

work in the maquilas is not a sustainable way of life; the maquila workers' purchasing power is too low. For maquila workers in Nogales, the basic necessities are out of reach. This begs the question, how do they survive?

In many cases, the maquila workers live one day at a time. They buy enough food and water for one day, and when their money runs out they simply do without. Cars sit on the street because they cannot afford gas. Dirty laundry piles up because they cannot afford to "waste" water for washing. Unlike the poor in the United States, they do not receive government relief—no food stamps, no housing vouchers, no unemployment insurance, and no Medicaid. This is probably the most shocking discovery uncovered during my fieldwork in Nogales. Since NAFTA the families of the female maquila workers, who worked very hard at least nine hours a day, six days a week, had to do without essentials that most American workers take for granted. Many families had not eaten meat for over a month, did not have running water, were without potable water in their homes, and were without clean and comfortable housing. Unsanitary living conditions meant children were often sick, and parents could not afford the medicine they knew would help their child feel better. The maquila women survived because they were committed to supporting their children—even if it meant sacrificing their own physical needs.

Beneath the warm and friendly exterior of Mexican women lies a host of coping mechanisms that give them tremendous strength in the face of adversity. Women are raised in Mexico to accept their fate and not complain. There is a Mexican saying, "Calladita te ves más bonita," "Quiet women are prettier." In other words, if women speak out against their abuse or their oppressors they are labeled "ugly" and ostracized from the *machismo* world.[17] The director of BorderLinks in Mexico, Jeannette Pazos, explained there are five reasons why women in Nogales do not complain. The first reason pertains to their culture; women are expected to accept life, however difficult, and make the most of their situation. As Jeannette said, "Complaining is not a part of their vocabulary." The second reason is that women are not highly educated and do not know their rights. It is rare to find parents in poor families who have attended high school. Neither girls nor boys learn about Mexican labor laws in secondary school. More often than not, multinationals do not include in their training programs a section on workers' rights. This makes it nearly impossible for workers to complain when violations take place since they are unaware of Mexican labor laws. The third reason for the complacency of women arises from their past. Many of the women feel they are better off now than when they were living in the southern states of Mexico. Despite the warmer weather and the fact that their families were intact, work was intermittent and the pay low. It was a hard life for the family. Some weeks the family earned enough to survive, and other weeks food and water were scarce. It was not uncommon for several children in the family to die from starvation, dehydration, and disease. Many women who moved to the border are just thankful to have a job in the maquiladoras and say, "Gracias a Dios porque yo tengo un trabajo" (Thank God because I have a job).[18] The absence of a true democracy is another explanation for workers' complacency. Most people in Mexico, except for the elite class, have been marginalized because their government was ruled by the PRI for seventy years. Political scientists have written a plethora of books on the corruption and exclusiveness of the PRI in Mexico.[19] After years of trying to effect change without success, many people no longer feel they can do anything to improve the way they live or work. They have, in essence, given up on the political process as a democratic mechanism to achieve economic progress and increase their standard of living. The fifth and final explanation for the fact that women are reluctant to complain stems from their faith. Pazos explained that the majority of women put their faith in the church and believe that God gives them what they need. The tenets of their faith say that they should be thankful for what they have and that God will provide what they need.[20]

Faith is an integral part of most Mexicans' lives. Their Roman Catholicism dates to the Spanish explorations of the fifteenth and sixteenth centuries. The influence of the conquistadors who came for fame and fortune also extended to their own religion and God. The impact of their faith is still evident to an outsider in everyday Mexican culture. Images of the Virgin Mary, the Last Supper, and the pope (el Papa) hang in many Mexican homes. Sunday Mass brings together the members of extended families. These traditions do not apply universally in the border city of Nogales, Sonora, as they would in southern parts of Mexico. On the border, religion conflicts with the stresses and obligations of everyday working life. Sunday Mass is no longer a religious mandate, as mothers frequently spend their Sundays in the maquilas and fathers enjoy their only day off tending to the children. In many households, Navidad (Christmas) and Semana Santa (Easter) are no longer weeklong celebrations of faith with family and friends but rather a brief occasion to share a meal together. The demanding work schedules of the maquiladoras have compromised the religious customs of many Mexicans living near the border. Rather than throw up their arms in despair or blame the government, the Mexican women hold on to their faith, giving thanks (gracias a Dios) for surviving each day.

Conclusion

[margin note: Border as 3rd country]

The Mexico-U.S. border is a country unto itself. It is the only place where the first world touches the third world. All five senses recognize its uniqueness. It has a different physical appearance from any city in the United States or Mexico. The streets and buildings on the U.S. side are clean, orderly, and uniform; those on the Mexican side are littered with trash, disorganized, and colorful. There are Mexican stores on the U.S. side and American stores on the Mexican side. People speak Spanish and English on both sides, and a blend of languages called "Spanglish" has evolved. In the middle of these two realities is a nine-foot metal fence built by the U.S. government. "¡Qué feo!"—"How ugly!"—many Nogales residents exclaim on looking at it. It artificially divides the two cities and its residents, appearing to "fence in" Mexicans—documented and undocumented alike.

It is hard to process the challenges of daily living for the maquila workers. The dual reality of working in a beautiful and modern maquila while living in a dirty and primitive home is difficult to fathom. The free trade agreement that created the modernized industrial zones ignored the squatter villages that grew around them. While the factories had electricity, indoor plumbing, and running water the day they opened for business, many of the colonias still have no electricity and no water more than ten years after NAFTA became law. The Free Trade Zones brought tremendous advantages to multinationals but hardship for the workers they hired. The lure of maquila jobs at the border prompted many families from rural southern Mexico to leave their farms and family enterprises and move to the border. Cities along the border grew rapidly; Nogales grew from a town of 30,000 to a city of over 400,000 in the ten years following NAFTA. The dramatic increase in the population pushed up the prices of goods and services while pushing down wages. Maquila workers found themselves trying to live on a declining real minimum wage. These workers became Mexico's working poor.

The "investment" of the developed world brought highways, railroads, airports, and ports of entry. Power generators, natural gas lines,

[margin note: only for industry — not community!]

and telephone networks were constructed along the border to ensure multinationals would have uninterrupted production. Mexican officials eagerly eliminated most obstacles, paperwork, taxes, and even unions to attract companies to their state. Nogales is ideal for this case study because the majority of its population works in maquiladoras. These workers, moreover, were willing to open up their hearts and homes. It was the perfect location to discover the truth about the working and living conditions of maquila workers.

CHAPTER 3

House to House: The Method of Analysis

The dual reality of the maquiladora workers in Mexico is not widely known. Most Americans do not know what type of working conditions exist in these "foreign" factories, nor do they know what type of people work there or why. Many Mexicans, except for those living along the border, have only a vague idea of how "good" these maquila jobs are or how the workers are treated by the American companies. Government officials in Mexico and the United States have pored over the actual NAFTA document in an attempt to identify all the potential benefits that can be realized for their countries. Policy makers and economists have provided projections based on theoretical analyses of the gains from free trade that NAFTA created. Multinationals have eagerly moved their production facilities to Mexico, hoping to boost profits by lowering costs. Families have voluntarily left their rural homes to work in the maquilas, hoping to increase their standard of living and provide a better future for their children. It has been more than fifteen years since NAFTA became law, promoting free trade between the United States, Mexico, and Canada. It is time now to weigh the costs and benefits and evaluate the long-term effects of this free trade agreement. It is time to collect and examine the evidence to decide what happened since NAFTA, who benefited, and at what cost. The best way to answer these questions and learn the truth about the maquiladora industry is to talk to the people who are the closest to it—those living it.

Interviewing Women in their Homes

In order to address the questions of the impact of the maquilas on the women, their families, and the economy, the perspectives of the women who work in the maquiladoras were examined. A survey was constructed containing some basic questions (personal history information) and several specific questions that focused on the role of the individual in the maquila industry. A copy of the survey (translated into English) is presented in Appendix 2. Certain questions required short numerical answers, for example, a person's age or education. Other questions were open-ended and called for elaboration, for example, what the workers did and did not like about their jobs. Ideally, the responses to these questions were expected to yield both quantitative and qualitative information that offers insight into the women's experiences as maquila workers.

The main objective of my research was to obtain information on the nature of work (hours, wages, and benefits) and working conditions from the women maquila workers. It was very difficult to enter most maquilas, and those that allowed access did not want outsiders speaking to the workers or taking pictures inside the plant. Female workers, moreover, would probably not be comfortable giving controversial or negative answers for fear of reprisal from their supervisors. Therefore, five Mexican women who were not currently working at the maquilas were hired to help conduct the surveys. Individually these women went *a casa en casa* (house to house) for a period of six weeks in March and April 2004. The advantages of this method are numerous. One of the greatest advantages is that it increased the sample size and improved the reliability of the responses. Since the five interviewers are Mexican women from the neighborhoods (colonias) in which they conducted the survey, they are more readily accepted into the workers' homes and accorded trust. This greatly enhanced the number of women who could be reached during the six weeks. This method also increased the likelihood that women would cooperate and answer truthfully because they felt more comfortable talking with a fellow resident than with a stranger who was a *gringa* (white woman). Finally, the interviewers were more likely to collect all the information necessary for each survey because they were invited into the homes of the workers and could sit down and talk. The response rate was extremely good; of all the women who were asked to participate in the survey, less than 10 percent declined. This is an extraordinary reply rate and can be attributed to a number of factors: the importance of community and cooperation among the Mexican poor, the interviewers' familiarity with the community, the interviewers' tenacity, and the desire of the workers to tell their stories.

The one constraint the five interviewers faced was that the only time they could interview the maquila workers in their homes was when their shifts were over. Fortunately the work schedules of the maquilas were fairly common knowledge among the residents of the community, and if the interviewers did not know, they could easily find out by asking a neighbor from the colonia. One of the interviewers knew where almost everyone worked in her colonia, their shifts, and who their friends were (in case they were not home when she stopped by). Others had less knowledge of the employment situations of the women in the various colonias so they simply went on foot house-to-house asking families if there was a woman at home who worked at one of the maquilas in town. In addition, several of the women went to bus stops and to the large supermarket, Casa Ley, in town. This was an ingenious way to gather a number of interviews at the same location and time, as long as the women did not mind waiting for their turn.

Several precautions and checks were put into place to improve the validity of the process, since the data from these surveys were a cornerstone of the research. I personally accompanied three of the five interviewers at some point while they completed the surveys in women's homes. This was useful not only for monitoring the authenticity of the data but also for giving the interviewers an opportunity to ask me questions they had about the surveys and what type of information I wanted. Two of the five interviewers, moreover, were accompanied on a consistent basis by me and my social work intern. The five Mexican women chosen as interviewers were from various walks of life. The women represented both sides of the issue of workers' rights. One was the leader of the Alianza Fronteriza de Obreros (AFO), a binational group trying to form an independent union in the maquilas, and another was a volunteer of the Confederación de Trabajadores Mexicanos (CTM), the official union established by the companies operating the maquilas. They were all recommended by the Mexican director of BorderLinks, Jeannette Pazos, who has lived in Nogales for over fifteen years and has worked at Hogar de Esperanza y Paz (HEPEC) for over ten years. The five women were chosen because they lived in Nogales, had some knowledge of the maquila industry, were educated sufficiently to conduct interviews, and were willing to meet once a week at HEPAC to review their surveys in the event I had questions about the answers they recorded or the meaning of the Spanish words they used. And finally, a formal contract was drawn up and signed by the interviewer and me.[1] The contract clearly stated the obligations of each interviewer, and each woman was given a copy.

The Resulting Sample

Statistically a sample must be random, reliable, and representative of the population it is drawn from if it is used to draw conclusions about the larger population. The method of sampling is crucial in the determination of the sample's validity. The interviews conducted by the five women resembled sampling from an infinite population. The population that could potentially be working in a maquiladora in Nogales is so large that it is impossible to list and count the number of individuals. The population can be considered infinite because there is continuous migration of families to the border from southern Mexico and considerable turnover of maquilas along the border. This suggests that the total number of individuals working in the maquilas is constantly changing. Even if this number were finite, it would be impossible to list the individuals in the population because those who live in the Nogales colonias do not have addresses. Given the reality of life along the border, the sampling procedure was devised to assure that the individuals interviewed were selected independently.

It was not possible to use formal methods of sampling to obtain a random sample because of the structure of the colonias in Mexico, especially along the border. A sample generated from interviewing individuals selected by computer-generated random numbers was not feasible in this situation. The homes have been built on squatter land in a disorderly fashion, often without street identification or mailboxes. The sample of maquila workers is random because of the informal sampling method and the checks and balances put in place. In order to produce a random sample it must be selected in such a way that the following two conditions are satisfied: each element selected comes from the same population; and each element is selected independently. The first criterion that each individual must be from the same population was met, since all the interviews took place in Nogales, Sonora. The second criterion may not have been met for each individual interviewer because for convenience they may have initially relied on asking friends, family members, and neighbors. In this case, it is not likely that each person was chosen independently. I would argue, however, that all the one hundred surveys collected by each interviewer could not have been filled out by workers whom the interviewer knew personally. This implies that for each interviewer there were many surveys completed by workers who were chosen at random. I would argue that they were randomly chosen because of the lack of organization in the placement of homes along a street as well as the frequent arrival of new homes and the vacancy of old ones. This constantly changing decentralized position of families made it nearly impossible to know who would be chosen, if they were home, and whether they worked in a maquiladora. Furthermore, the surveys that were obtained from the bus stops and grocery store would represent a variety of women because there is only one bus route to a given colonia and only one main commercial grocery store in *el centro*. Women who gathered at this location would likely be from different homes, from different colonias, and from a variety of maquilas. The randomness or independence of having one woman over another was further increased by the fact that there were five women going house-to-house. Thus the second condition is also met because the likelihood of interviewing any one woman was the same as interviewing any other.

The sample is reliable for several reasons. By hiring Mexican women from the community to do the interviews, the workers were more likely to cooperate and tell the truth. I can think of no incentive for the working women to lie about their answers; they were not getting paid for their responses, they were not at work and therefore not visible to their employers, and a member of their community was asking them the questions in the comfort of their own homes. Furthermore, if there was some pressure by the interviewer to answer a specific way that I was unaware of because of my lack of familiarity with the culture and language, it would show up in the data as outliers. The large size of the sample, 620 women, and the fact that the surveys were conducted by five interviewers who each contributed to the pool of interviews allow for problems to be tested by separating out the data obtained by one interviewer and comparing it with the others.

As I collected the surveys each week from the five interviewers, one problem arose that I had not anticipated. Some of the responses to the questions were difficult to understand. The Spanish I had learned was not always helpful in translating responses. I noticed after the first week that some words were missing letters, and many phrases and sentences were not grammatically correct. I also did not understand a few of the phrases that were used frequently as responses to certain questions. I asked the interviewers and discovered that many of the answers were written phonetically ("arness" for "harness" since the *h* is silent in Spanish) and as Spanish is spoken, not written. I attribute this to the fact that most of the interviewers and the maquila workers they surveyed had only a grade school education. I decided it would be best to translate the responses after I collected the surveys instead of waiting until I had the entire sample and had returned to the United States. This strategy allowed me to check my translations and comprehension with several members of the bilingual staff at HEPAC. It also helped me understand local expressions. For example, when asked what happened if they got pregnant while on the job, some women answered, "Te corre," which means "You ran." It turns out that along the border maquila workers use this expression to mean "You're fired." In order to maintain authenticity, the responses of the women used in this book are replicated exactly as they appear on the surveys. The quoted phrases used in chapters 6 and 7 have purposefully not been altered to conform to the grammatical rules of the Spanish language.

The potential errors in translating and reformatting the raw data from the sample of maquila workers to the Excel spreadsheet are minimal. The errors caused by incorrect translations from Spanish to English were reduced considerably with the help of the bilingual staff employed by BorderLinks at HEPAC in Mexico. Precautions were also taken to reduce coding and data input errors. There is the possibility of assigning the wrong code to information on a worker with a sample of this magnitude. I feel confident, however, that I corrected most of these types of errors when I checked the data on the Excel spreadsheet against the surveys and reviewed the means and ranges of each variable. Human error in transferring the information from the surveys to the spreadsheet can also occur. These errors may be harder to detect but are essential to minimize. I reduced these errors in data entry by having someone check each one against the original copy of the surveys. A handful of mistakes were discovered during this extremely time-consuming task. The end result, however, is a sample of data that I feel very confident using to draw conclusions about the workers and working conditions in the maquiladoras in Nogales.

The sample of 620 female maquila workers is representative of the population of maquiladora workers living along the Mexico-U.S. border. The overall significance of this sample, therefore, cannot be overstated. The large number of women interviewed, the authenticity of their responses, and the amount of detailed information exceeds that of any study to date. The results are not limited to women working in one or two maquilas. Instead these women worked in a variety of different maquilas, evident in table 3.1, which shows the range of products the women assembled (see Appendix 1 for the names of the companies that make these products). The women in this sample assembled pieces for cell phones for Motorola, locks for Master Lock, and suitcases for

Table 3.1. Products Made by Maquila Workers

Products Made	Number of Women	Percent of Women
Textiles	5	1.0
Medical equipment	79	16.5
Medical uniforms	14	2.9
Office equipment	27	5.6
Cell phones	27	5.6
Water pumps	9	1.9
Armor	11	2.3
Garage door openers	36	7.5
Cables	41	8.6
Coils	35	7.3
Circuit boards	49	10.2
Doors	7	1.5
Locks	33	6.9
Suitcases	12	2.5
Electronics	40	8.4
Chemicals	2	0.4
Fans	5	1.0
Plugs	5	1.0
Picture frames	3	0.6
Trophies	10	2.1
Other	24	5.0

Samsonite. These surveys are rich with quantitative and qualitative information on each woman's personal background and employment history. Documenting these women's experiences should contribute to the advancement of knowledge on workers' rights in the wake of free trade agreements. The data from this field research will help to set the record straight and uncover the truth about who wins and who loses as globalization sweeps through the world. These results have far-reaching implications and meaning for governments and workers in Latin America if this reality is replicated when CAFTA–DR spreads free trade to many Central American countries.

The descriptive statistics from this sample of 620 female maquila workers are representative of the overall population of maquila workers. Although this sample is from Nogales, there are multinationals employing women workers in maquiladoras all along the border. A few of the border cities such as Tijuana and Ciudad Juárez have more factories, while others such as Agua Prieta and Nuevo Laredo have fewer (see table 1.1). What is happening in Nogales is not unique or unusual. Workers in Ciudad Juárez and Agua Prieta lead similar lives, reside in similar homes, and have jobs that are similar to those in Nogales. The women who were interviewed ranged in age from fourteen to fifty-one, live in over twenty different colonias in Nogales, Sonora, and work for at least twenty-one different companies. Some of the women recently started working in a maquila; others have worked there as long as twenty-two years. The employment histories of these women are quite varied: some had previously helped on farms, worked in stores, and cleaned other people's homes. The responses of these women represent far more than the lives of workers in one town or one company. They document the working experiences of most women who work in maquiladoras owned by multinationals along the border.

It was far more difficult to interview supervisors and managers of the maquiladoras than I had anticipated. Originally, I had planned to interview as many managers as possible in order to accumulate at least fifty surveys. Identifying the supervisors in the population was not the problem. Most workers and neighbors knew who the managers of the maquilas were and where they lived. It was interviewing them that was the problem. I naively thought that I would be able to interview the employers in their homes, as I had done with the workers. This, it turned out, was unrealistic; I was not invited into any managers' homes. Not wanting to give up, I asked several Nogales residents to contact their managers to see if they would be willing to participate. They refused, despite some passionate pleas on my behalf. As a direct consequence of the lack of cooperation on the part of employers, the majority of information presented in this research is from the workers' perspective.[2] This book presents life in a maquiladora from the workers' perspective using the large, random, and reliable sample of 620 female workers.

I was able to conduct personal interviews with several longtime residents of Nogales, political officials in Nogales, union leaders in Nogales and Agua Prieta, and trip leaders from BorderLinks. Their names and positions are listed in the references. They offer the perspectives of individuals outside of the maquiladoras who have been affected by the growth of the maquila industry. The information from these interviews is used throughout the next four chapters as evidence of the impact of the maquiladoras on workers, their families, and the city of Nogales.

Conclusion

When I returned to the United States in May 2004, I had completed the major portion of my field research in Nogales, Sonora. With the help of five tenacious Mexican women, I had 620 completed surveys from women who currently worked in the maquiladoras. To ensure that the responses were truthful, the maquila workers were interviewed in the privacy of their homes. The interviewers went house-to-house in many of the colonias of Nogales, asking women of the household if they currently had a job in one of the maquiladoras. Almost all the women asked to participate agreed to do so and were forthcoming with their answers. We frequently spent over thirty minutes in a single home, beginning with introductions and casual conversation about the children, then conducting the fifteen-minute survey, and ending with a drink of water or something to eat before we thanked our host and left. The responses were written either by the interviewer I had hired or by the woman being interviewed. The significance of this sample is monumental. The large number of women interviewed, the authenticity of their responses, and the extent of detailed information exceeds that of any study to date. Much of the previous literature that made significant contributions to this topic predates NAFTA. Elizabeth Fussell (2000) uses a sample of 198 women from the 1993 Labor Trajectories Survey in her research. The results of her multivariate analysis describing the social and demographic characteristics of women working in maquiladoras in Tijuana are important but need to be revisited to determine whether the profile has changed since 1993. Kathryn Kopinak (1996) conducted a survey in 1991. She compiled information about the nature of the work and the conditions of work in the maquiladoras from conversations with the managers and from job advertisements. Kopinak also surveyed workers both inside and outside the plants. She focused on the transport equipment plants in Nogales and ended up with a very large sample of 216 workers. Susan Tiano's research (1994) surveyed women in specific factories in Mexicali from 1983 to 1984. She interviewed 66 women working in the electronics sector and 58 working in the apparel sector. Her groundbreaking work on gender issues in maquiladoras is very important but also quite dated. The study by Josiah Heyman (1991) was purposefully on a smaller scale. He spoke extensively to all the members of six families about their life and work experiences over two years, 1984 to 1986. The families lived in Agua Prieta and Douglas and worked in several maquiladoras. The fieldwork of Maria Fernandez-Kelly (1983) is the closest to my work in Nogales because of the number of women and maquilas it included. She interviewed 510 women working in fourteen different assembly plants. Fernandez-Kelly chose Ciudad Juárez as her fieldwork site because it has the largest number of maquiladoras along the border, while I chose Nogales, which has the third largest number of maquiladoras. Her research, however, was conducted in 1978–1979.

Surprisingly, there are few published studies on the workers in the maquiladoras along the border since 2003. The more recent research is vastly different from my own because it is more qualitative in nature. The scholars, primarily women, approach the issue from a variety of interesting perspectives. Leslie Salzinger in 2003 gathered information from a few maquiladoras in Ciudad Juárez. She worked alongside women in several factories to provide insight from personal experiences. Her research is extremely valuable because her observations were firsthand and her interviews were with people who confided in her. The obvious weakness is that her sample of workers is small. Her findings cannot be considered representative since she did not interview the workers from these plants in any systematic way. Martha Ojeda and Rosemary Hennessy in *NAFTA from Below* (2006) report on interviews with over twenty maquiladora workers and capture the impact of NAFTA on their daily lives. The workers, men and women, are employed in maquilas in all the border cities except Ciudad Juárez and Nogales. The combination of factual information and expressed emotion from the personal testimonies offers compelling evidence of the impact of free trade on maquila workers. The richness of this qualitative evidence provides an essential context to statistical analyses. Melissa Wright's research has spanned two decades, and her scholarship has become central in this literature. She interviews and tracks several women in maquilas as they transcend the traditional representation of Mexican maquiladora women. Wright (1997, 2006) demonstrates in her research that women can break the model of the "disposable woman" on assembly lines and become managers. Her findings, however, do not represent the situation for the majority of assembly line workers, as she admits. In her research on the health of women working in maquiladoras along the border, Catalina Denman (2008) conducted personal interviews with fourteen women in Nogales. The interviews, which took place from 1994 to 1997, focused on the women's reproductive health. Denman's research provides considerable depth on the issue of women's health along the border, whereas my research offers breadth by including other socioeconomic impacts. The perspectives offered by these sociologists, anthropologists, ethnographers, and union organizers make important contributions to the literature.

Given my training as an economic historian, my research offers yet another perspective and one that has been missing for decades. The last published study by a social scientist who did extensive fieldwork on maquila workers was in 1994. This study of 620 maquila workers in 2004 attempts to fill this void and update the literature on the maquila industry along the Mexican-American border. The mere size of this sample will silence critics who argue that the conclusions are not representative of reality but instead reflect a unique or exceptional experience in one maquila or one town. It is extremely unlikely that the words of 620 women are lies or exaggerations of the truth. The quantitative and qualitative information contained in this sample is extensive. It uncovers the truth about the maquiladora industry in Mexico by answering the following questions: Are the jobs in the maquilas better than other jobs in the economy? Are the maquila workers able to make a decent wage and provide for their families? Are the maquiladoras liberating the women or exploiting them?

CHAPTER 4

The History of the Maquila Industry

The first maquilas were built along the Mexico-U.S. border in 1965 with the commencement of the Border Industrialization Program. After touring Asia's export processing zone, Mexico's minister of industry and commerce, Octaviano Campos Salas, adapted this new development approach to Mexico's border by creating the maquiladoras (Kamel 1990, 36). The BIP established a twenty-one-kilometer free trade zone along the entire border. A maquila or maquiladora is defined as

> an entity operating under a special customs regime, which enables companies to import in-bond and duty-free raw materials, equipment, machinery, replacement parts, and other items needed for the assembly or manufacture of finished goods for subsequent export. Companies reexport the finished or semi finished product from Mexico and may sell it in the Mexican market subject to certain restrictions. Foreign investors may own 100 percent of the equity in a maquiladoras operation. (*Mexico's Bimonthly Economic News* 2000, 2)

Maquila defin [margin note]

The maquiladoras are also referred to as "twin plants" and in-bond industries.[1] Companies import machinery, parts, and raw materials duty-free and export finished products around the world. The Mexican government began the BIP as an aggressive regional promotion of capitalist industrial growth. In 1966 there were 57 maquilas employing 4,257 people, and by 2004 there were 2,800 maquilas employing over one million people. The number of maquilas and employees continued to climb until 2007, when the number of people employed had nearly doubled, to 1.9 million.

The idea of creating maquilas along the Mexican border did not originate with entrepreneurs and investors in the United States or Asia. It was the idea of the Mexican government, which needed to create lots of jobs quickly to put the country on the road to modernization. The government took advantage of U.S. tariff schedules 806 and 807, which allowed U.S. corporations to locate their manufacturing plants along the border and import machinery, parts, and raw materials without taxation. In the end this reduced the import duties on U.S. goods shipped abroad for assembly and then reimported into the United States for sale. The program was originally designed to provide employment for seasonal migrant laborers who had lost their jobs after the demise of the Bracero Program.[2] Initially, the growth of the maquiladora industry occurred only along the border in the Mexican states of Baja California, Sonora, Chihuahua (south of New Mexico and Texas), Coahuila (bordering Texas), Nuevo León (south of Texas), and Tamaulipas (bordering Texas). In 1972 the BIP became the Mexican Industrialization Program (MIP) because of its expansion beyond the border zones. Box 4.1 gives a timeline of the political and economic events that contributed to the growth of the maquila industry. In spite of two major setbacks, one in 1975 due to a recession in the United States and the other in 1982 created by a financial crisis in Mexico, the number of maquiladoras increased dramatically between 1978 and 2000, from 457 plants to 3,703 (table 4.1). Although multinational companies were eager to outsource their manufacturing in order to lower costs, the Mexican government sweetened the reward by passing laws that simplified the establishment of a maquila (1973), made workforces cheaper and more flexible (1975), and reduced taxes and eliminated tariffs and duties (1994). It should come as no surprise, then, that the Mexican government took the bold step of changing their constitution to clear the way for the maquiladora industry.

NAFTA and Maquiladora Growth

The North American Free Trade Agreement signed by U.S. President Bill Clinton and Mexican President Carlos Salinas de Gortari in 1994 broadened the scope of the BIP. NAFTA removed barriers to trade by eliminating custom duties and tariffs and offered "tax holidays" to foreign companies that established operations along the border and in the Mexican interior. As a result, the number of maquiladoras increased. As table 4.1 illustrates, the number of maquilas in Mexico grew steadily

BOX 4.1. HISTORICAL TIMELINE OF EVOLUTION OF MAQUILA INDUSTRY

1941   *Ley de Industrias de Transformación* (Manufacturing Industries Law)—Exempted "new" and "necessary" industries from a wide range of taxes, import licensing fees, and quotas.

1942–
1964   Bracero Program—Mexican migrants are officially assigned to temporary jobs, primarily agricultural (and some railroad construction jobs), in the United States in response to the World War II labor shortage.

1961   National Border Program (PRONAF)—A program during the administration of Adolfo López to promote commerce and enhance the natural beauty of the region. Objectives: to use more domestic goods, to increase exports, and to improve life on the border. PRONAF was rather unsuccessful but did help to increase the area's tourism.

1965   Border Industrialization Program (BIP)—The Mexican government begins this program due to the displaced Bracero workers and as a way to promote industrialization. By using the U.S. tariff schedules 806 and 807, U.S. corporations are able to locate their manufacturing plants along the border and can import machinery, parts, and raw materials without taxation. The use of these provisions allow for the beginnings of the maquiladora industry.

1967   First maquila in Nogales—The first maquila in the state of Sonora is established in Nogales. One story attributes R. Campbell Sr. as the owner of the new manufacturing plant. Campbell was a producer of plastic strawberry baskets on both sides of the border, but decided to focus on Sonora for the location of his industry because of the low cost and high quality of the Mexican workforce.

1967   United Nations Industrial Development Organization (UNIDO)—An organization created to promote industrial development in developing countries, facilitating their export production.

1969   Progress of BIP—A total of 147 companies are registered under the BIP and employed 17,000 workers.

1971   Mexico's Rules and Regulations—A list of specific objectives of the maquila program is created. These include the elimination of unemployment, industrial development along the border, and increased consumption of Mexican raw materials and services.

1972   Mexico changes name of BIP to MIP (Mexican Industrialization Program)—Free trade is expanded to nonborder areas.

1973   Paperwork is simplified—The establishment of a maquila factory becomes easier and quicker as import permits can be approved locally instead of needing authorization from Mexico City. Mexico changes

(continued)

the law that previously limited foreigners to only 49 percent ownership of Mexican firms. Foreign investors can now have 100 percent ownership of most maquilas.

1975 Economic Recession Affects Both Sides of the Border—A U.S. recession leads to a two-year economic downturn in Mexico. U.S. firms close thirty-nine maquilas and lay off 23,000 employees. Many rules are relaxed in order to try to keep the maquila industry going. These leniencies of rules include dismissal without severance pay, adjustment of workforce size and hours, and an increase in the retention of "temporary" workers from 30 days to 90 days.

1980s El Programa de Fomento Integral de Exportaciones (Integrated Plan to Promote Exports)—Mexico implemented four policies to increase exports: (1) the permanent under evaluation of the peso; (2) the elimination of barriers to foreign exchange for exporters; (3) the simplification of import and export permits; and (4) a subsidy on the importation of machinery and equipment used in export manufacture.

1982 Mexico has Financial Crisis—The government decides to devaluate the peso in response to the increasing inflation rates. This reduces Mexican wages and increases cost reductions for U.S. companies assembling products on the border.

1983 Domestic Sales Expand—Regulations are changed to allow maquilas to sell 20 percent of produced goods domestically if a certain amount of Mexican materials were used to make the goods. A government decree establishes regional development as a primary objective of the maquila industry.

1986 Mexico joins General Agreement on Tariffs and Trade (GATT)—Policies are implemented to make foreign investment easier, to allow for expansion of free trade, and to reduce the intervention of the state. Many taxes, tariffs, quotas, and licenses are reduced or eliminated.

1993 Maquila Products Surpass Domestic Goods—For the first time, maquila products outnumber domestic products.

1993 North American Labor Agreement—Pre-NAFTA agreement that establishes labor laws relevant under free trade agreement. The United States, Mexico, and Canada agree to uphold existing labor laws in basic areas of worker's rights. These rights include freedom of association; right to collective bargaining and strike; prohibition of forced labor; no child labor; no discrimination; health and safety; and minimum wage payment.

1994 North American Free Trade Agreement (NAFTA)—Continued liberalization of free trade to create the world's largest free trade zone. The treaty is formed to further integrate the countries' economies, specifically trade in the areas of investment, services, and goods. In addition, it hopes to aid in the elimination of illegal migration because of the new jobs that would be created in Canada, the United States, and Mexico.

2001   No Taxes on Value Added—Further changes in tariff laws allow for no taxes paid on value added which reduces total costs incurred by foreign producers operating in Mexico.

2004   NAFTA Extended—President Vicente Fox extends NAFTA tax holidays for another ten years.

2005   Free Trade in the Western Hemisphere Expands—Central American Free Trade Agreement–Dominican Republic (CAFTA-DR) is passed by the U.S. Congress and signed by President Bush in summer 2005. This new trade pact allows free trade among the United States, Costa Rica, the Dominican Republic, El Salvador, Guatemala, Honduras, and Nicaragua. Much like the BIP and NAFTA, CAFTA-DR removes trade barriers and facilitates investment in the free trade areas.

Sources: Kopinak 1996, 4, 8, 10, 14, 17, 33, 37, 207; Fernandez-Kelly 1983, 23, 24, 32; Fatemi 1990, 22, 77, 191, 207, 226.

---

from 1994 to 2000. After 2000, however, the growth of the maquila industry has not been steady, declining from 2000 to 2004, rising to a peak in 2008, and then declining again.[3] The growth rate of maquila establishments for the period from 1994 to 2005 was extremely high, 34 percent. The upward trend since 2004 surprised many American economists but not Mexican analysts, who claimed, "The automotive and Maquiladora industry programs have been highly successful for Mexico" (Ornelas 2006b, 14). The future also looks bright for Mexico's ability to attract foreign direct investment (FDI): "Mexico has recently been particularly competitive in the logistics, aerospace, and contract manufacturing sectors. At the bottom line, Mexico, with all of its shortcomings, is North America's low cost manufacturing platform" (Ornelas 2010, 38). Despite the current global financial crisis, real estate developers are hopeful, and Ornelas is "cautiously optimistic" that the worst of the economic downturn is over. He looks to the maquila industry as a gauge of the recovery and concludes, "In Mexico, positive signs are emerging as well as employment and production in the maquiladora plants and the auto industry has turned the corner. Most plants are reporting an increase in production orders" (2010, 38).

Twenty-seven of Mexico's thirty-two states—the exceptions are Nayarit, Colima, Chiapas, Tabasco, and Campeche—had plants in 1998. Those states that do not have maquilas are making preparations

Table 4.1. Growth of Maquilas in Mexico

Year	Number of Maquilas	Number of Workers	Year	Number of Maquilas	Number of Workers
1978	457	91,000	1995	2,267	681,251
1979	340	111,000	1996	2,553	799,347
1980	620	119,546	1997	2,867	938,825
1981	605	131,000	1998	3,130	1,043,483
1982	582	127,000	1999	3,436	1,195,371
1983	605	151,000	2000	3,703	1,310,026
1984	667	199,000	2001	3,279	1,071,488
1985	780	230,000	2002	2,976	1,067,948
1986	865	227,900	2003	2,802	1,050,210
1987	1,087	299,000	2004	2,800	1,131,612
1988	1,396	369,489	2005	3,049	1,185,000
1989	1,655	429,725	2006	2,805	1,224,000
1990	1,703	446,436	2007	5,138	1,938,593
1991	1,914	467,352	2008	5,257	1,857,362
1992	2,057	505,698	2009	5,210	1,616,998
1993	2,114	542,074	2010	5,111	1,818,455
1994	2,085	583,044			

Sources: 1978–1987: Fatemi 1990, table 13.1, 201; 1988–2009: INEGI 2010, 1999–2004, 1988–2000.

to attract them. In December 2006 Governor Pablo Salazar of Chiapas concluded:

> We offer our state for whoever is looking for a great strategic site, and we make the compromise as a government to support you with a blinding [*sic*] in your investment, great quality of incentives, acceleration and simplification of the paperwork that has to be made to establish your operations in Chiapas. We are a government open for business, and we are working hard on the creation of the infrastructure ideal for business. (Ornelas 2006b, 71)

Real estate companies are advertising Campeche as a new location for FDI from the United States. In *MexicoNow*'s Industrial Real Estate Market 2010 Outlook, Consorcio de Servicios Campeche placed a full-page advertisement. In addition to the lowest leasing rates, they claimed the following benefits of investing in Campeche: geographic proximity to the United States, a fully developed transportation infrastructure, the NAFTA alliance, and a one-stop shopping experience (*MexicoNow* 2010, 21). The majority of maquila plants (75 percent), however, still remain along the border and employ 79 percent of the workers (Wear 2002, 1). U.S. companies were not required to pay custom duties on the raw materials or machinery imported into Mexico or on the finished product exported out of Mexico. To further entice companies to move their manufacturing plants to Mexico, the companies were exempted from almost all taxes (real estate, corporate income, and profit). The only exception was the value-added tax, which was calculated from the low wages of the workers. The stages of growth and development of the maquilas industry are described below. By tracking certain political and economic events (or crises) in Mexico as well as the United States, the booms and busts of the industry are understandable.

Stages of the Maquila Industry Growth

Phase I: 1965–1973, Installation and Consolidation

The maquiladora industry had simple but steady growth under the BIP. In 1970 Mexico's populist president, Luis Echeverría Álvarez, introduced a federal labor law that provided significant improvements for maquila workers. Under this law the workers received paid vacations, Christmas bonuses, mandatory training, recreation programs, death and termination benefits, retirement benefits to be paid by the employer, employer-provided housing assistance, and a guarantee of the minimum wage. Though the BIP began primarily to reduce the number of unemployed braceros, the factories that were producing duty-free goods were actually hiring young women to work.

Phase II: 1974–1976, When the U.S. Economy Gets a Cold, Mexico's Economy Gets Pneumonia, Part 1

The steady growth ended as Mexico's economy experienced the backlash of a U.S. recession. There were massive layoffs, with employment in the maquila industry dropping 11.5 percent and leaving thousands unemployed. President José López Portillo allowed the CTM to regain control of the workers who were afraid of losing their jobs due to the recession in the United States. Many standards and regulations were relaxed in order to keep the industry alive and attract the U.S. investors who were not very interested in Mexico. As a result, employers were permitted to fire inefficient workers without severance pay, extend the thirty-day probationary period at below minimum wages to ninety days, and reduce their contributions to the social security fund.

Phase III: 1977–1982, a Booming Industry

Mexico changed its economic strategy from import substitution to export-led development, which favored the maquiladora industry. The industry experienced high rates of growth (over 13 percent annually) as even more regulations were simplified to attract foreign investment. In 1982 the Mexican government devalued the peso due to the debt and economic crisis. The International Monetary Fund (IMF) was placing external pressure on Mexico to undertake economic liberalization.

Phase IV: 1983–1989, Debt Crisis for Mexico

The devalued peso made Mexican labor even cheaper relative to other currencies. Foreign investment in maquilas increased dramatically, giving the industry some permanence. Growth of the industry hit new heights, with a new maquila opening for operation every five days on average. President Miguel de la Madrid had a strong neoliberal platform and joined GATT. He reduced protectionist tariffs, made it easier for foreign investment to operate in Mexico, cut public spending, reduced wages, controlled inflation, and sold off state enterprises. Real wages declined 40 percent during his term in office. He declared the maquiladora industry a priority sector for the economy. De la Madrid wanted to promote the industry primarily as a source of foreign exchange and jobs but also as a way to catalyze endogenous industrial development in Mexico.

Phase V: 1990–1994, Mexico Embraces Trade

As the maquila industry continued its steady growth, the beginnings of free trade were taking root. After the success and openness of GATT, Mexican officials explored other options of free trade, including agreements with Chile in 1992 and with the Asia-Pacific Economic Cooperation in 1993. NAFTA passed in 1994 and further expanded the free trade zone and reduced tariffs. Employment in the maquilas grew 6 percent per year.

Phase VI: 1995–2000, Post-NAFTA Growth

The reduced tariffs and tax holidays provided for by NAFTA generated an increase in foreign investment that stimulated another growth spurt in the maquila industry. The maquila industry became the fastest growing sector in the economy, an average rate of 14 percent annually. It surpassed oil and gas, migrant remittances, and tourism as the top foreign exchange generator.

Phase VII: 2000–2003, When the U.S. Economy Gets a Cold, Mexico's Economy Gets Pneumonia, Part 2

The maquiladora industry experienced its second major setback as a result of another U.S. recession. The industry lost over 240,000 jobs (20,000 to 40,000 layoffs a month) and experienced the closing of over four hundred plants. Foreign direct investment fell as U.S. firms waited for positive news on interest rates, inflation, and consumer confidence.

Phase VIII: 2004–2007, a Revival in the Industry

President Vicente Fox extended NAFTA for ten more years, giving U.S. firms the green light to continue outsourcing manufacturing to Mexico. The number of plants increased dramatically and the level of employment increased gradually, back to pre-recession totals. The industry secured several crucial automotive and aerospace contracts to build new production facilities. Free trade expanded as negotiations over the Free Trade Agreement of the Americas (FTAA) occurred, but the lack of support from South American countries generated a different agreement, known as the Central American Free Trade Agreement-Dominican Republic (CAFTA-DR), put into effect in 2005.

Phase IX: 2008–2010, the Great Recession Halts Growth

The maquila industry suffered considerably from the financial crisis in the United States and globally. Although fewer maquilas were closed, layoffs were staggering (321,595) and had an impact on all regions. Industry experts were cautious about the future because of wage competition from China and from signatories to CAFTA–DR.

Mexican or American Owned?

The idea of moving production from one region to another started at the turn of the nineteenth century as textile production began in the northern cities of Great Britain and crossed the Atlantic Ocean to settle in New England. The current transplanting of factories, however, is very different. Unlike the British and New England factories, the majority of the new factories in Mexico are not owned by Mexicans (see table 4.2 for a list of the top 100 maquilas in Mexico in 2004). Seventy percent are owned by Americans, 11 percent by Japanese, 3 percent by Germans, 3 percent by Koreans, and 5 percent by Mexicans (Maquila Portal 2004).

The high rate of foreign ownership has several important implications for the economy and the workers. In the short run the jobs that are created in the maquilas will increase the income of the workers and thereby increase consumption of goods and services in Mexico. American policy makers argued that Mexicans would now be able to afford U.S.-made goods. This has not been the case, however. Mexican workers receive the minimum wage in the maquilas (which was lowered since NAFTA) and can barely afford to buy food with their wages. Therefore, consumption will rise but not as much as predicted and not enough to boost the Mexican economy to full employment. Since the factories are foreign owned, most of the profits leave Mexico. It is reasonable to assume that most of the profits made will not be spent on Mexican goods and services, nor will they be deposited in a Mexican bank. Consequently, the initial investment in building and equipping the maquila will have no Keynesian multiplier effect[4] on the local or regional economy in Mexico. Conversely, it will boost the local economies where the CEOs, CFOs, managers, supervisors, and stockholders live. The FDI has a onetime impact on the Mexican economy when construction jobs are created to build the factories. If the multinationals lease existing buildings and/or import most of their machinery to equip the factories, however, the onetime impact on the Mexican economy is likely to be negligible. Therefore, in the long run there will be no economic growth in Mexico as a result of the expansion of the maquila industry. This is an important

Table 4.2. Top 100 Maquilas in Mexico in 2004 (based on number of employees)

No.	Company	Employees	Plants	Origin	Industrial Type
1	Delphi Automotive	68,000	54	USA	Automotive
2	Lear Corporation	34,000	8	USA	Automotive
3	General Electric	30,900	34	USA	Industrial
4	Yazaki North America	27,506	22	Japan	Automotive
5	ALCOA Fujikura Ltd.	25,700	19	Japan	Automotive
6	Takata	15,000	10	Japan	Automotive
7	Volkswagen	13,500	1	Germany	Automotive
8	The Offshore Group	13,270	3	USA	Shelter services
9	General Motors	12,200	3	USA	Automotive
10	Philips Electronics	11,500	16	Netherlands	Electronics
11	Visteon Corporation	11,200	15	USA	Automotive
12	RCA	10,874	6	USA	Electronics
13	Siemens AG	10,000	14	Germany	Automotive
14	Sony Corporation	9,679	4	Japan	Electronics
15	Ford Motor Company	9,150	3	USA	Automotive
16	Nissan Motor Co., Ltd	8,500	3	Japan	Automotive
17	Daimler Chrysler	8,200	6	Germany	Automotive
18	Jabil Circuit	8,000	3	USA	Electronics
19	Sumitomo Wiring Electric Systems	7,500	14	Japan	Electrical
20	Whirlpool	7,500	5	USA	Electronics
21	Kemet Corporation	7,005	5	USA	Electronics
22	Tyco International Ltd.	6,785	4	USA	Electronics, medical
23	A. O. Smith Corp.	6,598	8	USA	Electrical
24	Cardinal Health	6,500	5	USA	Medical
25	Flextronics Corp.	6,200	2	Singapore	Electronics
26	Sanmina-Sci	6,150	6	USA	Electronics
27	Motorola, Inc.	5,961	2	USA	Electronics
28	Sanyo North America Group	5,879	2	Japan	Electronics
29	Samsung	5,789	2	Korea	Electronics
30	Emerson Electrical Co.	5,678	7	USA	Electrical
31	Sanluis Rassini	5,030	4	Mexico	Automotive
32	Matsushita Electric Corp. of America	4,986	4	Japan	Electronics
33	Honeywell, Inc.	4,900	3	USA	Electronics

(continued)

Table 4.2. (*continued*)

No.	Company	Employees	Plants	Origin	Industrial Type
34	Daewoo Industrial Co.	4,856	3	Korea	Electronics
35	TRW Incorporation	4,554	11	USA	Automotive
36	Key Safety Systems	4,390	4	USA	Automotive
37	Bosch Group	4,320	7	USA	Automotive
38	Celestica, Inc.	4,150	5	Canada	Electronics
39	American Industries	4,138	22	Mexico	Shelter services
40	ITT Industries	3,845	4	USA	Automotive
41	LG Electronics	3,700	3	Korea	Electronics
42	Leviton Manufacturing	3,600	6	USA	Electrical
43	Johnson Controls, Inc.	3,589	7	USA	Automotive
44	Nova Link	3,549	8	Mexico	Shelter services
45	Am-Mex Products Co.	3,500	8	USA	Shelter services
46	Autoliv, Inc.	3,333	3	USA	Automotive
47	Molex	3,200	2	USA	Electronics
48	Trico Technologies	3,000	1	USA	Automotive
49	Scientific Atlanta Inc.	2,996	1	USA	Electronics
50	Plantronics, Inc.	2,855	1	USA	Electronics
51	Avery Dennison	2,830	2	USA	Office Products
52	Key Tronic Corp.	2,760	2	USA	Electronics
53	IBM	2,689	1	USA	Electronics
54	Ti Group Automotive	2,639	9	USA	Automotive
55	Hyundai Motor Co.	2,615	1	Korea	Automotive
56	Intermex Manufacturers	2,600	9	Mexico	Shelter services
57	Allied Signal Co.	2,589	4	USA	Automotive
58	Avx Corporation	2,587	2	USA	Electronics
59	Mattel, Inc.	2,578	1	USA	Toys
60	Skywork Solutions	2,400	1	USA	Semiconductors
61	Advance Transformer	2,387	3	USA/Holland	Electronics
62	Hamilton Proctor-Silex	2,331	3	USA	Appliances
63	Schlage de México	2,227	3	USA	Security
64	Tatung	2,200	1	Taiwan	Electronics
65	Yale de México	2,169	1	USA	Apparel
66	Avent	2,150	2	USA	Medical
67	Phelps Dodge Magnet	2,136	1	USA	Electrical
68	Eaton Corp.	2,113	2	USA	Automotive
69	EDS Manufacturing	2,100	1	USA	Electronics
70	VF Imagewear	2,100	2	USA	Apparel
71	Saturn Electronics & Engineering, Inc.	2,078	3	USA	Electronics

Table 4.2. (*continued*)

No.	Company	Employees	Plants	Origin	Industrial Type
72	Acco Brands, Inc.	2,063	2	USA	Stationery
73	Plamex	2,060	1	USA	Technology
74	Bose Corp.	2,050	2	USA	Electronics
75	Acustar, Inc.	2,003	1	Mexico	Automotive
76	National Processing	1,961	2	USA	Services
77	EDM International	1,948	2	USA	Services
78	Datamark, Inc.	1,865	2	USA	Electronics
79	Toshiba	1,780	1	Japan	Electronics
80	Irvin Industries, Inc.	1,633	2	USA	Automotive
81	Chamberlain Manufacturing	1,589	1	USA	Electrical
82	NCH Promotional Services	1,569	3	USA	Services
83	Coilcraft, Inc.	1,547	2	USA	Electronics
84	Cooper-Standard Automotive	1,520	3	USA	Automotive
85	Alpine Electronics	1,502	1	Japan	Electronics
86	Benchmark Electronics	1,500	1	USA	Electronics
87	Superior Industries International, Inc.	1,500	2	USA	Automotive
88	Sara Lee Corp.	1,489	2	USA	Apparel
89	Honda	1,450	1	Japan	Automotive
90	Invensys	1,420	6	USA	Electronics
91	Accuride International	1,355	2	USA	Steel Products
92	Strattec Security Corp.	1,300	1	USA	Automotive
93	Arvin Meritor	1,300	1	USA	Automotive
94	Automotive Safety Components International	1,250	2	USA	Automotive
95	Nokia	1,250	1	Finland	Electronics
96	Noma Appliance Electronic	1,235	2	Canada	Electronics
97	Plexus	1,211	1	USA	Electronics
98	Elcoteq Network Corp.	952	1	Finland	Electronics
99	Semtech Corp.	710	2	USA	Electronics
100	Mack Technologies	520	1	USA	Electronics

Source: Maquila Portal 2004, updated November 10, 2004.

lesson that Central American governments must learn when relying on FDI to stimulate domestic growth.

Although the special incentives offered to foreign companies as an enticement to move their manufacturing to Mexico have reduced the cost of doing business, they have crippled the infrastructure of the local border economies. Typically, corporations situated in rural towns or urban centers pay local property taxes and state income taxes that help finance the construction and maintenance of roads, bridges, sewers, water, public schools, public hospitals, and other public services. Unlike these corporations, the maquilas pay no property or state taxes, and they pay lower corporate taxes (6.5 percent compared to 30 percent).[5] The only taxes they pay are on the value added to the product by the worker, measured by their low wages. As a result, on one side of a road stands a maquila—a large cement structure with glass windows, a paved parking lot, electricity, and indoor plumbing—and on the other side of the road is a colonia—rough cardboard and wooden dwellings, dirt roads littered with trash, outhouses, and no electricity. This is how hundreds of thousands of people live (photos 10 and 11). The following description of Ciudad Juárez is representative of the dichotomy created by NAFTA.

> The U.S. corporations have built state-of-the-art manufacturing, assembly and packing plants in Juárez. Their Mexican partners have created modern industrial parks with huge truck parking facilities, powerful electric lights, and in some cases beautifully landscaped exteriors. The U.S. and Mexican governments and private industry have constructed superhighways, railroad tracks and terminals, and airports to serve the maquiladoras zone. . . . But the workers live in hovels, in shacks and shanties made of mud and the flotsam and jetsam of industrial production. Many of the streets remain unpaved, dusty and muddy, and some of the homes without running water, sewers or electricity. The schools have become over-crowded, rundown, and lacking in supplies, but in any case, many of the students don't go to school—they go to work. (La Botz 1999, 3)

Beneath these visual differences in working and living environments lie clashes of culture and work habits. Since the factories are foreign owned, the workers are exposed to another culture and are often asked to conform to cultural norms different from their own.[6] In the American-owned maquilas, the day begins and ends promptly, and tardiness or absences are penalized with fines. During a shift workers may not talk and must ask permission to use the bathroom. Workers are not permitted

Photo 10. Master Lock Maquila in Nogales.

Photo 11. The colonia Flores Magón in Nogales.

to bring their own lunch or snacks to work. They must work constantly and quickly during their shift, while standing the entire time. Having worked on a farm or for the family business, workers were accustomed to setting their own work schedules. Because of this work culture, they did not place the same value on promptness as their supervisors did. The work regimen of farming or a cottage industry, moreover, permitted conversation, bathroom breaks, occasional days off for illness, and flexible hours. There was not as much interdependence among workers, which gave workers more freedom. Many women like to bring their own meals to eat at work, because it is cheaper, it tastes better, it is a way to use leftovers, and it is something they like to eat. These new rules of the maquilas add yet another problem that might not have been present had the factory been owned by Mexicans. A similar factory regime was established in the nineteenth century by British factory owners: children toiled ten to twelve hours a day in the textile mills, and overseers of the Lowell boardinghouses worked the young women all day. A major difference was that they, their families, and their country benefited from the fruits of their labor until it was no longer necessary (or deemed appropriate) for them to work. Although maquila workers labor hours similar to those of their historical counterparts, they continue to starve, their families continue to be impoverished, and their country remains underdeveloped. Due to the peso crisis in 1995 and NAFTA, real wages for workers are well below their pre-NAFTA level. In 2003, nearly ten years after NAFTA, the Mexican government, moreover, estimated that over half of the population earns less than what is required to cover basic expenses (food, clothing, housing, health care, public transportation and education) (*Public Citizen* 2004, 2).

Production in Mexico versus Production in China

During the 1960s and 1970s the United States was suddenly competing with revitalized European and Japanese economies for a share of the world export market. Advances in communications (due to computers) and reductions in the costs of distribution (container ships and air travel) made it more profitable for Japan and parts of Europe to enter the global market. Profit rates for U.S. corporations plummeted from 15.5 percent in 1964–1966 to 10.1 percent in 1971–1974 to 4.5 percent in 1980 (Bluestone and Harrison 1982). American companies could respond in one of three ways: develop more efficient high-tech produc-

Table 4.3. Hourly Wage Rates in U.S. Dollars of McDonald's Cashier and Crew, 2000

Country	Wage in U.S. Dollars	Country	Wage in U.S. Dollars
Germany	5.33	Taiwan	2.20
Japan	7.33	Malaysia	1.59
United States	6.50	Indonesia	0.63
Canada	4.51	Thailand	0.57
United Kingdom	6.37	Philippines	0.56
Mexico	1.71[a]	China	0.55
Hong Kong	1.86	India	0.29
Singapore	2.31		

Source: Ashenfelter and Jurajda 2001, table 2.
[a]This level of compensation for Mexico is for the year 1999.

tion systems, support protectionist legislation against foreign competitors, or lower production costs by exporting labor-intensive operations abroad (22). Global outsourcing became profitable because of tariff reductions, foreign investment incentives, cheaper real-time communications, and cheaper transport. Free trade agreements such as GATT and NAFTA reduced tariffs and created export processing zones that offered tax exemptions and investment allowances for foreign direct investment. Advances in Internet-based software systems "made real-time information exchange possible and enabled just-in-time production and delivery coordination between producers and retailers on an international scale" (Oxfam 2004, 33). Reductions in sea freight costs of almost 70 percent between the 1980s and the mid-1990s as well as growth in air freight services decreased the cost of delivery across countries (33).

The Mexican maquiladoras kept corporate America competitive by lowering labor costs, distribution costs, custom duties, and corporate taxes. Motorola saved $4 million a year by moving from Phoenix to Nogales (NACLA 1979, 133). Wages were considerably lower in Mexico than in the United States (tables 4.3 and 4.4). A firm could save $30,000 per direct labor employee per year by hiring a worker in a maquila instead of a worker in a U.S. factory (Collectron n.d.). Multinationals producing in Mexico purchased their materials, components, and technology from the United States rather than from Far East suppliers if their plants were in China. Clearly, this would be cheaper than shipping raw

Table 4.4. Average Maquiladora Wages (includes benefits, direct labor only) (in U.S. dollars/hour)

1999	2000	2001	2002	2003	2004
$1.71	$1.88	$1.75	$1.79	$1.77	$1.82

Sources: Christman 2004, 5; IHS Global Insight, Inc.

materials and finished products between the United States and Asia. The multinationals could take advantage of several U.S. laws that encouraged companies to locate factories abroad. The Generalized System of Preferences (GSP) permitted duty-free imports of certain products from developing countries into the United States. This allowed U.S.-owned companies to assemble products in developing countries and ship them back into the United States without having to pay duties. In addition, since 1995 the Semiconductors Rule has permitted certain semiconductors to enter the United States duty-free from all countries that have the trade status of Most Favored Nations (Canada, Japan, France, and Mexico). This added another very important product used in many retail technologies (computers, cell phones, etc.) to be built by the cheaper foreign labor of Mexico. Finally, general tax incentives whereby corporations that pay income taxes to foreign governments can take a tax credit that permits them to subtract an equivalent amount from their U.S. corporate income taxes reduced taxable revenues in the United States. In addition, corporations can defer payments of U.S. income taxes on overseas profits until the profits enter the United States. This creates incentives for companies to shift operations abroad and reinvest their profits in foreign direct investment (Kamel 1990, 8–10).

In addition to the monetary incentives created by the BIP and NAFTA, there are other reasons U.S. companies set up assembly industries in Mexico. Despite the fact that wages in Mexico were double those in Asia in 1970, Mexico attracted large U.S. multinationals for geographic reasons and for diversification of their country risk. As Wilson points out in *Exports and Local Development* (1992), the proximity of Mexico to the United States lured U.S. firms that could not profit in Asia, small firms and firms whose products had low value-to-weight ratios (21). Although products that can be transported digitally may be more cheaply outsourced to China, heavier consumer durables are more costly because air transportation between the United States and China is more expensive than ground transportation between the United States and Mexico (Blinder 2006). Multinationals, moreover, did not want to locate all their plants in one area in case of social unrest or political instability and therefore put plants in Mexico to spread the risk (21). The advantages of locating within the "Asian tigers" gradually disappeared, and companies began to look to other countries to locate their plants. The low wage and an easily disciplined labor force disappeared as wage increases exceeded productivity and social unrest became rampant. Even government support could no longer guarantee cooperation of the workers (Wilson 1992, 30).

The BIP established the legal framework for promoting the creation of maquiladoras. A U.S. firm wanting to set up a maquiladora in Mexico has three options. It can set up a wholly owned Mexican subsidiary of a parent company such that the maquila in Mexico is owned by Mexicans, it can establish a joint venture with a Mexican partner, or it can use a shelter operation in which the foreign company or individual subcontracts with a Mexican company to assemble the goods and handle all the paperwork involving Mexican custom laws. In the latter case, the Mexican company is typically a full-time shelter operation, often with multiple foreign clients. A few examples of these are listed in table 4.2. The subcontractor recruits, hires, supervises, and pays the workers and deals with the Mexican government on all business-related issues.

Obviously, if the U.S. firm chooses the first option it has less control over the manufacturer in all realms of business: methods of production, purchase of raw materials and machinery, and recruitment, payment, and treatment of the workforce. At the same time the U.S. firm may perceive this loss of control as a lower commitment to stay with the subsidiary if problems arise. Given the nature of mobile manufacturing, a U.S. multinational can sever ties with one subsidiary in Mexico if conditions turn unfavorable and move operations to China almost overnight. The advantages of choosing this option would fall primarily to Mexicans and the Mexican economy. Since the plant would be Mexican owned, Mexican rules and laws would apply. Consequently, the Mexican managers, supervisors, and owners would reap the majority of the profits, which would help their families and local communities. Finally, the local economy where the plant is located will prosper from the fees and taxes collected.

The second option is likely to be the most difficult because it involves cooperation, sharing, and combining of different cultures. The advantages of this option are that each country shares liability in the event of failure and consequently shares an interest and commitment in the company's success. Specialization and improved efficiency is possible because the country and the firm are combining their expertise, skills, resources, and knowledge. On the other hand, there can be difficultly in combining different management styles from two countries with distinct cultures, dissimilar languages, and an antagonistic past. There may also be disputes regarding profit sharing. Was it the ingenuity of the product designer, the savvy of the marketing researcher, or the sweat of the worker that contributed most heavily to the profits?

In comparison to the first two, the third option is most popular when advantages and disadvantages are examined in light of the concerns of U.S. multinational interests. By using a subcontractor, the U.S. multinational has more control over costs, method of production, and profit margins. The multinational does not need to be an expert in Mexican law or know the local or national political scene; this is the responsibility of the subcontractor. This creates considerable distance between the employer and its employees, allowing multinationals to claim no responsibility for its own labor force. The firm does not hire, pay, or fire its workers. It has no contact with the laborers. Because it is working through a shelter company and does not own or lease a plant in Mexico, it can leave at any time. The corporations are interested in finding the most profitable contracts and have no location preference as long as costs are at a minimum. There are no loyalties to a country, a subcontractor, or a workforce under these new rules of mobile manufacturing. The disadvantages of this option fall mostly on the country where the work is being subcontracted, in this case Mexico. Workers are not directly connected to the U.S. company. The subcontracting arrangement by design breaks any sort of employer or employee relationship that could foster loyalty or goodwill between workers and the company. This disconnection can lead to lower productivity and higher absenteeism among workers and substandard working conditions and unfair labor contracts for the workers. Since the U.S. owners reap most of the profits from their company's success, the local Mexican economy will not benefit but actually suffer. The growing numbers of maquila workers put additional strain on the crumbling infrastructure and on the social services available at the border.

If the company uses a subcontractor or shelter service, the system is organized as illustrated by the pyramid in figure 4.1. The retailer places orders with a brand-name manufacturer. The brand-name manufacturer uses a subcontractor to get products made. The subcontractor recruits,

Figure 4.1. New model of manufacturing. The material is adapted by the publisher from *Trading Away Our Rights: Women Working in Global Supply Chains*, 2004, with the permission of Oxfam GB, Oxfam House, John Smith Drive, Cowley, Oxford OX4 2JY UK www.oxfam.org.uk. Oxfam GB does not necessarily endorse any text or activities that accompany the materials, nor has it approved the adapted text.

hires, and pays workers. In this supply chain the retailers and brand owners want lower prices from producers, fast and flexible production, high technical and quality standards, and better labor conditions (without making a long-term commitment to that supplier) (Oxfam 2004, 35). In attempting to meet these demands, the subcontractors keep labor costs low by hiring women and migrants and using short-term contracts to evade benefits, thereby putting workers under excessive pressure by establishing unreasonable production quotas, undermining unions, and hiding labor rights violations (35). Many retailers and brands, especially the popular discount warehouses such as Wal-Mart and Sam's Club, are constantly in search of lower costs, better quality, and faster delivery. By making short-term commitments, they can switch to a new producer that offers a better deal. Consequently, competition between subcontractors for business drives workers' wages down. Labor rights groups have blamed global competition for severely compromising the position of the worker at the bottom of the pyramid:

> In many countries, competitive bidding by these contractors for work drives contract prices down so low that they cannot pay minimum wages or overtime to their workers. In fact, in today's garment industry, very little competitive bidding takes place. Most contractors are put in a "take it or leave it" position and must accept whatever low price is given to them or see the work placed elsewhere. The contractors must "sweat" profits out of their workers, cut corners, and operate unsafe workplaces. (Sweatshop Watch 2001, 3)

Except for sewing labels on clothing or stamping products with company logos, workers are completely removed from the brand-name manufacturer. It is this distance and disconnection that allows the companies to rightfully claim that they do not have resident Mexicans on their payroll. The workers at the bottom end up insecure about the length of their employment, exhausted by long hours and high production quotas, and powerless to argue for their rights (Oxfam 2004, 35).

The Right to Organize: Unions in Maquiladoras

According to Article 357 of Ley Federal del Trabajo (LFT) each plant is allowed to have a union to ensure workers' rights and represent workers in disputes with management. The companies operating the maquilas along the border, however, have managed to create obstacles to organizing. According to Kamel (1990, 42), "Only a small minority of maquiladoras—perhaps as few as 10 percent—are unionized. In Tijuana, Mexicali, Nogales, and Ciudad Juárez, where most maquiladoras are located, there are few if any unions." The companies in Matamoros, Reynosa, and Piedras Negras have created "phantom unions" that protect the companies from strikes or uprisings. These unions are well known among both the employers and the employees who work in the maquilas. Most unions are under an umbrella organization called the Congress of Labor (Congreso del Trabajo [CT]):

> During August 1991, the CT confirmed its direct relationship with the government party in a document called the Political Agreement between the PRI and the Organization of the CT. The CT, considered the labor sector of the PRI, consists of more than thirty organizations encompass-

ing 85 percent of the unionized workforce. In the early 1990s, Mexico has an estimated 9.5 million unionized workers. The CT mediates between the labor unions and the government. At the same time, it provides the state with a formal mechanism for political manipulation of the labor force.[7]

The largest union, the Confederación de Trabajadores Mexicanos (CTM), was founded in 1936 and comprises over 11,000 labor unions with more than five million members.[8] Most of the members of the CTM are affiliated with the PRI. They are large landowners who wield economic and political power. The CTM supports the growth of the maquila industry and "cooperates with local officials and manufacturers to maintain a labor climate that is attractive to investors" (Kamel 1990, 42). The next largest organization in the CT is the Federación de Sindicatos de Trabajadores al Servicio del Estado (FSTSE), which was established in 1938 and is the association of unions for the federal civil system and other government-related organizations. The third largest labor union within the CT is the Confederación Revolucionaria de Obreros y Campesinos (CROC), which was founded in 1952 and had a membership of 600,000 during the 1990s.[9] Other important labor organizations are the Confederación Regional de Obreros Mexicanos (CROM); Federación Nacional de Sindicatos Independientes (FNSI); Confederación de Trabajadores y Campesinos (CTC); Movimiento Proletario Internacional (MPI); Confederación de Obreros Revolucionarios (COR); Confederación General de Trabajadores (CGT); Frente Auténtico del Trabajo (FAT); and the Confederación Revolucionaria de Trabajadores (CRT).[10] Another enemy of the workers is the government's arbitrator, Juntas Locales de Conciliación y Arbitraje (JLCA). Instead of mediating and resolving conflicts between companies and workers, it prevents labor negotiations in cases of collective bargaining and the registration of unions (CorpWatch 1999).

Many of the largest factories in Nogales have signed contracts, called "Company Union" contracts, with the CTM. The CTM, however, does not represent them or allow genuine collective bargaining. Rather it aligns itself with management and protects maquiladora owners from other labor unions and grassroots organizers (Cravey 1998, 87). As Avery Wear aptly puts it:

Today, as is typical of "global assembly line" sweatshops throughout developing countries, no authentic unions hold contracts in the maquiladoras. Rather, many maquiladoras operate under the "protection contract" system. In this system, plant owners sign "union" contract with Mexico's government-tied union federations—the CTM, the CROC, or the COR without knowledge of the workers. Known as charro unions in Mexico, after the autocratic and conservative leaders who rule them, these federations operate openly, and sometime even lead real struggles, in some parts of Mexico. But in the maquiladoras, they are strictly at the service of the employers. "We call the official unions in the maquiladoras *sindicatos blancos* [white unions]. They are worse than the charro unions—they are like no union at all," says ex-maquiladora worker Mauricio Higinio. (2002, 3)

It is essential for maquila workers to have access to unions because there is tremendous room for worker exploitation since employers are foreigners, workers are not educated, and the government has been plagued with corruption for over half a century. In addition, many women are hired by the multinational companies because they can be paid less than men, are naturally docile, are less educated, and will tolerate monotonous jobs of assembly work (Kamel 1990, 11). Therefore, an independent union is essential to educate the women and protect their rights under law.

There are several independent labor organizations that have been established specifically to help the maquila workers—some formal *sindicatos* (unions) and others informal *grupos* (groups). These organizations are staffed largely by volunteers who go house-to-house educating female workers about their rights under the federal law and asking if they are having problems with their employers (e.g., injuries with no disability, firing with no severance pay, or payment withheld for two weeks). Other staff members are paid a small salary on a part-time basis for maintaining an office and sending representatives out to the colonias to inform workers about their rights and sign them up for free workshops on occupational safety, Mexican federal labor law, and workers' obligations. La Coalición Pro Justicia en las Maquiladoras (CJM), a trinational organization of religious leaders, laborers, environmentalists, and women's groups, was established in 1989.[11] Its mission is to help the maquila workers and the communities on the border to improve their working conditions (*para mejorar sus condiciones de trabajo*), establish a healthy work environment (*establecer un ambiente saludable*), and a just standard of living (*un nivel de vida justo*) (CJM 2003). In Nogales and Agua Prieta female maquila workers sought help from the women of the Alianza Fronteriza de Obreros (AFO), an independent union first organized in Agua Prieta in 1996 and expanded to Nogales in 2001. A few of the other independent labor groups are Centro de Trabajadores y Comunidades (CETRAC) in Nuevo Laredo, Derechos Obreros y Democracia Sindical (DODS) in Reynosa, and Trabajadores/as de DURO in Rió Bravo. It is an uphill battle for these organizations because if companies find out that their workers have signed a petition to join the union they are immediately fired. Herein lies one of the major problems for the maquila workers: the union that exists in the plant does not represent their interests, and it is almost impossible[12] to form an independent union that will protect their rights and see that the labor laws are followed. If workers are unable to help themselves, who will protect their rights and enforce the labor laws?

CHAPTER 5

Are the Maquilas Sweatshops?

Proponents of NAFTA argued that the growing maquila industry in Mexico would help the country industrialize by providing jobs for thousands of Mexicans.[1] They believed that foreign direct investment by multinationals in the free trade zones would increase capital. The factories built with this capital would create new jobs and increase labor productivity, which would lead to higher wages. Critics of NAFTA, however, worried that workers' rights would be violated.[2] They focused instead on the dangers of outsourcing, believing that the multinationals' search for lower production costs and the Mexican government's desire to attract foreign capital would place workers in a precarious position. Mexican workers would have to compete with workers in other developing countries such as India and China where labor is even cheaper. They would be caught in a "race to the bottom" as wages and benefits were reduced to attract and keep multinationals. These two paths lead to extremely different outcomes for the workers and the country. Thus, in order to discern which reality exists at the border, it is necessary to examine the behavior of the multinationals. The questions I want to ask are the following: How are workers treated in the maquilas? Do maquilas offer good jobs with decent pay? Do multinationals obey the labor laws established by NAFTA?

As responsible global citizens in this world, we must be certain that American companies are not mistreating workers or violating basic human rights. But what standards or laws should we hold American companies to, American or Mexican? Skeptics argue that it is wrong to apply American standards to operations in other countries because their culture and political environment are dramatically different from those of the United States. What may be wrong or illegal in the United States may be a custom in Mexico. My aim here is not to tackle the philosophical question regarding which set of rules apply to companies that out-source. Instead, I want to document how workers are treated in foreign-owned maquilas. Consequently, I use the standards set by NAFTA and the Mexican government to evaluate the behavior of the multinationals with respect to workers' rights. The examination of evidence on work-ing hours, working conditions, and pay from the women's surveys reveal if multinationals are meeting the labor standards established by law.

Globalization and free trade have made goods and services produced in one country available for purchase in another. Consumers benefit be-cause they enjoy a greater variety of products and often pay less for the foreign-produced goods than domestically produced goods. Although the majority of consumers appear to be most interested in how much a product costs, there are consumers who care about how it was made. In the 1990s news stories surfaced about children sewing clothes in Bangla-desh for Wal-Mart, children stitching soccer balls in Pakistan for Nike, and children making children's pajamas in Haiti for Disney (Elliott and Freeman 2003, 111–115, 128).[3] Charles Kernaghan, an activist from the National Labor Committee, was relentless in his quest to expose multinationals that are exploiting workers. In 2004 Wal-Mart was ac-cused of employing children to make toys in China to be sold in the United States (National Labor Committee n.d.). As consumers of goods produced in Mexico, we are contributing to the profits of these multi-nationals when we purchase a toy or telephone *hecho en México*, made in Mexico. If multinationals are breaking labor laws in Mexico we as con-sumers are implicitly condoning their behavior. If American companies are mistreating workers and breaking the labor laws, then they are in fact operating sweatshops along the Mexico-U.S. border. A sweatshop, ac-cording to the U.S. General Accounting Office, is defined as a place of work that violates more than one labor law of the country in which it is located. Examples of labor laws that are often violated by employers are minimum age laws, minimum wage laws, maximum hour laws, overtime restrictions, provision of safety equipment, and distribution of benefits. Sweatshops can be large or small and are found in industrialized coun-tries as well as developing countries. They are usually detectable only in the formal economy.

NAFTA

Fifteen years after the passage of NAFTA the reality for both the United States and Mexico has been quite different from what was predicted.

Although multinationals were able to employ cheap labor to produce competitively priced goods in the global market, many working-class Americans have lost their jobs as factories closed and operations moved south. Despite creating hundreds of thousands of jobs along the border in maquiladoras, the Mexican economy has not grown substantially and the workers' standard of living has deteriorated. The new technology utilized in the maquiladoras is primarily labor-intensive. The transition to capital-intensive technology is necessary to prevent the maquilization of Mexico and to improve workers' standard of living. Capital-intensive technology requires higher skill levels and higher productivity, which is rewarded with higher wages. Mexican businesses, moreover, have not benefited from the growth of the maquila industry because the multinational companies continue to buy the majority of their raw materials, intermediate goods, and machinery from the United States.

NAFTA was a Mexican initiative designed to create a North American trade bloc that could compete globally with the European Common Market and the emerging markets of China. It was the first trade agreement of its kind, between a developing country and developed countries. This meant there was considerable asymmetry between Mexico and the United States and implied that Mexico had more to gain. As Cameron and Tomlin concluded:

> Mexico gains access to a massive market of 265 million people with an
> average per capita income of $27,000; in return the United States gets
> access to Mexico's smaller market of slightly over 90 million people with
> a per capita income of less than $7,000. Clearly, Mexico would have
> to do something to make the deal worthwhile for the United States.
> (2000, 225)

As the price of oil fell in the world market, the Mexican government recognized the need to develop other markets in the United States to sustain its export-led economic growth. The newly elected president of Mexico (1988–1994), Carlos Salinas de Gortari, made trade liberalization the centerpiece of his economic reforms. By spearheading NAFTA, Salinas went forward with the opening of the Mexican economy that his predecessor, Miguel de la Madrid Hurtado, had begun (Ganster and Lorey 2008, 188). Eager to attract foreign investment, Salinas pushed forward Mexico's membership in GATT and approached several European countries at the World Economic Forum in Davos, Switzerland, to consider doing business in Mexico. Unsuccessful, Salinas turned his efforts to establishing a bilateral free trade agreement with the United States.

He wanted to negotiate the pact as an effort to relieve the debt crisis and end economic hardship for millions of Mexicans by establishing closer ties with Washington. Salinas identified the opportunities for Mexico in attracting foreign investment and new technology and increasing employment. These jobs, whether in foreign- or Mexican-owned factories, would raise the incomes and standard of living of millions of Mexicans.

As a strong proponent of free trade U.S. President George H. W. Bush was receptive to the idea and made securing NAFTA a priority. Bush realized that "Mexico's ability to use its oil resources effectively and sustain a rapid growth rate in its economy [would] depend on its ability to expand non-oil exports to the United States" (Orme 1996, 38–39). He hoped to gain access to Mexico's oil and financial sector to reduce U.S. dependence on oil controlled by OPEC and give U.S. banks, investment firms, and insurance companies access to Mexican financial markets. Bush also recognized the advantage for other American businesses in employing cheaper labor for the production of U.S. goods and in gaining access to additional consumers willing to buy them.[4] President Bush believed free trade with Mexico would pull the U.S. economy out of its recession and secure his reelection. NAFTA appeared from the outset to be a win-win situation: both Mexico and the United States would prosper.[5]

The politics of NAFTA are unique because in the end it was a bipartisan agreement. It was developed by a Republican administration (George H. W. Bush) and passed and implemented by a Democratic administration (Bill Clinton). Interestingly, despite this bipartisanship neither party was enthusiastic about its passage, nor was the American public. Selling NAFTA to Congress and the public was much more difficult than the Bush administration had imagined. As the 1992 presidential campaign began in the United States, the agreement was portrayed by Bush as a massive domestic job creation plan. Believing the opposite would occur, Clinton reluctantly supported NAFTA in a campaign speech, hoping to appease the business community without annoying the unions. After the election the fate of NAFTA was uncertain and in the hands of a unified government, with Democrats controlling Congress and the White House. President Clinton was modestly pro-NAFTA and had to sell the agreement to an overwhelmingly protectionist (anti-NAFTA) Congress. Consequently, Clinton chose to minimize the effect of NAFTA on jobs in the United States and emphasize that its ratification was necessary to ensure both the economic stability of Mexico and the continued implementation of sound policy and governmental reforms on the part of that nation's leadership (Orme 1996, 54–55). Despite these arguments, the Clinton administration believed the vote would be a cliff-hanger, and there was an "unprecedented effort by the business community, the Mexican embassy in the United States, and other advocates to ensure NAFTA's passage (Hufbauer and Goodrich 2004, 41).

The North American Agreement on Labor Cooperation

NAFTA passed by a final vote of 234 to 200 in the House. It was viewed as the means to turn Mexico into a first world country. It has been identified as one of the greatest free trade agreements—an opportunity for investment, technology, and goods and services of neighboring countries to cross borders and create one common market. The document is approximately 406 pages and primarily contains information on which tariffs would be eliminated for a particular good and when it would happen. The removal of tariffs would reduce transaction costs, making it cheaper for Mexico, Canada, and the United States to export and import goods and services among themselves. The language was especially cumbersome because details had to be carefully spelled out. The movement of labor across borders and workers' rights, however, are absent from the historic agreement. Instead, the issue of labor rights is addressed in a much shorter (approximately forty-eight-page) companion agreement called the North American Agreement on Labor Cooperation (NAALC). This companion agreement, passed one year prior to NAFTA, was devoted entirely to labor and establishing labor standards. Responding to disgruntled Democrats in Congress, newly elected President Clinton insisted that two side agreements must be signed before he would consider NAFTA. One of these tackled environmental issues (the North American Agreement on Environmental Cooperation [NAAEC]), and the other, NAALC, addressed labor issues connected to free trade with Mexico and Canada.

In the NAALC negotiations, the United States wanted to create higher international standards, while Mexico and Canada preferred to retain their own existing labor laws. The United States compromised and agreed to "mutually recognize" each country's domestic labor laws as the relevant standard. As a result the objectives of the NAALC are to

a) improve working conditions and living standards in each Party's territory; b) promote to the maximum extent possible, the labor principles set out in Annex 1 [see box 5.1]; c) encourage cooperation to promote

BOX 5.1. LABOR PRINCIPLES OF NORTH AMERICAN AGREEMENT ON LABOR COOPERATION

The following are guiding principles that the Parties are committed to promote, subject to each Party's domestic law, but do not establish common minimum standards for their domestic law. They indicate broad areas of concern where the Parties have developed, each in its own way, laws, regulations, procedures and practices that protect the rights and interests of their respective workforces.

1. Freedom of association and protection of the right to organize

The right of workers exercised freely and without impediment to establish and join organizations of their own choosing to further and defend their interests.

2. The right to bargain collectively

The protection of the right of organized workers to freely engage in collective bargaining on matters concerning the terms and conditions of employment.

3. The right to strike

The protection of the right of workers to strike in order to defend their collective interests.

4. Prohibition of forced labor

The prohibition and suppression of all forms of forced or compulsory labor, except for types of compulsory work generally considered acceptable by the Parties, such as compulsory military service, certain civic obligations, prison labor not for private purposes and work exacted in cases of emergency.

5. Labor protection for children and young persons

The establishment of restrictions on the employment of children and young persons that may vary taking into consideration relevant factors likely to jeopardize the full physical, mental and moral development of young persons, including schooling and safety requirements.

6. Minimum employment standards

The establishment of minimum employment standards, such as minimum wages and overtime pay, for wage earners, including those not covered by collective agreements.

(continued)

7. Elimination of employment discrimination

Elimination of employment discrimination on such grounds as race, religion, age, sex or other grounds, subject to certain reasonable exceptions, such as, where applicable, *bona fide* occupational requirements or qualifications and established practices or rules governing retirement ages, and special measures of protection or assistance for particular groups designed to take into account the effects of discrimination.

8. Equal pay for women and men

Equal wages for women and men by applying the principle of equal pay for equal work in the same establishment.

9. Prevention of occupational injuries and illnesses

Prescribing and implementing standards to minimize the causes of occupational injuries and illnesses.

10. Compensation in cases of occupational injuries and illnesses

The establishment of a system providing benefits and compensation to workers or their dependents in cases of occupational injuries, accidents or fatalities arising out of, linked with, or occurring in the course of employment.

11. Protection of migrant workers

Providing migrant workers in a Party's territory with the same legal protection as the Party's nationals in respect of working conditions.

Source: The United States Department of Labor, The North American Agreement on Labor Cooperation, 1993, 38–40.

---

innovation and rising levels of productivity and quality; d) encourage publication and exchange of information, data development and coordination, and joint studies to enhance mutually beneficial understanding of the laws and institutions governing labor in each Party's territory; e) pursue cooperative labor-related activities on the basis of mutual benefit; f) promote compliance with, and effective enforcement by each Party of, its labor law and; g) foster transparency in the administration of labor law. (U.S. Department of Labor 1993, 3)

The objectives of NAALC were written with the welfare of workers in mind. Rather than focus on commercial and financial flows between countries, the Agreement articulates basic worker rights to work in a safe environment, receive a decent wage, and organize collectively when these rights are violated. The idea that the free trade agreement should "improve working conditions and living standards" ensures that workers will have better working conditions and be paid higher wages than they currently earn. At the heart of the agreement are the eleven principles listed in box 5.1. Based on these principles, the worker should be treated fairly, paid reasonably, and protected from exploitation. Since these objectives and principles pertain to employment in the formal economy, violations should be highly visible, making enforcement easier.

Although the principles are commendable, the agreement contains numerous structural flaws that render it ineffective. First, the NAALC fails to establish common minimum standards for labor. Reflecting the wishes of Mexico and Canada, the preamble, presented in box 5.1, states: "The following are guiding principles that the Parties are committed to promote, subject to each Party's domestic law, but do not establish common minimum standards for their domestic law" (U.S. Department of Labor 1993, 38). Instead, the labor principles are meant as guidelines that yield to each country's established labor laws when differences occur. Consequently, it is entirely within the letter of the law for workers in the United States to work a forty-hour week and workers in Mexico to work a fifty-hour week. In addition, overtime and overtime pay can be handled differently in Mexico than in the United States. This implies that it will be necessary to go beyond NAALC and review the labor laws of Mexico to determine whether the maquilas are sweatshops.

The second major flaw is that the system of enforcement is decentralized and the punishment for violators weak. The head of the Canadian Labor Congress, Bob White, called it a "tooth-less tiger" (Cameron and Tomlin 2000, 202). Unlike the trilateral enforcement mechanism created for the environmental agreement, the labor accord did not create a board or committee to process complaints or settle disputes if there were violations. Instead there are three separate and autonomous national offices to hear complaints. No one person or group is responsible or held accountable for ensuring the standards are adhered to by companies in each country. A country does not have to create a new judicial system because of NAALC, as clearly stated in Article 5(7): "Nothing in this Article shall be construed to require a Party to establish, or to prevent a Party from establishing, a judicial system for the enforcement of its labor law distinct from its system for the enforcement of laws in general" (U.S. Department of Labor 1993, 6). If a complaint is brought to one of the national offices, no sanctions or fines were established to deter or penalize violators. Hufbauer and Goodrich's (2004, 47) assessment of the dispute process casts considerable doubt that workers' rights will be protected: "Dispute proceeding under the labor side agreement are essentially a waste of time. There are no common standards, administrative barriers create serious difficulties, and potential remedies are very weak."

Third, there are no penalties for violators. In contrast to the NAAEC, violators of one or more of the labor principles do not face fines or sanctions. Although there is a detailed section on the resolution of disputes, that portion of the agreement goes into effect only when one country brings a complaint against another. Workers are not permitted to bring forth complaints but must appeal to their government officials to do so on their behalf. Even then, the implementation of any recommendations made to the violating nation is left to that nation's government, with a vague set of consequences applied if responsibilities are shirked. In the case of Mexico, the government and the most powerful union at the time, CTM, opposed U.S. or Canadian interference in their industrial relations. Cameron and Tomlin (2000) argue that official labor unions in Mexico liked the resulting labor accord because it did not challenge their privileged position within Mexico's corporatist system. Not surprisingly, Mexico has not filed any complaints on behalf of its maquiladora workers. On the other hand, labor unions and workers' rights groups in the United States have been successful in filing complaints:

> Only the U.S. NAO has pursued complaints against maquiladoras. . . .
> [T]hese complaints have served to call public attention to these problems in certain maquiladoras. The Mexican government, for its part, uses the mechanisms created under NAALC, such as public hearings or workshops . . . as a smokescreen, seeking to create the impression internationally that it is enforcing its own labor laws. Real maquila workers, however, are not invited to these events. (CFO 1999, 4)

Mexican Labor Laws

Since the NAALC lacks an enforcement mechanism, employers planning to move operations to Mexico must familiarize themselves with Mexican laws. The labor laws in Mexico set especially high standards for the treatment of both male and female workers. The Mexican Constitution of 1917 established the labor laws that are still in effect today. Mexican Federal Labor Law (LFT) regulates employee relationships in Mexico regardless of nationality or place of entry into the employment agreement. It regulates labor contracts, minimum wages, employee benefits, and union activity within Mexico. Unlike U.S. labor laws, those in Mexico are extensive in their coverage but specific in their provisions. Because of this there is very little room for misinterpretation. The labor laws cover four main areas of the work relationship: (1) mandatory employee benefits, (2) trade unions, (3) severance payments, and (4) employers' withholding obligations. Within each area there are a number of requirements placed on employers (box 5.2). A company is obligated to honor these regulations for all its employees, with or without a written contract.

There are a large number of employee benefits that are mandatory. Although wages are lower in comparison to the United States, benefits can substantially add to labor costs. Employers must pay workers at least the minimum wage as well as an overtime wage of twice the normal wage. In addition to their weekly wages, workers are paid annually a portion of the company's profits (10 percent), a Christmas bonus, a holiday premium, and a pension. Workers must receive nine days off a year with pay. Women are entitled to paid maternity leave of at least twelve weeks. Workers are not supposed to work more than forty-eight hours a week or eight hours a day, and overtime must not exceed nine hours a week. Most of the benefits workers receive are monetary; a few, however, such as training and safety, are nonmonetary.

The right to unionize was initially established in the constitution and has been reinforced in Mexican labor law. Workers have the right to unionize if there are more than twenty employees in the company. This implies that workers in the majority of maquilas may join a union. It is therefore illegal to fire a worker who has shown interest in or has signed up for a union. Unions can bargain collectively for their workers, and their contracts must be renegotiated every two years. Unions also have the right to strike during negotiations or encourage a slowdown on the production line. According to www.mexconnect.com, which publishes "Doing Business in Mexico," unions are popular and powerful. Under the subhead "Unions" the guide states, "If you are planning to hire Mexican workers, you must be prepared to deal with labor unions (*sindicatos*). Unions are an important and highly politicized component of the labor market that are especially strong within the public and indus-

BOX 5.2. MEXICAN LABOR LAWS

1. Mandatory Employee Benefits

- Workers receive 10% of the employer's pretax profit.
- Workers receive a Christmas bonus equal to at least 15 days' wages.
- Workers receive nine paid legal holidays each year.
- Workers receive an annual paid holiday of six working days after one full year of working.
- Workers must not work on 1/1, 2/5, 3/21, 9/16, 11/20, and 12/25.
- Employers must provide training.
- Employers must contribute to the Federal Workers Housing Fund (INFONAVIT).
- Employees must be paid a minimum wage with deductions on a weekly basis.
- Maximum number of work hours is 48 hours per week.
- First nine hours of overtime must be paid at 200 percent and anything over nine hours, 300 percent.
- Employers should provide a safe and sanitary environment for workers.
- Fully paid maternity leave of six weeks prior to and six weeks after the delivery date.
- Employers must pay 2 percent of the wage base to the Retirement Savings System (SAR).
- Schedule—day shifts are eight hours long, night shifts are seven hours long.
- Overtime cannot exceed shifts by more than three hours daily or three days a week.

2. Trade Unions

- Employees may unionize in any firm with more than 20 employees.
- Union contracts must be renegotiated every two years.
- Unions can strike or slow down production.

3. Severance Payments

- Employers may not dismiss employees without cause. Otherwise the employer must make the following payments (three months' salary, 20 days of salary for each year worked, a seniority premium equal to 12 days salary per year, back salary from the date of dismissal and accrued benefits).

4. Employer's Withholding Obligations

- All employers must register their employees in the IMSS (Mexican Social Security Institute)—Employees pay 5.25 percent and employer pays 17.7 percent.

- If workers earn minimum wage, the employer makes the entire IMSS contribution.
- No social security or income tax deductions for workers earning minimum wage.

Source: NAFTA Office of Mexico in Canada n.d.

---

trial sectors. The constitution and the LFT both favor unionization. Approximately 30 percent of the Mexican work force is unionized, about twice the U.S. rate" (Mexconnect n.d.b).

Workers are protected from unjustified firings and must be compensated accordingly. The third component of the labor law describes conditions under which workers can be fired and the severance payments that are required. The law forbids companies from freely dismissing employees without "just cause." It clearly outlines the employer's financial responsibility in terminating the work relationship. Employers who dismiss a worker for no specific reason must pay the worker three months salary, accrued benefits, twenty days of salary for each year of service, twelve days of salary per year, and back salary from the date of dismissal. Companies are not required to pay severance if the employee is fired because of immoral conduct, repeated absenteeism, unreasonable refusal to follow directions, or disclosure of trade secrets (considered "just cause"). The labor relationship between employer and employee may be terminated without either party being liable if there is mutual agreement of both sides; death of the employee; termination of the job; or the physical or mental incapacity of the employee.

The final component of the labor law covers the employer and employee obligations for withholdings from weekly pay. Employers are required to make deductions for social security and income taxes from the worker's paycheck. Both the employer and employee make contributions to the Mexican Social Security Institute (IMSS), which pays for medical expenses, disability, unemployment insurance, and retirement. Employers contribute 17.7 percent, and employees contribute 5.25 percent of their salaries to IMSS unless they earn the minimum wage. In the latter case employers cannot withhold social security contributions or income tax from their paychecks. If they earn above the minimum wage, employers are to withhold taxes according to the Income Tax Law (LISR) and pay the Mexican tax authorities on a monthly basis.

Factories, Dark Satanic Mills, or Sweatshops?

Mexican labor laws are clear and well established. Employers choosing to operate plants in Mexico and hire Mexicans to work in the plants are bound by them. American consumers, workers, stockholders, and politicians most likely expect that American companies—wherever they have production facilities—are law-abiding. Is this the case? What if some of the American companies are violating Mexican laws and treating workers poorly? Below I compare and contrast conditions in the maquilas as documented by the 620 women interviewed. The evidence presented provides a contemporary look at the physical conditions as well as the working environment. Given this complete view of the maquilas, we can discern whether U.S. multinationals have created factories, dark satanic mills, or sweatshops along the border.

The free trade zone, or "production corridor," puts foreign-owned factories in close proximity to each other and to the U.S. border. Almost all the maquiladoras in Nogales are located in two industrial parks. The roads leading to each park are public and do not prevent someone from stopping, looking, and photographing the exteriors. In most cases, however, this is as close as the public can get: tall fences and barbed wire enclose the factories. The entrances are gated and guarded by security personnel. The Old Industrial Park, in downtown Nogales near the train station, was developed in the late sixties and contains small maquilas. In 1968 Motorola was the first multinational company to locate assembly operations in Nogales. The buildings are cinder block or cement and have no windows. The owners of the companies that subcontract with the maquilas rent the land, which makes it easier for them to shut down and leave when conditions become unfavorable.

The New Industrial Park is located near the border but on the outskirts of town on a major road leading to Hermosillo. The buildings are large colorful structures constructed of glass and metal, with many windows at the front but unrelieved cement walls at the back and sides. High steel fences surround the buildings, and the entrances are guarded. Although the owners of the companies in this industrial park own the land, suggesting a long-term commitment, there is still considerable turnover. In the short time that I lived in Nogales, I witnessed two major plant closings, and in subsequent visits I have noticed new nameplates on the existing buildings.

Do these maquilas resemble the dark satanic mills of nineteenth-century Britain? Are the workers in the maquilas the modern-day version of the child laborers who toiled for ten hours a day in hot, stuffy, poorly lit cotton textile mills? I first address these questions using personal observation of the inside and outside of several maquilas. During the four and a half months that I lived in Nogales and participated in the BorderLinks program, I toured four maquiladoras with student groups. Although we were not allowed to take photos inside the factories, I kept detailed field notes of each tour and asked a number of questions at the end of each. This information gives us our first glimpse into the lives of the Mexican women working in the maquilas.

I visited Jeld Wen de México in the Old Industrial Park on March 24, 2004. This plant is called "Summit" by locals and everyone who works there because its affiliate company was located in Summit, Arizona. It employs between 50 and 100 people, only five of them women. It is a two-story cinderblock building with no windows and a front and back entrance. Like most plants in the Old Industrial Park, there were no fences or guards, but the doors were locked. At this plant the workers assemble doors, glass windows, sliding glass doors, and single- and double-pane windows. It had been in operation for nine years. The supervisor explained that most of the employees were men because the work was strenuous and making some of the doors required height. The plant was very clean (the workers were responsible for cleaning their own area once a week), well lit, properly ventilated, and a comfortable temperature. The workers did not have to wear uniforms but did have different colored jackets to identify what area they worked in. Most of the workers stood all day, but a few had stools to lean on. As we walked around the assembly line the only noise you could hear was the humming of the machines; the workers did not talk to one another. They wore safety goggles and thick jackets to prevent injury from cut glass. It was a labor-intensive process, and when asked why the company did not use more technology the supervisor replied, "It was cheaper to use more labor."

I visited the Steward maquiladora in the Old Industrial Park on April 16, 2004. It is a brick one-story building with no windows and a front and back entrance. The factory was not surrounded by a fence or gate, but a guard was posted in the back near the only door. The manager who gave us the tour remarked that it was one of the oldest maquilas in Nogales and that there was a plant in Tucson for storing the inventory. The company's headquarters is in Chattanooga, Tennessee, and it also has plants in China, Scotland, and Singapore. In Nogales the plant assembles motherboards for Ford, GM, Chrysler, Compaq, IBM, and

Hewlett Packard. It employs between 300 and 350 workers between the ages of twenty and forty, most of them women. The manager said that the United States provides all the inputs; 40 percent of their products are sold to the United States and 50 percent to Asia. Steward was among the first multinationals to arrive in Nogales. As we entered the plant, the manager pointed out that employees work with minerals, not chemicals, and that the "production process produces no toxic waste." He commented that the work is hard on the eyes and back, especially when the pieces are inspected. One of the main rooms was hot and smelled of metal, but it was clean. Many workers used gloves and wore glasses in the first room, but very few wore masks or earplugs in the second room. As we walked around the assembly line we saw a number of drums containing chemicals that released an oily odor. Chromium was used to polish the materials, which is hazardous for workers touching or inhaling it without protective gear. The toxic material containing chromium was shipped to the United States for disposal (as dictated by NAFTA). In a few areas the workers had music playing. In most areas the machines were so loud it was almost impossible to hear the tour guide. The manager was proud to list the benefits the workers received: free breakfast and lunch, food coupons, transportation, and a wage of 150 pesos a day. He remarked that the going market rate was 100 pesos a day. When asked if this was enough to live on comfortably, he replied honestly, "No, this is not much. I play baseball with many of the workers, and I know they spend 90 percent of their salary on food." The manager said that workers receive a ninety-day contract and if they are productive will receive a permanent contract. He said that some workers had been there more than five years and that roughly 4 percent leave after receiving their Christmas bonus. He told us that he was on a U.S. payroll and paid in U.S. dollars, not pesos like the assembly workers.

A female human resources employee at the maquila Osborn International in the New Industrial Park was extremely proud of the company's relationship with its workers. The company was built twelve years ago in Nogales to make industrial brushes of all sizes. It is a smaller maquila that employs up to fifty people at any given time. During the tour on April 14, 2004, our guide spent considerable time describing the annual company parties and field trips paid for by management. On Mother's Day and Children's Day the company hosts a party with food and games for all the workers. She said that this maquila was clean and operated according to a Japanese system that rewarded cleanliness and quality. We were not allowed to see this for ourselves, however, because we were not permitted in the plant, on the grounds that it was "too noisy." Instead operations and contracts with workers were described to us in the lunch-room. She felt the benefits were quite generous and believed they went beyond what the law required. The workers at Osborn regularly worked ten hours and fifteen minutes Monday through Friday but had recently put in a lot of overtime because they had just received a contract from Wal-Mart. The assembly line workers received 650 pesos a week and were paid double for overtime. They also received *médico* or social secu-rity and extensive training. Training occurs monthly and emphasizes se-curity and safety. In response to a question, our guide said that it is not necessary for women to have a pregnancy test before they work in the plant. There is, however, drug and alcohol testing but only once a year.

These maquilas clearly do not resemble Hobsbawn's description of the "dark satanic mills" of the British industrial revolution. The red brick cotton mill with its tall smokestack is a relic of the past. The condi-tions inside, moreover, have improved in almost all the factories of the twenty-first century.[6] Even in the oldest maquilas the working environ-ment is clean and comfortable. Although there is no natural light from windows, bright lighting hangs above every work space. Most plants have central air-conditioning, which keeps the inside air cool and dry and the whole plant ventilated. The machines may not be modern, but it appears that some maquila owners provide their workers with safety equipment to prevent injury. The plants have bathrooms with a waste disposal system, and some even have hot showers for the workers. Pho-tos 12 and 13 capture the front of Samson and Crescent in the Old In-dustrial Park; photos 14 and 15 show the outside of Master Lock and Otis in the New Industrial Park.

Despite the pristine physical environment of the maquilas, the work-ing conditions have improved little from those that existed in the "dark satanic mills" of nineteenth-century Great Britain. In the 1830s British children worked long days (often eleven hours), six days a week, with two short breaks for meals under the strict supervision of overseers in textile factories. In 2004 Mexican women worked long days (nine to twelve hours), six days a week, with two short breaks for meals under the strict supervision of *jefes* (supervisors) in maquilas. The employees at Summit work a ten and a half hour day and are paid on a seven-day wage scale. The starting salary is 87 pesos a day, or roughly 9 pesos an hour. Pregnancy tests are mandatory for women who want to work there, and if a woman gets pregnant in the first three months Summit will dismiss

Photo 12. Maquila Samson in the Old Industrial Park.

Photo 13. Maquila Crescent in the Old Industrial Park.

Photo 14. Maquila Master Lock in the New Industrial Park.

Photo 15. Maquila Otis in the New Industrial Park.

her. Workers receive only three paid sick days a year and four holidays (Christmas Eve, Christmas, New Year's Eve, and New Year's Day). Employees at Steward work twelve hours a day on a four-day schedule. The starting salary is 480 pesos a week, or roughly 10 pesos an hour. Pregnancy tests are mandatory for women who want to work there, but workers are not required to take contraceptives. The workers receive eight paid vacation days and a Christmas bonus. Initially, assembly line workers are put on a ninety-day contract so that they can easily be dismissed if there are any problems. The assembly line workers at Osborn work ten hours and fifteen minutes a day, five days a week. The average salary is 650 pesos a week, or a little over 13 pesos an hour. Many workers have to put in overtime because Osborn practices just-in-time production. Pregnancy tests are not mandatory, but drug testing is required once a year.[7] Long hours, low pay, little time off, and human rights violations are among the types of injustices that Hobsbawm attributed to the "dark satanic mills." How widespread are these injustices?

Injustices against workers are widespread in the maquilas along the Mexico-U.S. border. This research has produced considerable documentation demonstrating that the work relationship between the Mexican women and the companies that own the maquiladoras in Nogales violates several components of the LFT. Many of the multinationals abide by only two of the long list of requirements: they pay at least minimum wage and contribute to IMSS. Several labor rights groups and social activists have been denouncing the violations for a decade but with little reaction from consumers or multinationals.[8] As Valadez and Cota (1996, 3) have written, "The conditions in and outside the maquila, as well as the malnutrition caused by low salaries, produce skin illnesses, cancer, irregularities in menstruation, abortions, tumors, intoxication and birth of undernourished or disabled babies." The CFO, an independent union trying to organize maquiladora workers, compiled a report that

cites numerous illegal practices that are widespread in the maquiladoras, many of which involve the violation of rights guaranteed by Mexico's constitution as well as the country's labor code. Examples include illegal payments in merchandise or scrip; illegally excluding so-called bonus payments from calculations of pension and health benefits; involuntary overtime and failure to calculate overtime pay according to legal norms; and routine evasion of legally mandated benefits, including profit-sharing, compensation to laid-off workers, and compensation to workers affected by plant closings. (CFO 1999, 3)

Many of the maquilas that employ the women surveyed are guilty of breaking five or more Mexican labor laws. They do not fulfill many of their obligations under mandatory benefits, they actively discourage union activity, they fire people without just cause, and they do not give severance pay. Statistics from the workers' surveys confirm that most of the maquilas do not provide their workers with profit sharing, holiday premiums, paid legal holidays, or overtime pay. Thus, with their complete disregard for mandatory benefits, many multinationals broke four labor laws. Very few women, moreover, received maternity leave and were instead required to take pregnancy tests before they were hired, and they were fired if they became pregnant. This is clearly against the law and, more seriously, violates the women's human rights. The results from the workers' surveys also reveal that the majority of women worked more than the maximum hours permitted in a day and were rarely paid overtime. To make matters worse, union membership was discouraged and union activity severely curtailed by managers of the maquilas. It is not an accident that there are no unions in Nogales; rather, it is the consequence of a well-executed plan to keep them out. This may go a long way toward explaining why maquilas continue to violate labor laws without penalties or fines.

Minimum Wages and Mandatory Benefits

The vast majority of women who work in the maquilas in Nogales are earning more than the minimum wage. This means that most of the maquilas in Nogales are in compliance with Mexico's minimum wage law. A general minimum daily wage, which covers all Mexican workers, is set by the government every year. Initially, the system was conceived at the municipal level, and minimum wages were fixed for 2,300 municipalities. This created a highly decentralized and complicated system that took considerable time to update. The minimum wage fixing structure evolved from this decentralized system for municipalities to a regional system and then became a centralized system based on geographic areas. The current system divides the country into three geographic areas (A, B, and C), each of which has a general minimum wage. The National Commission of Minimum Wages also sets minimum wages for eighty-eight occupations, ranging from accountant to handyman. The general minimum wage for Zone A, which includes Nogales, is used here for maquila workers since it is not listed among the eighty-eight occupations. The minimum wage in 2004 for Nogales was 45.24 pesos a day, or approximately 317 pesos per week (National Commission of Minimum Wages 2004).[9] Supervisors and HR personnel reported they paid workers considerably more than the minimum: Summit paid workers 609 pesos a week, Osborn 650 pesos a week, and Steward 900 pesos a week. In an article in the *Arizona Daily Star*, a spokesman for the maquiladora industry claimed this practice was widespread: "Production workers at the maquiladoras earn 2.5 times the minimum wage for the region. That makes the more than two million workers in Mexico's 4,000 maquila factories among the highest-paid unskilled workers in Mexico" (Ibarra 2000, 1). The level of these weekly salaries is consistent with what the 620 women reported in the surveys. An average weekly wage of 644 pesos was reported by the maquila workers who were surveyed in Nogales. This is more than double the minimum wage set by the government, indicating the maquilas are following this regulation of the LFT. The vast majority of maquila workers (94 percent) are earning considerably more than the minimum wage, and a few earn as much as 1,526 pesos a week. There are, however, a few maquilas violating this portion of the law; 6 percent of the women reported earnings as low as 300 pesos a week.

The maquilas are not as compliant in providing the required benefits to workers. The survey asked women to list the benefits they received while working in the maquilas. Not one of the women mentioned profit sharing or pensions.[10] Fewer than ten women mentioned receiving a Christmas bonus, while the majority commented that a worker received a Christmas bonus if she had a perfect attendance record for the year. Surprisingly, most of the maquilas along the border in Nogales provide only two of the six mandatory employee benefits required by law. Employers register their employees with the IMSS and give workers legal holidays. Even with these two benefits, however, maquilas do not offer the amount required by law. Nearly all the women, 92.75 percent, confirmed receiving social security, a form of health care in Mexico. This was the only consistent response in all the surveys. A few women showed me their pay stubs indicating the deductions for IMSS. One worker's paycheck showed a deduction of 23.90 pesos from a base weekly salary of 408.89 pesos. Another worker's paycheck showed a deduction of 17.67 pesos from a base weekly salary of 707.55 pesos. Although social security in Mexico officially includes both health coverage and old age payments, health coverage was the only part workers commented on.

The social security system runs several clinics and one hospital that provide free health services. This is an extremely important benefit, and

many workers said they left higher-paying jobs to work for the maquiladoras because they provided *médico*, or social security. This benefit,
however, was not as good as it appeared because the services were limited and the coverage was basic. Major surgeries and expensive operations would be avoided at all cost by the company, through various measures. A few women mentioned this on their surveys. For example, one
woman said, "Que tengas que esperar hasta que me dan el contrato para
hacerme una operación de vesicula porque si falto no me dan mi contrato" (I must wait until they give me a contract to have my gallbladder
operation because if I miss a day they won't give me a contract). Under-
handed methods such as the hiring of on-site doctors to evaluate pa-
tients based on specific criteria mandated by the company result in ma-
nipulating diagnoses and ignoring workers' well-being in order to save
the company money. Many workers who are caught up in this debacle
seek legal help. One of the women reported, "No podia salira comer, es-
tuvo accidentada por su trabajo y tuvo que pelear legalmente el salario
para que le pagaran su incapacidad" (I don't like that I can't leave to go
eat lunch, and once I had an accident at work and had to fight my case
in court so that they would pay my disability).

Medical care was plagued, moreover, with the same problems of any
"free" public good: the staff and facilities were overburdened because
demand far exceeded supply. In Nogales, for example, in 1994 there was
one large public hospital in the city that served the families of maquila
workers. Ten years later, when the population of Nogales had increased
from 40,000 to 400,000, there was still only one public hospital. The
mayor of Acuña, Eduardo Ramón Valdez, realized the limitations of his
town's public services: "Acuña's sixty-year-old Social Security hospital,
the basic health service for most factory workers, is outdated and over-
whelmed. It has forty-five beds; the city needs several times that many.
And Acuña's 135 schools lack, well, nearly everything. They need windows, toilets, drinking water. They want desks. They want a flag. It's
an endless list" (qtd. in Dillon 2001, 6). Workers have access to emergency care and some preventive care but often no treatment for chronic
illnesses (e.g., diabetes, migraine, and cancer). The other component
of the IMSS, the Retirement Savings System, offered only promises to
workers because it was still in its infancy. Time will tell if the promise of
old age payments becomes a reality.

All the maquilas gave workers time off for vacation, but the specific
terms varied widely across plants. Mexican labor law clearly states that
workers must receive six working days of paid vacation after one year of

[handwritten margin note: public services did not keep up w/ pop. growth brought by maquiladoras]

employment. Women from this sample worked at maquilas that adopted variations of this benefit—giving the required number of days off but without pay; giving fewer than six days but with pay; and giving two days without pay. Three-fourths (75.25 percent) of the women surveyed received six vacation days. Because it wasn't specified on the survey whether vacations were paid, it cannot be assumed that they were not paid. Many of the women surveyed had not been at the maquila for a full year and therefore had not yet taken time off. A number of women commented during the interviews that they were unable to take their vacation days because they could not afford to lose one week's wages, implying their vacation days were not paid. Other women complained that they did not even receive the legal holidays off. During a visit to Nogales in June 2007 a new twist was placed on the vacation benefit. Workers told me they did get one week of vacation, but it was unpaid and the supervisor determined when it would be. The workers were infuriated about this practice because usually the "assigned week" did not coincide with Easter or Christmas when their children would be off from school. For workers, the "vacation benefit" was a mixed blessing: although it offered much-needed time to rest and spend with their family, it could make it tough for the family to survive if it wasn't paid.

Instead of receiving the benefits required by law, workers in the maquiladoras got other benefits. It became apparent during the interviews that many maquilas provided food, transportation, and, in a few rare cases, day care for the women workers. This may at first glance seem like odd behavior for profit-maximizing companies in a capitalist system. Why would any company offer benefits to their workers that weren't required by law, especially if many of the mandatory benefits weren't offered? Benefits add to labor costs and can be very expensive to provide, and many firms outsourced to minimize costs. The two benefits offered, transportation to and from work and food, were in fact self-serving for companies. By providing transportation and food, workers could be more efficient and productive. When workers are more efficient and productive, costs per unit fall and profits increase. Although these two benefits were certainly helpful to workers, they did not improve their situation as much as bonuses and profit sharing might. The quality of the benefit, moreover, was often poor and unacceptable.

Sixty-three percent of women reported receiving food through the maquila. Unlike many factory jobs in the United States, workers were not allowed to bring food into the plant or leave the premises to buy lunch. Several women expressed their discontent with the lack of freedom to leave their work site in order to buy lunch: "Que necesario me dan permiso" (that I have to get permission); "No podia salira comer" (I don't like that I can't leave to go eat lunch). Because of this restriction, many of the maquilas provided food in a designated lunchroom. The responses from workers and supervisors conflicted most regarding whether the food was free. During the tours, supervisors cited "free lunch" as one of the benefits they offered their workers. In the surveys, many of the women remarked that they had to pay for this "free" food. The workers' pay stubs from three different maquilas showed deductions for food from the base salary. For one woman who worked forty-eight hours, 58.44 pesos were deducted for food and indicated "retención café" from her base salary of 408.89 pesos. For another woman, 54.55 pesos were deducted for "cafeteria" from her base salary of 707.55 pesos. Comments on the quality of the food available were mixed and varied considerably from maquila to maquila. When women workers were asked to comment on the likes and dislikes of their jobs, many women chose to comment on the poor quality of the food: "La comida muy mala y tienen cabello suesta salada tortillas duras de otras dias" (The food is really bad, there's hair in it and it's salty, and the tortillas are old and hard); "Comida, estar parade todo el dia" (The food is hard all day). Many stated bluntly that the one aspect of their jobs they disliked was *la comida*, the food. Some went so far as to describe their frustration with the food: "La comida, los tacos mislo y no mas los olia y bomitaba" (The food, just smelling the tacos made me want to vomit).

Some maquilas offered transportation in company buses to and from work. This was a good way to make sure that people got to work on time since many families do not own cars and the public transportation system is extremely slow. It was not uncommon to see white schoolbuses marked with company names picking up and dropping off workers as the shifts changed (photo 16). This benefit, however, was much less prevalent than the food benefit. Only 16.65 percent of the women surveyed received transportation to and from work. Some women expressed gratitude for having a ride to work; others expressed disappointment. The women who were happy to take the bus responded simply that they liked "que tienen transporte que los vanos" (that they have transportation) and "servicioda camiones y cafeteria" (the bus service and the cafeteria). Other women complained that the buses did not have convenient routes and were not dependable. In addition, one woman said, "La banda camine porque se me pasan las piezas y tengo que corer a ponerselas" (The bus passes too fast, and I have to run to get on it); and

Photo 16. Bus service for residents and maquila workers in *el centro*.

another said, "Lo q' me gusta es q' no hay camiones al la salida" (What I don't like is that there aren't buses when we leave). Some women wished that their companies did provide transportation and did not like "que no tiene transport y hay veces que esta loviendo y tiene que caminar" (that there's no transportation, and sometimes it's raining and we have to walk). Others did not like paying for a benefit: "que tenga que pagar el transporte" (that you have to pay for the bus). Many women preferred living within walking distance of the maquila so as to avoid dependence on the maquila's transportation services.[11]

Work Schedules and Hours

The majority of workers in the maquilas work more hours in a day than mandated by law. Work hours and schedules are established by the LFT under the heading "Mandatory Employee Benefits." A normal day shift is eight hours, a night shift seven hours. The mean number of hours worked in the sample of 620 women was 9.47 hours, roughly 1.5 hours more than allowed by law. The median and mode were 9 hours, with a minimum of 5 hours and a maximum of 16. The majority of women (71 percent) in the maquilas are working long days, above the maximum 8 hours set by the government. Sixty-six of these women are working 12-hour days, the maximum allowed under the law with overtime. In conversations with supervisors and workers, two types of shifts exist in the maquiladoras. One type of shift works six days a week, nine hours a day. The workers get paid for a total of 48 hours a week even though they worked 54 hours. The other type of shift works four days a week (usually Thursday through Sunday) for 12 hours a day, for a total of 48 hours a week. This sample contains women who work each type of shift. Clearly, the majority of maquilas are guilty of having their employees work longer days than permitted by law. Interestingly, most maquilas abide by the law for the total number of hours worked in a week. The mean number of hours worked in a week in this sample is 47.56, under the maximum allowed by law. It appears, moreover, when reviewing the distribution of weekly hours, that the median and mode are 48, exactly equal to the limit set by the law. There are far fewer maquilas that break the law on weekly hours than on daily hours. In this sample, 70.65 percent worked exactly 48 hours, 83.37 percent worked 48 hours or less, and only 16.63 percent worked more than 48 hours. The physical consequences of working long days were poor health, and the emotional consequences were the destruction of the family's cohesiveness.

If companies are abiding by the law, we would expect to find a lot of women in this sample earning overtime wages since many of them work in excess of the maximum hours allowed in a day. Mexican law even goes so far as to limit the total number of overtime hours in a day and a week. Workers are not permitted to work more than three hours of overtime a day and for only three days a week. The typical nine-hour shift found in many maquilas does not break this law as workers are working only one hour a day overtime. As long as the women receive overtime pay for these hours, the maquilas are operating within the law. The second type of shift by design completely violates the law. The women work three hours of overtime a day (which is the maximum permitted) for four consecutive days (when the limit is three days). Therefore, a maquila that has employees working a four-day shift is breaking the law. Not only do maquilas make employees work longer hours than permitted by law, but they do not pay their workers for these additional hours. Not one of the women interviewed reported receiving overtime wages. According to many of the workers, they are told to work overtime if they want to keep their jobs. On surveys women revealed this truth; for example, "No te dejan escojer si quieres o no trabajar tiempo extra, te exijen trabajar el dia que ellos quieren y asta que les da la gana nos dejan salir" (They don't let you choose if you want to work overtime or not, they make you work whenever they want and they let you leave whenever they feel like it); "[Ellos] obligan a trabajar tiempo extra no se portan amables con toda la gente" ([They] make you work overtime, they aren't nice to everyone); "Despues la obligan a trabajar tiempo extra diciendo le que si la corren no puede conseguir genete trabajo en trabajo en ortra maquila por suedad" (They make me work overtime, saying that if I get fired I'm not going to be able to find work in another maquila because of my age); "No le gusta que obligan a la gente a trabajar tiempo extra y las mujeres muchas veces no pueden quedarse porque sus hijos los tienen que recojer de la guarderia" (I don't like that they make everyone work extra, and a lot of times we women can't stay because we have to pick up our kids from day care). The blatant disregard for the laws governing hours and overtime is unconscionable.

Union Representation

In theory maquila workers have the right to belong to a union that represents their interests to employers. In reality, the unions established by the maquila represent the interests of the employers and the Mexican government, not the workers. Recently scholars have begun to distinguish between government-subordinated unions and authentic unions (Fernández 2002; Hathaway 2002; Murillo 2001; and Núñez 2002). This is especially true along the border, where "traditional corporatist unions" have a stronger presence than independent unions. Mexico's largest and most politically powerful union is the Confederation of Mexican Workers. The CTM claims to represent 85 percent of the workers in the private sector. In Agua Prieta and Nogales, the CTM is the government-recognized union, or what residents call the *sindicato official*, "shadow union" or "*charro* union." In Agua Prieta if an individual wants to work, he or she must first register with the CTM. On employment, CTM dues of 4 to 5 pesos (1–1.5 percent of weekly pay) are automatically deducted by the government from the worker's pay.[12] As Hathaway (2002, 427) has remarked, "Nowadays unions are even formed before maquilas open their doors. Thus the issue at hand is not simply unionizing maquiladoras. Rather it has to do with securing unions that authentically represent the interests of their workers and that have the ability to protect those interests." This creates tremendous difficulty for the workers: to the outside world it appears they are being protected when in fact they are not. Workers have nowhere to go when they have grievances or experience sexual harassment or discrimination. Workers have no recourse when they do not receive the mandatory benefits stated by federal law. Because of the imbalance of power between the employer (multinational company) and employee (Mexican worker), even a strong, aggressive worker will not be heard. A single voice is drowned out by the supervisors, managers, and owners who control the paychecks. Given this predicament, workers may want to form an alternative independent union, one that represents their interests. The process of opening and operating a maquila in Mexico makes it almost impossible to do so, because according to federal law companies can establish relations with only one union. The process has been aptly described by Jorge Alberto Fernández:

> When a company decides to establish a maquiladora in Mexico, a meeting takes place with local authorities in which the company is presented with a catalog of central labor councils. The company proceeds to choose one, signs a collective contract committing to minimal conditions required by law (by merely signing the contract, a *charro* union leader receives a percentage of the total of the amount projected and is given a commitment of a percentage of each annual salary revision, which is usually 2–5 percent), and this is only until the plant opens and contracts personnel who come in to work paying these dues never even knowing about the *charro* union. It is not until workers attempt to hold a company accountable by demanding collective bargaining or by establishing a union that workers discover that a contract has already been registered with authorities by the *charro* union. (2002, 463)

In addition, it is more difficult to form an authentic union, such as FAT, in maquilas, because "people on the border generally do not trust people from Mexico City. The border has its own culture, and resentment against the capital is an important part of it" (Hathaway 2002, 433).

The anti-union environment should not be surprising since many multinationals blame rising costs in the United States on unions. One of the main reasons companies outsource is to reduce labor costs and avoid "hostile unions." Even Mexican supervisors and managers understand the preferences of multinationals. This was confirmed during a wildcat strike in Reynosa in 2005 when an article appeared in *Prensa de Reynosa* stating, "In Mexico, workers at foreign-owned assembly plants known as maquiladoras frequently complain about being left in the dark of the affairs of their union—when one exists. Sometimes called 'charro' unions, they are criticized for being too cozy to management at the expense of labor" (Hernández and Tirana 2005).

There have been numerous attempts to organize the maquila workers in an independent union, one not associated with CTM. They have been unsuccessful because workers are afraid to sign the petitions that are necessary to register a new union. They don't want to lose their jobs, they can't afford to lose their jobs, and they can't survive without their jobs. Workers were fired in Chihuahua when FAT tried to organize in the Honeywell plant (Hathaway 2002, 430) and in Ciudad Juárez when FAT tried to organize at the General Electric plant (429). I personally met, interviewed, and accompanied women working for the AFO in Agua Prieta and Nogales. When the AFO was first formed in Agua Prieta in 1996, everything was kept secret—the name, its objective, and its employees. Within a year it was registered and known by the government. Elisa said that initially the goal of AFO was to educate workers about their rights and obligations. Elisa and Pola went house to house using two booklets published by the Coalición por Justicia en las Maquiladoras (CJM) to teach women about their rights. These booklets, *¿Cuáles son mis derechos en el trabajo?* (What Are My Rights at Work?) and *Conozco mis derechos en el trabajo, pero ¿Cuáles son mis obligaciones?* (I Know What My Rights Are at Work, But What Are My Obligations?) used illustrations and conversations between employers and female employees to explain a worker's rights under the LFT (CJM 1999, 2000). After successfully speaking with many workers, the AFO began to focus on forming an independent union among the maquila workers in 2001. Elisa sees the work they are doing as "seeds for a fruit that is produced later." Since she and Pola were unsuccessful in forming an independent union by 2004, the little money left went to Nogales, where there was more hope of organizing. She admitted sadly that both she and Pola were currently working on a volunteer basis because of the lack of funds.[13]

The AFO in Nogales has shared a similar fate. Despite the optimism and hard work of the two part-time employees of the AFO, Juana and Polita, no independent union was formed after three years of organizing. Funding for the project began in 2002 and ended in 2004. Both Juana and Polita, however, saw progress. Juana believed the objectives of AFO were to educate women about their rights as workers and women. She believed that "the federal laws were supposed to be the best in the world but are dead laws because they are not enforced." She felt AFO was necessary because if women complain on their own they are threatened or fired and their lives are made very difficult. She recalled one of their accomplishments in Nogales: "There was a strike at ICT because the workers had worked three days for twelve hours a day and the company wanted them to work the fourth day for the same pay instead of paying overtime. They had a strike and the company paid them overtime."[14] Polita recalled an experience that made a lasting impression on her. She and Juana had successfully convinced twenty-one individuals to sign a petition to form the first independent union in Nogales. They had just gotten the last two signatures and were planning the trip to Hermosillo when they heard that three people on the list had gotten fired by the maquila. Polita and I drove to the home of one of the workers whom she knew personally. The women were distraught because someone had told the company about the list, and the manager fired three workers—all from the same family. Polita was almost speechless. Although Polita was disappointed, she was encouraging to the father of the family. She knew once word got around no one else would sign the petition. She comforted the family and told them she would help them find other jobs.[15]

The prospects for maquila workers to join an authentic union are slim. The maquila industry is not free from the repression of unions for which Mexico has become infamous. Foreign multinationals face the same challenges that Mexican companies do when it comes to recognizing and working with unions. The "unholy trinity of company-government-*charro* union" is pervasive in the maquilas, and "sweetheart contracts" are the norm (Fernández 2002, 461, 463). As Fernández's research reveals, "It merits emphasizing once more that such corruption, union repression, and the fact of putting the interests of leaders above those of workers constitutes the essence of official unionism in Mexico, and in no manner are these 'isolated actions' or 'deviations' that could be corrected" (462). The fact that American companies are complicit in signing contracts with these charro unions is unfortunate but clearly not completely within their control. Thus although American companies are breaking the law that gives workers the right to unionize and collectively bargain, there may be little they can do to correct this situation.

Conclusion

The critics of NAFTA are correct. As multinationals moved to the free trade zone, hundreds of thousands of jobs were created in Mexico. American companies found cheaper labor and Mexican workers found steady jobs in manufacturing. The jobs, however, were not as good as everyone predicted. They did not improve workers' standard of living. The grim reality for the Mexican worker is undeniable. Mexican workers are caught in a race to the bottom—accepting working conditions that are substandard due to insecurity about losing their jobs. The only real guarantees in the maquila jobs were the long hours, little vacation, and tough production standards. But most workers could also count on receiving a wage above the minimum and medical services.

Workers desperate to feed their families accepted the maquila jobs since there were so few opportunities. Internal migration had caused an excess labor supply, and competition for the jobs was fierce. Families that had sold their farms or closed their family businesses to move north were now stranded in the border cities trying to find work. They had no other options since they could not go back to where they came from. As the number of people looking for work increased, the equilibrium wage fell, and the need to attract workers by offering good benefits disappeared. If one worker didn't want to accept the working conditions offered, there were hundreds in line who would. This drove labor standards down. Many employers offered a wage and a work schedule, and desperate workers accepted them. Workers were happy to have jobs, and companies were happy to have a workforce.

The problem arises when companies use their advantage in the labor market to exploit their workers. History has witnessed this again and again as countries have industrialized. Men, women, and children suffered in the textile factories in Europe. They also suffered in the glassworks and pottery factories and coal mines. The mechanized assembly line is extremely demanding and terribly monotonous. Unemployed workers with few skills are eager to get these jobs and have regular paychecks. Companies eager to increase production and profits push workers beyond what is humanly possible. Workers, acting independently, cannot push back and attempt to meet the expectations of their employers. Unions evolved to give workers more power and the ability to push back when the demands seemed unreasonable. Along the Mexican border the owners of the maquilas have pushed workers too far, and the unions have not pushed back.

As Graciela Bensusan notes:

[Experience] indicates that labor asymmetries will persist and that neither NAFTA nor NAALC has fulfilled its objective of improving living and working conditions in the region. NAALC has not coerced the

Mexican government to level the playing field among the different union options, though it does constitute a requirement for a true representative trade union movement and the need for more strict application of the present regulations. In this sense, Mexican opposition to the inclusion of a labor clause in NAFTA and other trade agreements and safeguards against the artificial lowering of salaries and the absence of true union formation is being exposed as a short-term and inadequate strategy. (2004, 145)

The current situation along the U.S.-Mexico border is inexcusable. ✂ [Many of the maquilas owned by multinationals are in fact sweatshops.] ✂ They are mistreating workers and breaking several, even most, of Mexico's labor laws. The only two laws that seem to be universally respected are the minimum wage law and access to medical care. The majority of women in the sample reported earning on average twice the government-mandated minimum wage, 644 pesos. Three-fourths of the women reported their employers contribute to the IMSS, which gives them access to the public hospital and other health care services. Many women felt strongly that the health benefit was very valuable to their families. The remaining benefits, although not as essential for day-to-day survival, would improve workers' living standards considerably. The fact that almost none of the women received any portion of profits, a Christmas bonus, a holiday premium, or a pension is troubling. These benefits are required by law. This additional income would go a long way to help the families who barely survive on the pay they receive (see chapter 2).

Unfortunately the exploitation does not end there. The women who work in the maquilas are exploited because they must work more hours each day than required by law and do not receive additional pay for these hours. In fact, one of the shifts used by many of the maquilas breaks the law. Many women work twelve hours a day for four consecutive days at the same daily rate. It is irrelevant that women may choose to work this shift because they can spend more time with their children during the week; it is against the law. One may wonder how companies can get away with breaking so many laws. Why don't workers strike or report the violations? There are several explanations. NAFTA says nothing about labor or labor rights. The NAALC, which does say something about labor rights, did not establish minimum labor standards. In addition, the NAALC did not create a new judicial system or board to hear workers' grievances. In this environment the only voice a worker has is her union. The unions established at most maquilas, however, are usually controlled by the corporations. These official unions are not the collective voice of workers but instead represent the interests of the company and the government. The maquila workers, therefore, have no voice. The next chapter gives the workers a voice and tells the stories of the women who work in the maquilas.

CHAPTER 6

Liberation or Exploitation of Women Workers?

As globalization spreads and connects developed and developing countries, the winners and losers are easy to identify. Free trade agreements have created *zonas libres*, or free trade zones, and a new production model—that of mobile manufacturing. The free movement of capital (both direct and indirect), technology, ideas, and labor is supposed to improve economic efficiencies and reduce production costs. Consumers benefit in two ways. First, they have access to an increased number and variety of goods. Second, they experience an increase in their purchasing power as goods become cheaper. Consumers are able to enjoy an increase in their standard of living. Companies who move capital and technology across borders benefit in a number of ways as well. They have access to more raw materials and cheaper labor, which allows them to reduce production costs and lower prices. These cheaper goods can be sold to millions of consumers in poorer developing countries, which increases the company's revenues. Profits will increase as well because total revenues rise as total costs fall. These successes imply that the salaries of management and the earnings of stockholders will rise. Clearly, globalization benefits the consumer and the producer. Do the workers benefit as well? At first glance it appears they do because many unemployed or underemployed workers receive jobs that pay a steady wage. With these higher earnings poor families can move out of poverty and into the working class. A closer examination, however, reveals considerable hardship for many workers. In Mexico, this hardship falls on the women who work in the maquiladoras.

Do these modern-day factories provide opportunities for women to become independent and liberated, or are they as exploited as their historical counterparts were two centuries ago? There are two theories that give conflicting answers to these questions. The integration thesis, originally developed by Esther Boserup (1970), argues that industrialization leads to female liberation and sexual equality by involving women in the labor market and eventually the political process. Both single and married women work outside the home, earning a wage in the formal economy. Initially women are marginal in their society's developmental efforts because they are typically confined to their traditional roles in the household or in the informal economy. This is interpreted by economists, however, as a waste of human resources for the country. The existence of assembly plants is seen as a source of stable employment that yields income and benefits. This provides economic security for women and their families. In addition, women gain productive skills that increase their competitiveness in the labor market, which promotes upward mobility among industrial firms (which translates into higher earnings). These jobs expand women's opportunities and offer them an alternative to early marriage and child rearing (Tiano 1991, 78).

In contrast, the exploitation thesis, primarily developed by Tiano (1994), argues that industrialization creates a female proletariat by supplying low-wage labor. Instead of offering women new and exciting opportunities to learn useful skills, assembly plants place women within capitalist relations of production, exploiting them and deepening pre-existing patriarchal relations that oppress women. Women do not take jobs because they want to and are behaving independently but instead are being directed by their husbands and working just to survive. They accept low wages and poor working conditions to uphold the subordinate and obedient role of women in the family and on the factory floor. Young women especially may be forced to quit school to take assembly jobs and often must hand over their wages to their parents or husbands.

Thesis I: The Maquila Industry Liberates Mexican Women

Employment in the maquiladoras can offer women an opportunity to leave home and work in a key industry in the formal economy. Depending on the situation at home, women may feel their independence as liberating. Several scholars have developed this perspective in their research on gender and production along the Mexican border. Ellwyn Stoddard (1987) claims "the ladies of the assembly line" are liberated from all three sources of oppression in their lives—their husbands, their bosses, and society. Stoddard goes even further and asserts that the assembly line jobs in the maquilas have liberated women from a life of poverty. He believes that most researchers, scholars, and observers are misguided in their conclusion that maquiladoras are sweatshops and argues that all current literature on maquiladoras incorrectly compares their wages, working conditions, and alienation issues with the wages, working conditions, and issues of factories in industrialized countries (in particular, the United States). Instead, he claims, if one compares work in the maquiladoras with other workplaces in Mexico an entirely different conclusion will be reached. Maquiladoras offer higher wages and better working conditions than other opportunities in the formal and informal economy of Mexico. He finds that although wages are low, the "average maquiladora's wages have been higher than minimum wages everywhere, and minimum wages at the border are still well above those in the rest of the country" (43–47). Stoddard surveys American-owned maquiladoras and shows that they voluntarily offer benefits that are not provided by other maquilas or other employers in the formal economy. The benefits include a hiring bonus, attendance bonuses, a production bonus, a medical plan (in-plant nurse/medical aid with on-call physician or transportation to the Social Security national health care center), a cafeteria subsidy, a transportation subsidy, a savings plan, and an education refund (45).

Stoddard argues that the maquila industry offers a positive opportunity and congenial workplace, which is not common in other occupations available to Mexican women (66). Women needed to find jobs when economic crises hit Mexico and their husbands' incomes were no longer sufficient to provide for a family. Women could work as domestic servants in the informal economy or in maquiladoras in the formal economy. The maquiladoras did absorb many of the women looking for work but did not pull them from their homes and wreak havoc on their family life. Stoddard believes that maquiladoras helped more than hurt women by offering steady employment and paying the minimum wage. Family poverty and local unemployment would have been much worse with the growing population and migration if maquilas did not use Mexico's surplus labor (62–63).

Stoddard concludes his book by identifying the winners and losers from the proliferation of the maquiladoras. He believes the groups who gained from the growth of the industry are (1) local Mexican politicians who use the assessments from the border maquilas for public services; (2) local Mexican politicians who have more jobs and lower unemployment in their areas; (3) Mexican investors who earn more income by leasing their industrial park facilities to foreign operations; (4) private transportation companies that transport workers and materials; (5) U.S. border retail merchants who profit from the workers' wages spent on U.S. clothing, food, and recreation; and (6) American maquiladora managers who live in the United States while working in a "foreign" plant just across the border (Stoddard 1987, chap. 6). His list of losers, although shorter, suggests a much broader and deeper impact on the income of American workers than Mexican workers. The losers are (1) Mexican women who are exploited; (2) U.S. workers in unions who have lost their jobs when factories closed and moved out of the country; and (3) Mexican workers who are paid lower wages relative to American workers. Stoddard concludes with a request for more accurate descriptions of the maquila industry and offers two conclusions: "multinational corporation maquiladoras provide extra-wage benefits, a better workplace (safety and comfort), and better worker relationships than do Mexican-owned factories or those formed around labor cooperatives"; and "worker satisfaction and working conditions in multinational maquiladoras are better than in factories in the U.S." (68–71).

Although Stoddard does bring attention to the humane maquilas that exist along the border, his data are outdated and could be considered biased. The data on border maquiladoras he uses were obtained in 1983 and 1984—a period of rapid expansion of the maquila industry and rapid contraction of workers' real wages. Consequently, it may have been more common for U.S. multinationals to offer additional benefits such as attendance bonuses and cafeteria and transportation subsidies when wages were low. Furthermore, the large number of people leaving their jobs because of low wages cannot be entirely blamed on the Mexican government's ability to set a low minimum wage. U.S. multinationals can pay a wage higher than the national minimum but not lower. His conclusions are based on responses from a survey given to current and former workers on their reason(s) for staying or quitting their jobs at a maquiladora. Stoddard obtained his data on why people quit from the exit interviews that workers must submit in order to collect their final paychecks. It is highly probable that the workers felt pressured to respond in ways that would not upset or offend the supervisor who holds their last paycheck. Thus his conclusions use statistics that are derived from data that may not be current, accurate, or representative.

Offering a feminist interpretation, Patricia Wilson (1992) argues that employment in the maquiladoras freed women from the patriarchal structures at home and in society. According to her view, women confined to their traditional roles in the household and informal economy were marginalized by society. Employment in the formal market offered these women new opportunities and an alternative to early marriage and childrearing (78). Women were now able to make a contribution to the economy and by doing so enhanced their role in the public sphere. Maquiladoras are viewed as a source of stable employment that provides economic security for women and their families. Employers recruit and hire according to productivity and technical skills, not reproductive roles in society. Women, both single and married, are capable of making a significant contribution in the public sphere as well as the private sphere. The maquila owners want highly motivated, hardworking employees with a strong need for personal attachment (Tiano 1994, 74). Women were not only considered "acceptable" as workers, but they were preferred. Gay Young (1991) found that many maquila managers in Ciudad Juárez believed "that women possess 'innate' capacities and personality traits that make them more productive workers. They have 'naturally' nimble fingers as well as greater patience and discipline, and thus, this manual dexterity and docility makes them better suited to the tedious, monotonous routine of assembly work" (Ruiz and Tiano 1991, 109). As a result, women hired to work in the maquilas earned higher wages and received important health benefits. These wages allowed them to become more independent or at least to have more of a say in where the money is spent. This liberates them from their dependence on men and integrates them into the economy. The work experience, moreover, gives the women a sense of accountability, responsibility, and skills that will promote upward mobility in industrial firms. In many ways, the jobs in the maquiladoras offer great opportunities for women to improve both their present and future standard of living.

Recent feminist research reveals that some women have taken this independence a step further and have become supervisors and managers. Wright (1997, 2006) argues that it is possible for women to break through the traditionally defined role of female maquila workers to earn promotions within a company. She follows the paths of a few women working in U.S.-owned maquilas in Ciudad Juárez who challenge the American male view that Mexican women are not trainable. The women, already liberated by their assembly line jobs in the maquila, are confident that they will be promoted. Two of the four women Wright interviewed were successful, earning a higher wage and more respect from both Mexican and American managers. Although this upward mobility clearly implies women have been liberated, the new *maquiladora mestiza* is the exception rather than the rule.[1] Surprisingly, even in an empowering organizational structure, women allowed gender to dominate their actions over education and experience. Salzinger (2003, 60–66) found that women working in a unique maquila where a participatory management program had been implemented did not try to become managers. Male Mexican managers complained that women acted as followers and "won't make the leap" to become coordinators (68). The managers of the maquila had hoped to move the work paradigm away from docility toward assertiveness but were unsuccessful. In these cases as well as others, there is a consensus among scholars that most women work in traditional roles in maquilas. Wright (2006, 120) herself admits, "The majority of Mexicans in the maquiladoras continue to work for poverty wages and live in economically strained conditions."

The victories of the maquiladora mestizas can offer hope to some women but not to the majority. It is possible, however, that the women working on the assembly line can become more skilled and better paid. It is clear that the type of production utilized in a maquila, the development of the industry, and its integration into the country's economy will dictate the level of skilled labor that is needed. Wilson's thesis that host countries can shape and utilize the global assembly industry to further their own internal development offers a promising future for their workers and economy. She (1992, 34) argues that through linkages— buying inputs from local markets, selling products domestically, and producing products domestically—a country can use the government's export-led strategy to create a comparative advantage beyond that of cheap labor. Wilson claims that the assembly industry, as experienced in Mexico, has changed dramatically since the 1980s, from one based on a low-skilled labor-intensive workforce to a highly skilled, more capital-intensive workforce. After studying the maquila industry from the macroeconomic perspective, she concludes that the largely low paid female workforce has been replaced by a primarily higher paid male workforce that has adopted some of the flexible manufacturing methods of the successful "Asian Tigers" (4). Consequently, as the emerging corporate strategy becomes one of flexible production, workers become more highly skilled, more productive, and higher paid. Rather than work in a dead-end job year after year, there is room for upward mobility. Workers employed in this system can learn more and be rewarded with interesting job opportunities and higher pay. Unlike their previous jobs on an assembly line, where tasks were specialized and the principle of the division of labor was strictly applied, workers are not alienated, bored, or uninterested in quality. Instead they are encouraged and rewarded for improving quality and catching errors (53, 55). The new method of flexible producers uses capital-intensive production processes. Workers rotate through a variety of tasks, work in quality circles, and use just-in-time inventory to keep down costs.[2] Wilson predicts that as firms continue with their flexible production strategy there will be less of a need for cheap labor and firms will no longer need to place plants in Mexico where the greatest comparative advantage is cheap labor (56).

This does not appear to be the case in Nogales. Although the number of maquilas have declined in Mexico from the peak in 2008 (see table 4.2), there were 5,111 maquilas employing over 1.8 million workers in 2010. The workers in these maquilas, moreover, did not experience an increase in their wages but instead a decrease (see table 4.5). Along the border the comparative advantage of Mexican workers as cheap labor continues into the twenty-first century. Not surprisingly, flexible production has not replaced the labor-intensive production methods. This reality defies Wilson's predictions because the majority of maquilas along the border still use labor-intensive technology, or first-generation maquilas. A review of the list of maquilas in Nogales reveals primarily companies using assembly line production: Samsonite, Moen, Master Lock, Black and Decker, Ford, Motorola, and General Electric. Kathryn Kopinak (1996) studied transport-equipment maquiladoras in Nogales, Sonora, in 1988. She interviewed workers, managers of maquilas, and the former leader of the maquila association to discern whether or not the labor-intensive type of maquilas were replaced by the capital-intensive type of maquilas. This would mean that higher-paid skilled labor would replace lower-paid unskilled labor. The concern is that cheap labor may promote antiquated and simple technologies as cost-effective, which hinders modernization. She identifies four dimensions of the labor-intensive type of maquilas: (1) feminizing the labor force; (2) highly segmenting skill categories with the majority of workers in the unskilled category; (3) lowering of real wages; and (4) introducing a nonunion orientation (13). The central premise of modernization is that developing countries begin with a small modern sector with high productivity and high wages, which transforms the larger, more traditional agricultural sector with low productivity and low wages (18). Kopinak found that there was "technological heterogeneity" and that both the labor-intensive and capital-intensive types of maquila existed side-by-side (26). She documented many maquilas using the old system ("fordism," i.e., assembly line, specialization and division of labor, unskilled labor, and employee/employer conflict) and only a few using the new system ("post-fordism," i.e., flexible specialization or lean production, skilled workers who work in groups or quality circles, no inherent conflict between employee/employer). She concluded that "the majority of the maquiladora sector [in Nogales] is the traditional maquila doing labor-intensive assembly" (42). She argued that Stage 2, or the second generation of maquilas, has not yet arrived in Nogales. This stage goes beyond the assembly line technique to flexible production with sophisticated machinery and work groups. The production process is more capital-intensive, and the products use advanced technology. The labor force is older, more skilled, and usually male (9).

A few scholars have challenged this view, arguing that second- and third-generation maquilas dominate the northern border of Mexico (Carrillo and Gomis 2003; Hansen and Mattingly 2008; Tiano 2006). They believe that the first-generation maquilas have moved out of Mexico to other Central American or Asian countries. As competition forces companies to search for places where they can pay even lower wages, first-generation maquilas leave and are replaced by second-generation maquilas. The companies owning these newer maquilas continue to import raw materials and export the finished product. The maquilas require more advanced machinery, however, since the products are more complex. The workers using these machines are both semiskilled and skilled. These second-generation maquilas hire mostly men, typically men who are older and married (Tiano 2006, 83–90). Finally, the most advanced stage of the maquiladora industry, the third generation, occurs when companies move research and development centers offshore. Trade magazines and websites are purposely targeting this market because it attracts larger investment expenditures, higher levels of technology, and professional workers. These third-generation maquilas hire highly skilled, older, and educated men. Many of these companies are located farther south in Mexico, although a few exist along the border (Carrillo and Hualde 1996; Carrillo and Gomis 2003). Examples of companies in this most advanced stage are GM, Ford, Boeing, Honeywell, and Precision Aerospace.

It is difficult to discern the exact stage of the maquila industry in Nogales and whether second- and third-generation maquilas have arrived and to what extent. As Kopinak observed, first- and second-generation maquilas can and do exist side-by-side. It is clear, however, that first-generation maquilas are predominant in the free trade zone of Nogales. Companies use female labor in assembly production. The masculinization of the maquila workforce on the border has yet to take place. This suggests that Tiano's (2006, 89) convenient assumption that "if women are increasingly marginalized from the maquiladora workforce, the working conditions in maquiladora firms will be less and less relevant for them," cannot be applied to Nogales. Does this make Nogales unique and my research less representative? It appears more likely that most developing countries in the early stages of industrialization will attract first-generation factories in their free trade zones. Evidence of this type of foreign direct investment has already surfaced in several Latin American countries and has spread rapidly in China. Although second-generation factories have developed in Mexico and other developing countries and will continue to do so, their arrival does not preclude the continued operation of first-generation maquilas. Fussell (2000) offers four valid reasons why the female workforce has persisted despite a decade of maquila expansion along the border. She identifies factors affecting the demand and supply of labor for the maquiladora industry. On the demand side, it is a buyer's market, and employers hold all the power. Consequently, their preference for women (over men) and their threat to move production bias employment toward women. On the supply side, high unemployment and an increase in migration to the border create a large supply of unemployed workers competing for jobs. The women in this research are primarily employed in the first-generation maquilas in a labor market where employers hire them because they are "ideal" maquila workers.

In summary, some researchers believe the job opportunities available in the new maquila industry located along the Mexico-U.S. border have liberated the Mexican woman from her oppressed status within the family and society. According to Stoddard, the jobs offer women higher wages and better benefits than any other job in the formal or informal economy for women with very little education and training. Wilson argues that the maquila industry does not liberate women immediately; it must go through a stage in which some exploitation takes place. But once all the efficiencies have been exhausted from the division of labor and specialization, she believes, maquilas will adopt flexible production strategies and move from first-generation to second- and third-generation maquilas in which workers learn new skills and earn higher wages. In the case of Mexico, the female worker becomes a productive and contributing member of the family and economy, which is a new and challenging role. As most of the feminist literature has pointed out, however, the arrival of second-generation maquilas brings about "the masculinization of the border maquiladora workforce" (Tiano 2006, 90). Employers prefer men because they believe that women are not capable of performing complicated tasks or operating sophisticated machines. Consequently, societal gender roles are reinforced within the foreign factories and women are pushed out of the formal economy. As Fussell (2000, 77) concludes, "The payoff of working in a maquiladora is not improving as the industry becomes established."

Thesis II: The Maquila Industry Exploits Mexican Women

A number of scholars believe that women do not benefit and are actually harmed by the maquilas. This exploitation thesis was developed by Fernandez-Kelly (1983a) and has been supported by Cravey (1998) and Tiano (1994). According to this view, maquilas exploit women by placing them in an unequal relationship with managers and supervisors, thereby deepening preexisting patriarchal relations that oppress women. Industrialization creates a female proletariat that supplies low-wage labor for accumulating capital at minimal cost (Elson and Pearson 1989). Instead of acting independently and deciding willingly to take a job, many women have to take a job. The first two layers of oppression originate in the home between husband and wife and between fathers and children. A wife feels she has no choice but to work because of pressures from her husband and the hunger of her children. Children may also have to work because their fathers tell them their contribution is essential. Young women, especially, may be forced to quit school to take maquila jobs and give their wages to their parents. The third layer of oppression occurs in the maquila. Once on the job a woman is confronted by the rules and regulations of the maquila set by management. A woman accepts the low wages and poor working conditions because she accepts this extension of her obedient role in the family to the factory floor. The boss, or *jefe*, uses this obedience to his advantage by pushing women to meet unreasonable quotas or production standards. Women are oppressed rather than liberated by their jobs in the maquilas.

Fernandez-Kelly (1983a) examined the impact of globalization on Mexican women. She argued that competition created by globalization lead multinationals to further oppress women in the economy as well as at home. Consequently, multinationals invested in developing countries exploit inexpensive female labor, thereby taking advantage of and reinforcing women's inferior position in the labor market and household

(Fernandez-Kelly 1983b, 219). She explained that patriarchal ideologies have defined appropriate roles for Mexican women in the economy. During industrialization employers did not recruit or hire older married women because their primary duties were in the home, or private sphere. Mexican society and culture perpetuated and protected the belief that married women were entirely responsible for childbearing, child rearing, cleaning, cooking, and caring for the sick and elderly (Fernandez-Kelly 1983a, 116; Fuentes and Ehrenreich 1983, 13; Safa 1983, 97). This exclusion from the formal labor market meant their contribution to society in the public sphere was minimal. Consequently, married women were not liberated from the home or integrated into the economy by industrialization. Single women were not liberated either, despite their participation in the formal economy. Employers' preferences were for young single women. Their employment in the maquilas led to exploitation instead of liberation. According to Fernandez-Kelly, the economic development of Mexico created by the growth of the maquiladora industry placed the burden on young single women. They performed tedious and monotonous tasks for low wages. They had little job security, minimal training, and few advancement opportunities in the maquilas (1983b, 220). She concludes that "the incorporation of women with acute economic needs into the maquiladora industry represents, in objective terms, the use of the most vulnerable sector of the population to achieve greater productivity and larger profits" (219).

Fernandez-Kelly's conclusions are based on data she collected in four stages in Ciudad Juárez between 1978 and 1979. Her research made a tremendous contribution to the literature because of the breadth and depth of the data she collected. In the first stage she secured a job in a maquila. This unique approach provided participant observation on the working conditions and hiring/firing policies within maquiladoras. Working on the inside, moreover, allowed her to initiate contact with working women and gain their trust. Subsequently she surveyed 510 women working in fourteen different assembly plants. The information she gathered in this manner, however, is suspect because her interviews took place during work shifts in the plant. It is highly probable that many of the women did not respond honestly because they feared retribution from their supervisors or management. This was not a concern, however, with the third stage of her data collection in which she obtained the information in the women's homes. The fifty-five ethnographic recordings she derived from these conversations provide candid and honest responses of the women's perceptions and attitudes toward their employment in the maquila. Conclusions based on the ethnographies are both reliable and authentic. In the final stage, she interviewed several government officials, promoters of maquiladoras, and upper and mid-level management to put the women's responses in context (6).

Tiano's work (1991, 91; 1994) supports Fernandez-Kelly's conclusion that women are victims working against their will. Tiano interviewed female workers, managers, and personnel directors of maquilas in Mexicali in 1983 and 1984. She hired students to administer a questionnaire to sixty-six women in U.S. multinational maquilas and fifty-eight women in Mexican-owned garment maquilas. Her findings indicate that the maquila workers did not *choose* to work but felt pressured by hungry, sick, and disabled husbands and family members. Tiano's findings support the exploitation thesis because (1) women worked out of economic need; (2) women were unlikely to earn above the minimum wage despite skill level or seniority; (3) electronic maquila workers' benefits were not any better than service worker benefits; (4) maquila workers were more likely to experience layoffs; and (5) their jobs did not teach them useful skills (1991, 97, 98). As Tiano concluded, "Maquiladoras have not enhanced northern Mexican women's position in the labor force" (35). She does not believe, however, that the women are weak, obedient, and submissive. She sees hope in the future for female workers in the maquilas as they discover informal ways to protest, through work slowdowns (*tortuosidad*) or sabotage, rather than the formal way of forming a union.

Cravey (1998) studied the maquilas in Nogales, Sonora, and concluded that the new factory regime (1978–present) exploits the women who work in them. Her research supports the exploitation thesis because she finds that during post-NAFTA market-led industrialization, women are paid below minimum wages, work long hours, are not permitted to unionize, and are not given the benefits workers received during the old factory regime (1930–1978). Housing, health care, and child care are no longer considered a worker's right (1998, 89). Because workers were struggling to stay alive, the employers had the upper hand and would often pay below minimum wage in exchange for offering some of the social services needed for survival. Workers would be more willing to accept these low wages and poor working conditions if losing their jobs also meant losing their housing or access to health care. Cravey concludes that the maquiladora industry hurts both the workers and their families. She argues that since employers have the power, union contracts represent the employer's interests, and there is minimal enforcement of labor laws. As a result, the maquilas employ workers under the minimum legal age, pay below the minimum wage, fire workers without compensation, offer no job security, and disregard occupational health regulations:

> U.S. producers are using the maquiladoras industry primarily for mass production manufacturing operations as well as more traditional labor intensive assembly in order to reduce costs without fundamentally restructuring operations. The most rapidly growing segments of the maquiladora industry are the manufacturers—especially in the interior—and the labor intensive assembly plants—especially along the border. (1998, 72)

In summary, researchers have concluded that the new job opportunities in the maquila industry located along the Mexico-U.S. border have led to the further oppression of Mexican women. Employment in the maquiladoras often meant the movement of women from the informal economy, where they had been cleaning homes, making or selling clothes, or growing and preparing food, into the formal economy. Consequently, women must submit to the patriarchal structure at work as well as at home, in the economy and in society. In developing the exploitation thesis, Fernandez-Kelly (1994, 192) interpreted the entrance of women into the paid industrial labor force as a symptom of their economic vulnerability rather than an improvement of their lower status as individuals in society or within the family. According to Kopinak (1996, 15, 39), women were being exploited because the labor-intensive maquilas paid low real wages for repetitive monotonous work and signed "official contracts" with the CTM without the workers' consent. For Cravey (1998, 89), the exploitation went beyond wages; with the expansion of the maquila industry, health care, child care, housing, and subsidized or free meals were no longer considered a "right" of the worker. Tiano (1994, 124) found that whether young or middle-aged, single or married, childless or with children, the majority of women worked because their wages were essential to their families' financial survival. The "push factors" that suggest the exploitation thesis is operative in Mexico include the economic need of the family due to an increase in the number of female-headed households and the absence or underemployment of the husband; Mexico's economic crisis, which has eroded workers' purchasing power; and submission to patriarchal authority (Tiano 1994, 55). According to these researchers, these new maquila jobs were not "good, decent jobs" but instead another form of exploitation.

Profile of Female Maquila Workers

The female maquila workers in Mexico are a heterogeneous group of individuals with one common objective—survival. Almost all the women have families that they help support with their wages. Their wages are spent on the most basic goods and services: food, clothing, and school for their children. Although they all resided and worked in Nogales, Sonora, many had migrated to this border town for work. The female maquila workers in Nogales are older and married with children. Most women are educated and have two children in school whom they support with their earnings. At the point they were interviewed, the women had already spent considerable time with their current employers. For most women, moreover, it was not their first time in the labor force, although many had previously worked in the informal economy. They bring with them a multitude of work experiences—ranging from small local stores to large multinational factories.

News traveled fast about the new job opportunities along the border in the maquiladoras. Men, women, and entire families gathered together their belongings and moved closer to the border hoping to secure one of these new jobs. Many of the women in this sample were not born where they currently resided. Many had migrated to Nogales, Sonora, from the southern states of Chihuahua, Michoacán, and Veracruz (table 6.1). A few of the women came from as far as Tabasco and Chiapas, while the majority of women were born in Sonora and Sinaloa. No one in this sample was from Coahuila, Aguascalientes, Hidalgo, Tlaxcala, Colima, or Campeche.

The conventional image of the female workforce in maquiladoras is that of a homogeneous group of young, single, childless women with little work experience. Tiano (1994) explains this result by examining women's role in the economy from a cultural perspective. She believes this type of workforce is a direct result of the (primarily male) employers' stereotypes of women. She argues that employers assume young women tend to view wage work as a temporary activity before marriage, which makes it easier for companies to lay off workers and offer short-term contracts. High turnover allows companies to avoid the additional

Table 6.1. Birthplace of Female Workers in Nogales

Name of State	Number of Workers Born in State	Name of State	Number of Workers Born in State
Baja California	7	Oaxaca	11
Chihuahua	17	Puebla	7
Chiapas	3	San Luis Potosí	1
Durango	7	Sinaloa	156
Guanajuato	2	Sonora	188
Guerrero	7	Tabasco	1
Jalisco	7	Tamaulipas	2
México, D.F.	12	Quintana Roo	1
Michoacán	15	Veracruz	13
Moiles	1	Yucatán	1
Nayarit	13	Zacatecas	1
Nuevo León	1	Other Countries (U.S.)	3

labor costs—higher wages and accumulated benefits—associated with seniority. The other stereotype is based on the strong system of patriarchy in Mexico. Employers believe young women who still live at home with their families are more docile and compliant than older women (73). Carrillo and Hernández (1985) explain these management preferences in maquilas from an economic perspective. They argue that employers hire younger single women to reduce costs and turnover. It is assumed they are not supporting children or families and work merely to make money for nonessential items such as dances or dining out. Single women, moreover, are less likely to be mothers, so companies do not have to pay maternity leave or day care. Companies can also lower absenteeism by hiring single women. The balancing act for mothers between work and family can be extremely difficult to manage. Women who have a spouse or dependents are more likely to need time off because of unpreventable and unpredictable family situations (illness, school conferences, etc.). Employers act as profit-maximizing economic agents when they recruit and hire young, single, and childless female workers (Carrillo and Hernández 1985, 116).

Research on the maquiladoras in Mexicali and Baja California by Tiano (1994) and Ciudad Juárez by Fernandez-Kelly (1983), Pena

(1987), and Young (1991) supports the conventional view. Tiano's research separates workers according to the type of maquila that employed them—electronics and apparel. She discovered that the ideal maquila worker was young (twenty-three in electronics and twenty-eight in apparel) and predominantly single (65 percent in electronics and 52 percent in apparel) (1994, 81). The assemblers in these maquilas had small families: the mean number of children in electronics was 0.74 and in apparel slightly higher at 1.65 (81). For the entire sample, the maquila workers were on average twenty-six years old, single, and had one child. Fernandez-Kelly found this description applied to the workforce in Ciudad Juárez as well. She also separated workers according to the type of product produced by the maquila. The women were young, ranging in age from seventeen to twenty-five, and single (61 percent in electronics and 54 percent in apparel) (1983, 50, 52). The households in her sample were considerably larger, with an average of seven members, but only 53 percent of the households had children aged three and under. Her statistics revealed that most of the families were composed of relatives rather than children.

The conventional view also argues that employers sought women who were uneducated and had little experience in the labor market. The literature suggests that women with little education made ideal maquila workers because they were less likely to know their rights as workers and less likely to take the initiative to secure them (Carrillo and Hernández 1985; Fernandez-Kelly 1983). These women therefore would not pose a threat to management by organizing themselves into a union to claim their rights or strike when their rights had been violated. According to this view, women are preferred over men because they have no reason to doubt the validity of their employers' interpretation of their rights under the law and are therefore more docile in the workplace. This aspect of the conventional view is not uniformly supported by the existing literature; the workers in Ciudad Juárez fit this characterization, while the workers in Mexicali do not. The majority of the women surveyed in Fernandez-Kelly's research had completed only sixth grade (55 percent) and had never worked before in the formal economy (60 percent in electronic and 30 percent in apparel) (1983, 52, 53). Although there were clearly more educated and more experienced women in the electronic and apparel maquilas, it was not the norm.[3] The women surveyed by Tiano in Mexicali, however, tended to be more educated and have more labor market experience than purported by the conventional view. They had on average eight years of schooling (8.7 years in electronics and

6.53 in apparel) and eight years of experience in the labor force (5.53 in electronics and 9.84 in apparel) (1994, 81, 108).

The profile of the female maquila worker in Nogales based on my research does not fit the conventional view. In my sample, the mean age of a maquila worker was thirty, with some women as young as fourteen and as old as fifty-one. Although there were some young and childless women working, the vast majority had surpassed this stage of their lives and had become mature middle-aged women. In their thirties they tended to be married and have children who were dependent on their earnings. There was an average of five people in a family, with two under the age of sixteen. The family usually consisted of two adults and three children, two of which were young and dependent on others for survival. The two adults, however, were often family members (siblings, cousins, and parents) or friends but not husbands. Surprisingly, men were absent in a large number of households, and the women were the head of the household. Going house-to-house, it quickly became evident that current circumstances made the maquila woman the breadwinner of the family. Frequently, mothers holding infants came to the door, admitting their husbands or boyfriends were not living with them. Although a variety of explanations were given,[4] the consequences were the same: the woman of the household was the main income earner. As the breadwinner, each female worker supported on average three people on their salary, with some supporting as many as eleven and as few as one.

The maquila workers in Nogales had better credentials than most female minimum wage workers in Mexico. The average number of years of school completed by the female maquila workers was eight, while the average education level for Mexican workers in general is 3.8 years (World Development Report 2009). The women in Nogales were better educated, had previous work experience, and had earned seniority, which is the antithesis of the conventional view. In the sample almost all women had completed a basic education, and nearly half went further and completed pre-college degrees. There were a few women at the extremes; one woman completed seventeen years of schooling and found herself working alongside women who had not completed primary school. Figure 6.1 illustrates that an overwhelming majority (82 percent) of the women working on the assembly lines in the maquilas have completed, on average, eight years of schooling. This would be considered a good education in Mexico as six years is common. In the Mexican educational system eight years is equivalent to finishing primary and secondary school. Unlike the United States, in Mexico education is compulsory

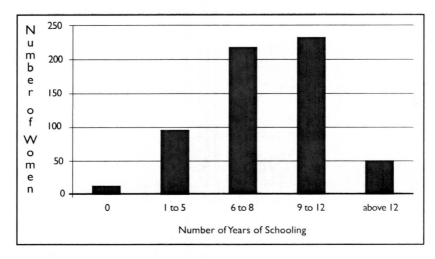

Figure 6.1. Educational attainments for maquila women.

and free only up through eighth grade. Thus in poor families it is common for children to begin working at the age of sixteen instead of attending preparatory school (pre-college or high school). It is simply too costly for families to send children to preparatory school. Families incur explicit (out-of-pocket) costs because they must pay for teachers, supplies, and books. They also incur implicit (opportunity) costs because they lose the wages children would have earned. Therefore it is interesting to find that almost half (**46** percent) of the women in this sample had nine or more years of schooling. As a result, many women were overqualified for their assembly line jobs, which required at most a secondary school certificate. Instead of preferring workers with little education, as the conventional view purports, employers appear to want more educated women. According to human capital theory, a worker with a higher education will be easier to train and will be more productive. More productive workers on an assembly line yield more output and larger revenues for the employers and company. It is a profitable strategy for companies to hire more educated women in this new global economy of mobile manufacturing.

The older age and extensive work experience of this female workforce suggests that young women stayed in the maquilas (although they may have moved from one to another) as they aged and did not see themselves as temporary members of the labor force. The permanence in employment status contrasts with the prevailing view that maquila workers are temporary participants in the workforce. Scholars espousing this perspective argue that women intend to be employed only a short time before they return to their more traditional domestic role in the home. Regardless of the circumstances that led them to seek employment in the maquilas,[5] they planned to return home and resume their roles as wives and mothers. Fernandez-Kelly (1983, 53–54) finds in her sample of women that 60 percent of the electronic workers and 30 percent of the apparel workers had not held previous jobs. Carrillo and Hernández (1985) also found that maquila workers were new to the workforce. In their research, the majority of women (69 percent) had no previous job experience. Even the women who had worked before were also new to formal employment; 75 percent had previously held only one job (121). The women I interviewed in Nogales were far from temporary. They had been working for most of their adult lives and planned to continue working. Some women had worked in the maquilas for years, while others were in their first month of work. The women had considerable experience on the job and had worked on average 3.88 or 4.0 years for a specific maquila. This average, however, includes varying lengths of seniority, from a few days to up to twenty-two years. Since outliers may have biased the mean in this case, the median and mode were also calculated. The most frequent response from women in this sample was four years (mode), and the middle value (or median) was three years. These summary statistics tell the same story: women did not voluntarily move from one job to another or from one maquila to another. These women were clearly permanent members of the workforce. This is further supported by the statistics on the employment history of the women. Of the 620 women, 91 percent had worked before and 57 percent had worked in another maquila. This is an extremely high labor force participation rate for women in developing or developed countries. These Mexican women worked in both the formal and informal economies. Women were clearly not being dragged into the labor market by maquilas if only fifteen women had previously been in school and thirty-seven women had been at home. Not surprisingly, many women previously worked in the more traditional female occupations, domestic service (7 percent), cottage industry or *casa* (12 percent), and sales or *tienda* and restaurant (8 percent) (figure 6.2). These jobs are primarily in the informal economy, whereas the maquiladora jobs are in the formal economy.

In summary, our image of the maquila worker must be altered to reflect the fact that the women are older and more educated and have young children. They are not young, single, childless women who con-

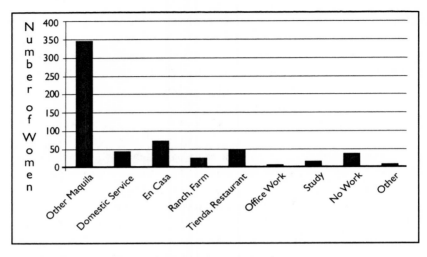

Figure 6.2. Previous work experiences of women workers.

sider their labor force participation temporary. This new image of the ideal maquila worker discovered by Tiano (1994) when she conducted follow-up interviews in 1990 has become the prevailing reality. The managers she interviewed revealed hiring practices that favored older, more mature women, preferably with children (92). Fussell's (2000) multivariate analysis uncovered similar results for maquilas in Tijuana. She found that employers continued to hire the cheapest and most vulnerable labor force available. In her sample, women working in maquilas tended to be over twenty-five, had a child under five years old, and had only a primary education (72–74). This is clearly a dramatic change from the past and suggests that the conventional view is no longer the norm. The profile of the maquila worker in Nogales reflects this change in preference. The women in my sample are older and have children to support. They are not new to the demands and routines of formal employment and have been employed a considerable part of their adult lives. Instead of viewing children as a distraction for the mother, maquila owners view them as assets, giving mothers strong motivation to work hard. Women with children are less likely to quit because they have the responsibilities of child care and are in desperate need of the wages to feed their families (Tiano 1994, 94). As Tiano points out, employers believed "children were an asset to a woman's successful job performance because the responsibilities of childcare made her more reliable in all aspects of their lives" (92). Many managers she interviewed voiced their preference for older, more mature women. They felt older women were more dependable and were less likely to be absent from work (92). This implied lower turnover and more consistency along the assembly line, which generates higher output.

Why Do Women Work?

It is important to establish the women's motivations for working in the maquiladoras in order to understand from their perspective whether it was *por necesidad* (for necessity) or *porque le gusta* (because they like it). Proponents of the integration thesis argue that the growth of the ma-quila industry has provided women with jobs that liberate them from dependence on their husbands and society. Women will be able to leave their homes where their traditional role has left them demoralized and marginalized and enter the labor market where they become empowered and productive members of society. According to this theory, women enter the workforce because they want to and not because they have to. Women accept employment voluntarily because they are more ed-ucated and want to learn skills that help them become financially inde-pendent. They enjoy the work, hope to be promoted, and can leave if it doesn't meet their expectations. In sharp contrast, the exploitation the-sis argues that the jobs in the maquilas have created another layer of op-pression of women. Women leave the oppression of their fathers and husbands at home to accept the oppression of an employer in the ma-quiladora. Rather than enter voluntarily, women must work in the ma-quilas because of the economic need of their families. Women can be exploited by employers because they have to work, they are desperate, and they cannot afford to complain. They may enjoy their work and hope for promotions, but they cannot leave if the job falls short of their expectations.

The results from my research indicate that it is survival instincts that push a vast majority of the women assemblers into the maquilas day after day and month after month. The women work to feed and clothe their families. It is that simple. The women do not feel they have a choice. They have to work. They know the bills have piled up—food, purified water, tortillas, transportation, electricity, phone, school supplies, school fees, nonpotable water for bathing. . . . The list is endless. The results of the 620 surveys refute the integration thesis that women worked be-cause they want to. Only five responses to the question "What do you like about your work?" reveal a woman's desire to gain transferable skills and/or to become independent:

> "Todo pero mas la costura y lo que" (Everything but especially sewing and that)
> "Tener responsavilidad" (Having responsibility)
> "Que me agradecen el trabajo porque saldo muy bien me vin de mucho" (That they appreciate my work, because I have a good salary and it goes a long way)
> "Que tenia oportunidad de subir de puesto oportunidad de seguir pre-paran dose" (That I had the opportunity to move up and the opportunity for more training)
> "Las cosas q'uno v aprendiendo las cosas que va conociendo" (All the things that you learn and get to know)

Instead, the more common response was that they didn't like anything ("nada") about the job but needed the money to provide for their family ("nada pero tengo que trabajar"). Based on my visits to many of the homes of the workers, it is clear that these women workers are now the breadwinners of the family because their husbands are ill, incarcerated, or with another woman or seeking employment illegally across the border in the United States. The responses to the surveys make it clear that women's wages are essential for the survival of the family, especially the children. In some cases the women work because their husbands' earnings are insufficient; in others, the women work because they are the head of the household. This sentiment is revealed in a number of responses to "What don't you like about your work?" A few of their responses reveal the pressure the women feel as breadwinners:

> "No le gusta el salario, ni el jefe es muy presionante ella tiene que mantenera sus niñas y a sus papas." (I don't like the salary, or the manager because he really pressures us. I'm the one who has to support my little girls and my parents.)
> "No le alcanza para mantenera sus hijos ella esta solo mantiene a sus 4 hijos." (It's not enough to support my kids, and I'm on my own and I take care of four kids by myself.)
> "Nada pero tiene que trabajar porque mi esposo esta en la carcel." (Nothing, but I have to work because my husband is in jail.)
> "Ella trabajar y mantiene a su esposo y hijos porque su esposo es invidente." (I work and support my husband and children because my husband is blind.)

"Yo tengo a mi hija estudiando en prepartoria si no trabajo el salario de mi esposo no me alcanzaria" (My daughter is in high school, and if I don't work my husband's salary isn't enough).

"No me gusta trabajar de noche, pero tengo que trabajar porque dos de mis hijos tienen ataques epileptico y tienen que tomar pastilles de por vida." (I don't like working at night, but I have to work because two of my sons have epileptic attacks and they have to take pills for the rest of their life.)

They frequently lamented that they did not get to see their children as much as they would like because they were always working. Examples of the common responses are the following:

"No le gusta que su jefe la presione para que haga el trabajo mas a prisa y que no le den permiso cuando alguno de sus hijos se enferma y como no tiene familia esta sola con mis hijos." (I don't like that the boss pressures me to do the job more quickly and that they don't give me permission to leave when one of my children is sick and since I don't have any family and I am by myself with my kids.)

"El tener que trabajar mucho tiempo y no poder ver a mis hijos como yo quisiera, el que nos tengan trabajando entra bajos muy pesados y no nos den descansos." (Having to work so much and not being able to see my kids as much as I would like, I also don't like that they make us work really tough jobs and they don't give us any breaks.)

A Typical Day in the Life of a Maquiladora Worker

Whatever the motivation, work in the maquiladora had a profound influence on the women's lives. What follows is a description of a "typical" workday for a woman working in a maquila in Mexico. I based this description on personal observations obtained from three different sources that represented reality as closely as possible. The first source of information was the family I lived with during my home stay in Nogales. The woman in the family worked at a maquila packing cucumbers and peppers in boxes. As a member of the household, I watched her every day for three months as she got up and went to work in the morning and returned home in the evening. At night she shared her reflections about the day with me and her oldest daughter. I kept a personal journal about what I saw and heard. I realize that this was only one woman's experience and could have been the exception rather than the rule. I put her comments in context and discerned their representativeness during the interview process. My second source of information was the women I had the privilege to interview in their homes. A pattern quickly emerged from the multitude of experiences expressed by the women. The work-day in the majority of the maquilas was identical, the only variation be-ing the shift women worked. And finally, I was a silent observer dur-ing many of the conversations between the women who sought counsel from Juana or Polita, paid employees of AFO. The rules set by employ-ers concerning breaks, absenteeism, injuries, and contracts were revealed as they shared their frustrations and problems. After hearing the same things over and over, I constructed the following daily routine of a ma-quila worker.

Women, beginning at the age of sixteen, wake up at 4:00 A.M. to have a cup of instant Nescafé and a warm flour tortilla. If they have children, as many of them do, they prepare a breakfast of eggs and beans for their children, who are still asleep. They iron their clothes, usually a skirt, and then get dressed, washing their hair only if there is time. Within thirty minutes of rising they are out the door and walking to the bus stop where the company bus will pick them up and take them to work. They arrive at the maquila by 5:00 A.M., after riding silently in a hot, sticky, dusty bus.

Their shift begins at 5:00 A.M. and ends at 5:00 P.M.—a long, twelve-hour day. They do not receive overtime for the hours they work over the legal limit (Mexican law states that no worker should have to work more than eight hours a day). They do not complain because they desperately need the wages they will receive at the end of the week. Although forty-eight hours is a typical workweek, some women work fewer hours and others work more. It depends on the production "standards" or quotas for a given week.

The work is tedious and physically demanding. Typically the work-stations have no chairs, so women have to stand all day. Their hands grow sore and stiff as they repeat the same motion over and over again. Supervisors say, "If you can move your hands you can work." The women are allowed two ten-minute breaks, one in the morning and one in the afternoon, and thirty minutes for lunch. The only time work-ers can get something to drink is during the breaks, despite the need for water. In addition, workers are allowed to talk only during breaks and lunch and are fined if they do so while working. The maquilas pro-vide lunch for the workers in a lunchroom; the menu varies from ramen noodles to rice and beans. The quality of the food is often poor. Many women remarked on their surveys that they often found hair, fingernails, and rocks in their "free" lunch.

At the end of the day, supervisors check each station's production and compare it to the quota. If it falls short the women are told to stay until their output matches the quota. Others pack up their belongings, take off their work jackets, and are searched as they leave the assembly line to prevent theft. Exhausted and barely able to walk, they trudge toward the large doors of the maquila and go outside. They locate their bus, climb aboard, and are relieved to sit down for the first time that day. As the buses make their way through the dusty and bumpy unpaved streets, some women chat, while others, exhausted to the bone, remain silent or doze briefly until they reach their stop.

The women walk home and greet their spouse or children as they enter their house. Their "second shift" begins as they prepare dinner and tidy up the house. As they fall asleep around 10:00 P.M., they know a new day will begin at four o'clock the next morning.

A Liberating or Humiliating Experience?

It is far too simplistic to argue that every woman's experience in the maquilas was the same, day in and day out. Some women may have enjoyed getting out of the house and working; others may have suffered physically and emotionally at the hands of the jefe. The statistics, quotes, and stories of women's work experiences reveal the extent to which women felt liberated or exploited by the maquilas that employed them. I attempt here to interpret the qualitative data gathered during the interviews in order to distinguish between everyday practices and rare events in the work lives of the Mexican women. How were women treated by their supervisors? Did they feel empowered or enslaved? What sort of hiring practices did maquilas follow? Did they abuse their power in the employer-employee relationship? By documenting these women's experiences, we are able to look inside the maquilas. These women's voices give us a rare glimpse of the triumphs and struggles they experience working for U.S. multinational companies.

In order to put the women's responses into proper perspective, it is necessary to understand the dynamics within the maquilas as well as the individuals responsible for enforcing regulations and setting the production standards. Many of the maquilas along the border have an organizational structure placing the plant manager at the top and the workers

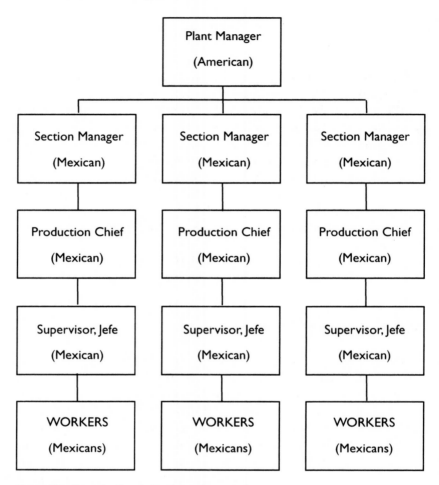

Figure 6.3. Organizational structure of a maquila.

at the bottom of the hierarchy (figure 6.3). The plant manager or general manager gives orders to the section managers, who relay them to the production chiefs or superintendents. The supervisors are the next in line, and they have direct and daily contact with the workers. Workers fear the plant supervisor, or jefe, much more than the manager, who is often American and has little contact with them. The supervisor has considerable control over the workers' lives and time: when they work, when their break is over, whether they can use the bathroom, if they have met the production quota, whether they must work overtime or are allowed to leave early. The supervisors communicate with the assembly line managers, who often work alongside the workers checking production quotas, or "standards" as they are called, and the quality of the work (Prieto 1997, 18).

Positive Work Experiences

Although the majority of women in this sample expressed negative feelings about their job in the maquila, there were many women with positive remarks about their work experience. Their responses to question 14 on the survey, "What do you like about your job?," yielded a number of common answers and a few uncommon ones. The common answers were placed into more general categories and are shown in figure 6.4. The three most frequent responses were "the environment" (20 percent), "everything" (16 percent), and "type of work" (12 percent). In many cases women responded simply with "el ambiente" (the environment) or "el ambiente de la maquiladora" (the environment of the maquiladora), while others elaborated on what they meant by "the environment." Although some women were referring to the physical environment, most were referring to something less tangible—camaraderie. Workers commenting on the actual physical environment inside the maquila painted a picture quite different from the "dark satanic mill" of nineteenth-century Britain. They described a well-lit factory with a

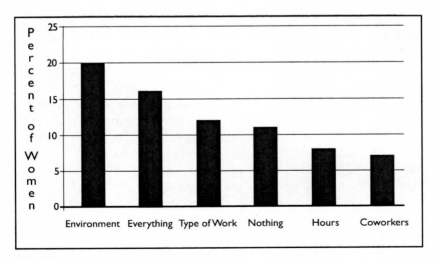

Figure 6.4. What workers liked about their jobs.

pleasant atmosphere and modern amenities. For several workers the maquila served as a haven where they could escape to an air-conditioned facility with water fountains, clean bathrooms, and sometimes even showers. For many other women, something much less tangible put a smile on their faces as they began their workday. For them, the benefits of a group environment, meeting new people, and forming friendships with other workers made work enjoyable.[6] This sentiment was expressed in a variety of ways: "las amistades que a ocho con algunas compañeras" (friendship with other workers); "muy buenos compañeros" (very good company); "la convivencia con las demas personas" (the camraderie with other people); "que es tranquilo" (that it is relaxing); "hasta ahoy el ambiente muy buen os compañeros" (until today, the environment, very good companions); "el compañerismo de las mujeres" (the companionship of the women). By establishing friendships with coworkers, these women create a personal attachment to the maquila. For women who previously worked on farms, in homes, or in small stores, this was a definite advantage.

Quite a number of women expressed satisfaction with the specific type of work they performed. When asked what they like about their work they responded by describing the task they completed on the assembly line. The comments reveal a general appreciation for technical as well as nontechnical assembly tasks. The women felt good about contributing to production. Women responded that they liked "hacer las piezas" (to make the parts); "utilizar la maquina de acabado" (use the machine to finish); "soldar" (to weld); "la costura" (the sewing); "hacer lo oberoles mas bien coserlos y doblarlos y los descansos" (to sew well and fold the overalls, and the breaks); "la magia de agarrar el monton de tela y sacar un aprendame gusta coser y pegarle la espumita y lo rasponsito para que se abroche la prenda" (the magic of taking a bunch of cloth and turning it into a piece of clothing and also sewing and putting the nylon and the other material together so that the clothes button up). These types of responses are grouped together under the category "Type of Work" in figure 6.4. Seventy-six women (12 percent of the sample) seemed to take pride in their jobs and felt productive and useful. These women believed their contribution to the maquila industry and to the formal economy was significant. Some of them felt they were learning useful skills. For example, one woman replied that she liked her work because of "las cosas q'uno v aprendiendo las cosas que be conociendo" (the things that you learn and get to know along the way), and another responded, "me agradecen el trabajo porque saldo muy bien y me vin de mucho" (the work enhances my skills, and I like this type of work). Other women gave responses indicating they felt they were acquiring good work habits on the job: "tener responsavilidad" (having responsibility); "se hace uno mas sociable" (it makes you more sociable). One plausible interpretation of these positive sentiments is that these women felt empowered and liberated by their jobs in the maquila.

It is very difficult to interpret the one-word responses—"todos" (everything), "nada" (nothing)—and the lack of responses to this question. Sixteen percent of the women reported they liked everything about their work, which indicates an overall positive work experience. These women had no complaints, no problems, no concerns; they were satisfied with their work. Common responses expressing this sentiment were "todos" (everything), "me gusta mi trabajo" (I like my work), and "todo me gusta" (I like everything). Other responses were more specific, identifying hours, friends, and benefits as things they liked about their job. Eleven percent (seventy women) responded negatively to the question, "What do you like about your work?" by simply saying, "Nada." Clearly these women were completely dissatisfied with their work experience. It is a bit more puzzling, however, to interpret the 14 percent who left the question blank. Perhaps they did not know what to say or did not like anything about their job. Given this ambiguity in interpretation, it is reasonable to conclude that at least 48 percent of the women interviewed liked one or more aspects of working in a maquiladora.[7] This does not mean, however, that 48 percent of the women interviewed felt liberated by their job. Instead, it means that nearly half of the women liked at least one aspect of their assembly line job. Based on the responses, it can be concluded that only the 16 percent who said they liked "everything" were satisfied with their job and had no complaints or concerns. This group of women clearly had a positive work experience in the maquiladoras. In the context of the literature, these women were liberated by their jobs in the maquilas.

The qualitative data provide essential information about how the women felt about their jobs. Unlike statistics that give averages, ranges, and frequencies, the candid responses of women provide insight into how women viewed their jobs and work experiences. Based on the responses of women to question 14, "What do you like about your job?" it is clear there are women who chose to work in the maquilas and believe it is a good job. These women, instead of being forced to toil away their days, feel empowered by their current jobs. They are thankful to have a job and did not feel exploited by a multinational corporation.

Negative Work Experiences

Mexican women are given the opportunity to work and earn a wage in the maquila industry. The oppressive nature of many of these multinationals, however, often leaves them disillusioned, exploited, and even humiliated. Why then would women take these jobs or continue to work for the multinationals if the situation is so horrible? An economist would argue that since they are not forced or bonded into working in the maquiladoras, the women must be better off than they were previously. In weighing their options, the women are acting rationally when they choose to work in the maquiladora even if they are mistreated. If they do not like it, they can leave at any time. But is this a reality for most of these women? What kind of options do they have? In most cases these women have exhausted all their viable options, and the only alternative is starvation. In reality there are no "choices" or options to consider. Sadly, most of these women are controlled by their desperate financial situations. Some money, no matter how little, is better than no money at all. Many women would admit that a job in the maquila is better than no job at all. Unfortunately this job does not always fulfill its obligations according to Mexican law. Rather than the "decent job" they expected, it was a demeaning and dead-end job. Over half (54 percent) of the women earned less in their current job than in their previous job. Benefits that would go a long way toward buying necessities are withheld. Access to health care, one of the few benefits given, is limited when the injuries or illnesses are work-related. Living in fear of losing their jobs and without a union to back them, the women acquiesce. The multinationals that conduct business in the maquilas have almost complete control over the worker. They determine how much money these women receive, the amount of time spent with family members, and the number and length of breaks these women have throughout the day. In some cases the multinationals even determine, indirectly, when these women can have children. Admittedly these women are fortunate to have a job, but they would clearly be better off if companies were to follow the labor laws and give them what they have a legal right to.

For the majority of women in Nogales, working in the maquiladoras along the border is a humiliating experience. The maquilas engage in illegal practices, the supervisors are inhumane, and the multinationals engage in unethical behavior. The illegal practices of the maquilas leave women unable to support their families and provide health care for their children. The inhumane treatment by the assembly line jefes results in forced overtime, inadequate breaks, unjustified firings, and unreasonable wage deductions. The multinational companies that own the maquilas engage in unethical behavior by stripping the women of their reproductive rights. The types and number of complaints expressed by these women during interviews supports this conclusion.

Short-Term Contracts and Job Security

Unlike most factory jobs in the United States, many women working in the maquilas often have no contract stating their wage, their hours, or their term of employment. They have no contract explaining their rights as workers by Mexican law or their obligations as workers to the employer. Simply put, one woman responded to what she didn't like about her job, "No el que no me dan contracto" (They didn't give me a contract). Although this may be common in the informal economy where many people are self-employed, it is uncommon in the formal economy where national labor laws dictate specifics about the employer-employee relationship. In the United States, if workers do not receive a contract on securing employment with a company, their union steps in and holds the company accountable until the violation is corrected. In Mexico, if workers do not receive a contract when they are hired there is nobody to correct the situation. It is therefore not surprising to find that many multinationals outsourcing in Mexico do not offer contracts to their workers. As a result, workers are powerless against the multinationals. The situation is ideal for employers to take advantage of their employees: few workers know their rights, no independent unions exist, and the Mexican government overlooks violations. Without a contract, anything is possible. Wages can be lowered, hours can be increased, and employment can be terminated. Understandably, many of the women working in the maquilas worry that they will be terminated without cause and without advance notice. Women in this precarious position were more likely to be compliant on the factory floor. This benefits the maquilas because they are able to keep the size of their workforce flexible and the workers highly productive.

Even women who had contracts with their employers lacked job security. The length of contracts has been constantly changing in the maquilas over the past six years. During the earlier stages of the maquila industry, workers received one-year contracts that were often extended. Many of the older workers interviewed mentioned they were given one-year contracts. If they successfully completed the year they became permanent workers, or their contract was "indefinido" (indefinite). Women of all ages agreed that this situation was preferable because it gave them both job security and social security (medical care). By the time I arrived in Nogales to conduct my interviews in February 2004, most maquilas were offering six-month contracts to newly hired workers. For many women, this meant fewer benefits since they were no longer permanent employees with respect to the law.

Several women shared their frustrations and pointed out that shorter contracts allowed the companies to change their wages and hours every six months. The situation worsened by the time I returned in May 2006: maquilas were only offering three-month contracts. The companies argued it was necessary to adjust the size of the workforce, especially when the U.S. economy experienced a recession. The women claimed it allowed companies to redefine their workforces from "permanent" to "temporary." A common response was, "No me gusta que me vayan hacer firmar otro contrato por tres meses" (I don't like that they are going to make me sign another three-month contract). Workers argued this allowed companies to further reduce costs because employers did not have to pay the higher wages that accompanied seniority or any benefits, including medical care. Companies, depending on orders, would then rehire existing workers for another three months. This hire-rehire process continued for several years. During a visit in February 2007 many maquilas were offering twenty-eight-day, or monthly, contracts. This put women in a most precarious position—in constant fear of losing their jobs. Although these contracts offered very little job security, many women were compelled to accept them. Some maquilas used the short contracts to threaten their workers, increasing their anxiety about having no money to feed their families. A few examples of the women's responses are as follows: "Nos obligan a trabajar tiempo extra diciendo que pueden cancelar el trato" (They make us work extra time and say that if we don't, they can cancel our contract); "Si falto no me dan mi contrato" (If I miss work they won't give me a contract); "a mi cunao lo despi dieron después de 6 meses porque se lo vencio según ellos el contrato" (They laid off my brother-in-law after six months because according to them his contract had expired). Labor rights advocates recognize the difficult predicament short-term contracts create. Francisca Acuña Hernández from the CFO realized the situation had deteriorated since NAFTA at the release of their report:

> In Miami they asked us why we were demonstrating against the FTAA.
> I said that free trade was supposed to benefit everybody. It's been quite

a while now, and the reality is that we are poorer than we were before. We working people used to earn good wages, but now they're falling. Working conditions are not like they were before. You used to become permanent after working for a month. Now, they're giving us month-to-month contracts, so that we can never earn seniority or health benefits. Our other benefits are also disappearing. (CFO 1999, 1)

Inadequate Wages and Substandard Living Conditions

One of the strongest justifications given for the creation of hundreds of maquiladoras along Mexico's border was that they would provide good wages and benefits. The maquilas along the border, however, do not pay a living wage or provide the benefits necessary for survival. Though the women surveyed in Nogales earned salaries greater than the minimum wage, the salaries fail to cover basic needs. According to Mexican law in 2004, the minimum wage is approximately 44 pesos per day, or 308 pesos per week. An average pay of 644 pesos per week was reported by the maquila workers who were surveyed in Nogales. When examined from a purely numerical perspective, the average pay is more than double the federal minimum wage, which creates the perception that these women are earning high wages for low-skilled labor. These wages, however, fall short of what is necessary to climb out of poverty. According to Mexican labor law, the daily minimum wage should represent purchasing power for a basic standard of living. A living wage, as it is called in the literature, requires enough money to purchase the amount of food, housing, clothing, and nonconsumables necessary for survival. It is widely acknowledged that a worker needs to earn four times the legal minimum wage to afford the goods and services necessary for survival. As reported by the CFO from a study by the Center for Reflection, Education, and Action (CREA), "In the cities surveyed, it would take between four and five minimum wage salaries to meet the basic needs of a family of four" (CFO n.d.a). At the 2004 minimum wage level, that would mean that maquila workers' weekly salaries should be between 1,232 pesos and 1,540 pesos. Using the mean earnings of the 620 women, the "average" woman must earn 588 to 896 pesos more than they are currently earning.[8] This figure is almost double what they are currently being paid. Undoubtedly such significant additional earnings would have a dramatic impact on their families' standard of living.

As heads of households and major contributors to family income, the women are well aware that the money they earn falls short of what they

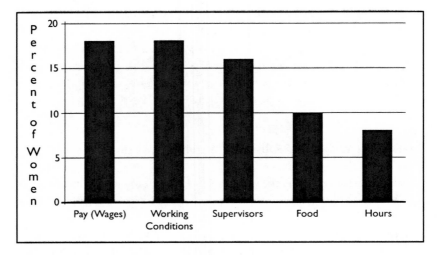

Figure 6.5. What workers disliked about their jobs.

need. It doesn't seem to matter how hard or how long they work, their wages barely pay for food and water. Common among the qualitative data gathered was the complaint of nonsustainable wages. As figure 6.5 reveals, the most frequent answer to the question, "What don't you like about your job?" was "el salario" or "el sueldo," the pay.[9] Eighteen percent of the 620 women responded they were dissatisfied with their pay. In one form or another, the most frequent response boiled down to frank statements such as "Lo que no me gusta es el bajo salario que la empresa nos brinda" (I don't like the low salary that the firm offers us) or "Es muy poco de lo que me pagan" (It's very little that they pay me). A number of women were candid about their predicament, admitting that their husbands had sought higher wages in the United States, for example, "El salario que es muy poco y su marido tuvo que emigarlo Estado Unidos por falta dinero" (The salary is very little, and my husband had to migrate to the United States because there wasn't enough money). Other women confessed they couldn't make ends meet, for example, "No le gusta el salario, ni el jefe que es muy presionante ella tiene que mantener a sus niñas y a sus papas" (I don't like the salary or the boss because he really pressures us, and I'm the one who has to support my little girls and my parents); and "El salario que ya no se lo han subido y no le alcanza para manterera sus hijos ella esta sola mantiene a sus 4 hijos" (You can't get an increase, and you don't make enough to support your four children).

This may not come as a surprise to anyone in business who would without hesitation say that workers as a whole are generally dissatisfied with their pay.[10] However, it would be a mistake to interpret this result from an American perspective. The maquila industry and the jobs they create are pushing the country forward to first world status. The jobs created in the maquilas are the main source of employment for unskilled workers. Employment of the masses can eliminate poverty and raise families' standard of living. The initial stages of industrialization, however, are often associated with sweatshop conditions and worker exploitation (Bhagwati 2004; Sachs 2005; Tuttle 1999). The complaints of the Mexican maquila workers are therefore not unique, but they are unusual. Complaining, especially among women, is not common in the Mexican culture. A possible testimony to this fact is that 23 percent of the women left the answer to this question blank (this response is not included in figure 6.5). Thus it is more remarkable that they complained at all since their culture has taught them to cope, compromise, and be thankful for what they have instead of worrying about something they don't have.

Concerns over inadequate wages reveal there has been very little progress in the past two decades. The CFO and several researchers (Carrillo and Hernández 1985, 131; Tiano 1994, 149) uncovered this problem ten to twenty years ago. According to the CFO, "The cost of the official 'market basket' of food, housing, and essential services has risen by 247 percent since 1994. Many products, including gasoline, telephone service, milk, chicken, bread, and even beans are more expensive on the Mexican side of the border than on the U.S. side. For us, simply feeding our families is becoming more difficult every day" (CFO 1999, 2). As one worker testified, "In 1993, even with a single salary and two children in school, I could buy more. It used to provide enough to send your children to school and eat better" (CFO, 2009, 1). Several workers' comments reveal just how difficult it is to provide for a family and that they used to be able to live month to month but now live from day to day. Many women must supplement their wages earned at the maquila to buy essentials for their families. The CFO reported that "to eke out their wages and provide a little extra for their families, women workers are particularly likely to supplement their income from shift work by selling sweets or other goods during their breaks; by selling their blood to blood banks on the other side of the border; by selling products at weekend flea markets; and sometimes, by casual prostitution" (CFO 1999, 5). As one woman testified, "I have to take in other peo-

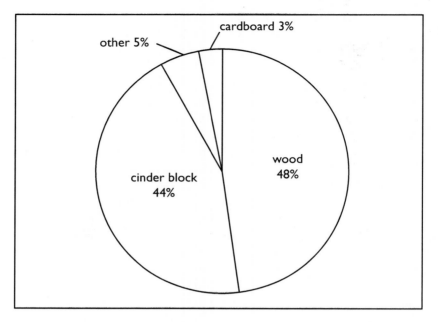

Figure 6.6. Material of house.

ple's washing, and I am still only half way to meeting expenses" (CREA 2001, 71). And it isn't an isolated problem experienced only by maquila workers in Nogales. Mexican workers all along the border feel the pinch. The CREA study in 2001 concluded that maquiladora workers needed four to five times the minimum wage in order to attain a very modest standard of living. Detailed calculations of earnings and essential expenses revealed that the legal minimum wage provided only 25 percent of a sustainable living wage in Piedras Negras and only 27 percent in Ciudad Acuña (CFO n.d.a).

The consequence of such low wages is visible in the homes of the maquila workers. One needs only to step into the realm of a border town to understand that these wages are not supporting the maquila workers. A visit to a worker's home in any of the colonias, except those that are government subsidized, sheds light on their daily struggles. Most maquila workers live in homes made from wood or cinder block, as illustrated in figure 6.6. Almost half, 48 percent, of the workers live in homes constructed from wood. These wooden homes are typically a combination of two-by-fours, plywood, and scraps (see photos 17 and 18). Forty-four percent live in homes constructed of cinder blocks. These are typically

Photos 17 and 18. Homes made primarily of wood in Nogales.

one story high with two openings, one for a window and the other for a door (photos 19 and 20). The remaining workers live in homes made of cardboard (3 percent) or other materials (5 percent) such as tar or roof shingles. Roofs of the homes vary widely from a flimsy plastic tarp or a blanket to a firm piece of plywood or plastic. Some homes have no roof at all, habitable because of the desert climate but not optimal. Owners explain that they ran out of funds before construction was complete.

The homes are small and the rooms multifunctional. The homes have, on average, two rooms. Ninety-three women surveyed live in a home with only one room, and only one woman has a home with as many as seven rooms. The rooms are small and contain all the family's material possessions. The floors are unfinished and consist of either dirt or cement (figure 6.7). Fifty-two percent of the homes had dirt floors, 42 percent had cement floors, and 5 percent had wood floors. A few floors were made of asphalt (0.38 percent) or tile (0.75 percent). Keeping these floors clean, whatever the material, is a challenge because the water used to mop is nonpotable.[11] There were, on average, two consumer durables per household. This ranged from a phone to a gas stove, from a TV to a refrigerator, or from a radio to a microwave. Many, if not all, of these appliances were secondhand, *estufa segunda* or *refri segunda*. A few households owned only one appliance; only one household enjoyed as many as seven. It was common to find that a two-room home had a refrigerator and stove in one room and a large bed in the other. It was customary for an entire family to sleep together in one king-size bed.

Owning just barely enough to survive, these maquila workers had very few material comforts or modern conveniences to enjoy when they returned home after a day of hard work. Fortunately, almost 90 percent of the women live in homes that have electricity. Electricity makes it possible to have light when it is dark, to keep food cold in refrigerators, and to operate most household appliances. Almost all the homes had a television, although most were old, secondhand, and small. The majority of households lacked running water and proper drainage. As illustrated in figure 6.8, as many as 66 percent of the households had no running water in their home, and 67 percent had no method to dispose of *any* type of waste. Life without running water causes many simple daily chores to become major time-consuming projects. Some daily activities simply take more time, effort, or money, while others are not even possible and lead to unhealthy outcomes. For example, life-sustaining activities

Photos 19 and 20. Homes made primarily of cinder block in Nogales.

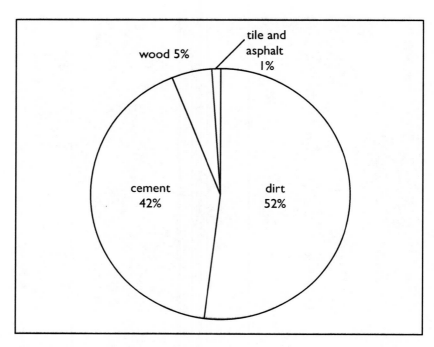

Figure 6.7. Types of floors in house.

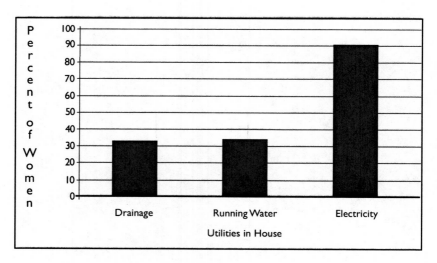

Figure 6.8. Living conditions in the colonias.

such as drinking water and washing hands require buying and transporting purified water, and urination and elimination of solid waste requires the cheaper nonpotable water. Similarly, daily routines for personal hygiene such as showering, washing hair, and brushing teeth can damage a person's health. Many families cannot afford large quantities of drinking water and therefore resort to using nonpotable water for these activities. Consequently, most families must dedicate a significant portion of their wages to buy bins of nonpotable water in order to bathe and clean dishes as well as purified water to drink and wash their hands. The CFO reported, "Over the past ten years, overall conditions and the quality of life in Mexico have deteriorated. Maquiladora workers who make electronic products or auto parts don't earn enough to buy what they make. Communities that house global companies such as Alcoa, Delphi, or GE should be enjoying good economic conditions. Instead, they don't even have basic services like running water, sewage, electricity, or paved roads. Squatters keep opening up new land because there isn't enough housing" (1999, 6).

Working Conditions

The second most common complaint of the workers was the working conditions. Eighteen percent of the women mentioned some aspect of the working conditions when asked what they did not like about their work. Collectively their comments reveal that the working conditions in the maquilas resemble those in nineteenth-century British factories. In these twenty-first-century sweatshops, workers are treated like cogs in a machine, resources to utilize fully, and not as human beings. This inhumane treatment left workers exhausted, sick, and sometimes permanently disabled. Tremendous pressure was placed on workers to perform consistently at very high levels, ignoring physical and mental limitations. The number and the length of breaks were limited. Workers were asked on a daily basis to ignore normal and necessary bodily functions in order to perform beyond what is physically possible. Workers had to ignore fatigue and continue working until break time. Workers often had to ignore urges to use the bathroom. Workers were fined or punished if they used the bathroom longer than the allotted time. One woman we interviewed was fired because she took seven minutes for a bathroom break. She told us she was suspended for using part of her bathroom break to call her husband (who was in the hospital). She said she took three minutes to use the bathroom and talked for four minutes on the phone. The supervisor disapproved and told her she was suspended and had to leave the maquila immediately. She refused to leave, whereupon the supervisor called the police. The supervisor then told her she was fired. She was forced to leave the maquila without getting her belongings from her locker. She was very upset because she was suspended and fired for a reason not on the list (lateness, illness, talking, and not meeting the quota). Workers had to get permission to get a drink of water. They were not allowed to talk to one another while on the assembly line. These relentless physical and emotional demands left the women feeling enslaved to their work. As two women so aptly put it, "Es muy esclavizado el trabajo" (The work is very enslaving), and "Los jefes te esclavizan al trabajo" (The bosses enslave you at work).

Unfortunately this type of mistreatment was not rare among the maquilas at the border. One hundred twenty women in the sample mentioned working conditions when asked what they disliked about their job. Women particularly complained that bathroom breaks were too short: "El tiempo dan para ir al baño 5 minutos" (The time they give to go to the bathroom is five minutes); "enojones y no puede ir al baño cuando le dan ganas tiene que aguantarse" (angry people, and I can't go the bathroom when I need to, I have to wait); and "5 minutos para tomar agua 2 veces puede ir al baño y 1 sola vez tomar agua" (you can go to the bathroom twice, and you only have five minutes once a day to get a drink of water). Several women recalled the consequences of taking bathroom breaks longer than allotted: "No le dan permiso para ir al baño y le levantaron un reporte porque duro 11 minutos en el baño" (They don't give me permission to go to the bathroom, and they even filed a complaint against me once because I was in the bathroom for eleven minutes); "que nos dentan poco tiempo par ir al baño site dilatas 1 minuto mas del tiempo te levatan una reporte" (that they don't give you much time to use the bathroom, and if you stay one minute more than you are supposed to, they file a complaint). Most women reported they were written up; others lost their "bonus"[12]; and a few were fired. Many women complained that the breaks were too short: "No me gusta es los descansos de 10 minutos no alcanza hacer nada en 10 minutos" (I don't like the ten-minute breaks, you can't do anything in ten minutes); "los descansos de 5 minutos" (the breaks of five minutes). One woman's frustrations with the working conditions are clear in her response: "Las reglas muy duras que pone, no puedes platicar, tienes 10 minutos para ir al baño y a mi no me al cansa" (The rules that they have are very strict, you can't talk, you have ten minutes to go to the bathroom, and that's not enough for me).

These and similar responses document the inhumane treatment of the women working in the maquilas. Unions fought long and hard for these basic labor rights in the United States. These same labor rights must be extended to workers in Mexico, especially in the multinational corporations owned and operated by Americans. Denying workers basic labor rights is wrong and illegal. No firm has the right to deny or limit the number of lavatory visits for a worker. It is unnatural and poses a health risk to workers. Furthermore, firms should give adequate breaks and sufficient time for meals in order for workers to stay physically and mentally healthy as well as perform their jobs to the best of their ability.

Pressure from Supervisors

The third most common complaint about working in the maquilas focused on the behavior of supervisors. Sixteen percent of the sample disliked their jobs because of their supervisors' harsh treatment. Some felt their supervisors acted arrogantly on the plant floor, making unreasonable demands without any consideration for the workers' plight. Common responses were "la preparencia de los supervisores" (the arrogance of the supervisors) and "el abuso y que nos exijan estandar nos quieren tener como robots sin abler" (the abuse and that we have a quota they want us to be like robots without talking all day). One woman was frustrated with the increased hours and no additional pay: "que ahora estamos trabajando doce horas y media segun para apoyo de la empireza peroes por el mismo sueldo" (that now we are working twelve and a half hours supposedly to support the company but for the same pay). Many women felt powerless and vulnerable in their job and acquiesced to the demands of their superiors: "el trato de los jefes se expresan mal de nosotros" (the treatment of the bosses, they treat us bad); "Los jefes son muy prepotentes y abusan de nosotros" (The bosses are very arrogant and take advantage of us); "La jefe de linea es muy enojona y exigente" (The line boss is angry and demanding). They described their supervisors as despots, unnecessarily punishing them for tardiness or talking while showing favoritism toward other workers. These candid responses to what they didn't like about their jobs reveal the pressure felt by the women:

"el despotismote los jefes y la preferencia de los jefes por algunos em-
pleados" (the tyranny of the managers and the favoritism that they show
for some employees)

"Mi supervisor que es muy despota no sabe tratar a la gente." (My supervisor is a tyrant and doesn't know how to treat people.)

"que no por falta te quitan muchos benefisios" (that even if you don't
miss work they take away our bonuses)

"que son muy estrictos y 1 minuto que lleguen tarde nos quitan los bo-
nos" (that they are very strict and if you arrive even a minute late they
take your bonuses)

"que si llego tarde un minuto no nos reciben y nos descuentan $300"
(that if I arrive late they don't give us 300 pesos)

"Lo que no me gusta es que no nos dejan platicar ni reirnos muchos me-
nos comernos un dulce." (What I don't like is that they don't allow us
to talk or laugh and we definitely can't eat a snack or anything.)

"los problema con los jefes faboritismo" (the problem with the bosses'
over-favoritism)

"No me gusta es la presion y la preferensia que tienen los jefes con algun
personal." (I don't like the pressure or the favoritism that the manager
show toward some people.)

"Lo que no me gusta, es que hay mucho favoritism entre el personal." (I
don't like that there is a lot of favoritism among supervisors.)

Many of the workers said that their supervisors would do whatever it
took to make sure the quota for the day was reached. The response of
one woman revealed the constant stress:

No le gusta el trato de los patrones exigent el estandar y lo quieren muy
bien nos carrerean todo el dia por llegar 30 minutos tarde me quitan
lo de un dia entero, no les pagan como en otras maquilas sabado y do-
mingo. (I don't like how the bosses treat us, they require a quota [stan-
dard] and they want it done really well so they push us all day. Just for
arriving 30 minutes late they take away a whole work day, they don't pay
like they do in other maquilas for working on Saturday and Sunday.)

Methods of control used by maquila superiors tended to make many
women feel pressured and stressed at work rather than productive —"hay
mucha preción" (there is a lot of pressure). A number of women complained about the mental and physical anguish forced on them: "No me
gusta las reglas que estan poniendo en la maquila y la prepotencia con la

que nos las estan obligando creo que quieren que muncho gente renuncie" (I don't like the rules that they have in the maquilas, and how rude they are about making us follow them, I think they want a lot of people to quit).

One woman expressed her feelings about her supervisor quite passionately:

> No me gusta la prepotencia, la esclavitud dentro de la planta, el nepotismo, la forma de tartar la vulgaridad con quese expresa el gerente ante nosotros (todos los empleados en juntas general). Lo estrictos que son. Y tratan de exprimir al trabajador todo lo que se pueda. (I don't like the bossiness, the slavery inside the plant, the nepotism, the way they treat us, and how in general meetings the manager is really vulgar in front of all of the employees. I don't like how strict they are. And they try to squeeze as much as they possibly can out of the worker.)

Supervisors would publicly scold workers and threaten them with fines or dismissal: "el supervisor que es muy regnon" (the supervisor scolds me); "muy prepotente y sangron" (very arrogant and snobby); "que me regañaban por nada" (that they scold me for nothing). Put simply, many women felt their supervisors lacked human qualities: "Los supervisors tan inhumanos que les piden un permiso porque su hijo se enferma no se lo quieren dar" (The supervisors are so inhumane that if you ask permission to leave because your child is sick, they don't want to give it [time off] to you).

A few women reported that they had been sexually harassed and that they knew women who performed sex acts to keep their jobs. Although this did not happen in every maquila, it was pronounced in the maquilas where it did take place. In a handful of maquilas, the most common response to what they disliked about their job was "acoso sexual" (sexual harassment). It was clear by their responses that many women were uncomfortable with the sexual overtones on the assembly line. One woman remarked, "que es tratas de ser amable con algunos jefes mal interpreten nuestra amabilidad pensando que queremos sexo con ellos" (that when you try to be nice with some of the managers they misinterpret our friendliness and they think that we want to have sex with them). Another said, "Mis jefes inmediatos son muy prepontes, su jefe le ofrecio un aumento de sueldo si axedia a sus peticiones indecorosas" (My immediate supervisors are very arrogant, one of my bosses offered me a raise if I agreed to his inappropriate requests). As one woman explained:

Pero los jefes de linea se protaban prepotentes y la acosaron sexual-
mente, no los tener contacto con sus compañeros de trabajo a un com-
pañero lo corrieron por auxiliary a una compañera que se des mayo.
(The line bosses are very arrogant, and they sexually harassed me, they
keep the women and men separate and they fired one of my male coworkers for helping out a female coworker who fainted.)

Although it is not uncommon for assembly line workers to have dis-
dain for their supervisors even in industrialized countries, this type of
abuse is reminiscent of the dark satanic mills of the British industrial
revolution. The maquila laborer, like the child laborer, was pushed to
work beyond what was physically possible by the "blows from the heavy
hands and feet of the merciless overlookers" (Alfred 1857, 21–22). Although it is the supervisor's responsibility to make sure that workers are
productive and that the quota is met, a variety of rewards and penalties
have shown to be effective in industrialized countries. The tactics used
by the Mexican supervisors in the maquilas, however, are extraordinarily
severe. Not surprisingly, these sordid managerial tactics took its toll on
the women. The maquila women were exhausted—physically from long
hours and forced overtime, emotionally from the harassment of the supervisor, and mentally from the external and internal pressures to keep
their jobs. For many women, working in a maquiladora was a humiliating experience endured to support their families.

Long Hours and Neglected Families

The days and nights are long for the women who work in the maquilas.
Seventy-seven percent of the women in this sample worked at least one
hour more than the maximum of eight hours per day, and 15.5 percent
worked as many as twelve hours per day. Eight percent of the women
in this sample responded that they did not like "el horario" (the hours)
they worked. Their comments reveal their frustrations over long hours,
forced overtime, and few breaks. Many women complained about standing on their feet, with few breaks to sit down and rest. By the end of
the day they were exhausted—with sore feet, aching backs, and swollen
joints from performing the same repetitive motion hundreds of times.
The jobs did not require much skill but did require considerable stam-
ina. Common responses on the physical demands of the work were, "no
me gusta que trabajamos de pie" (I don't like that we work on our feet)

and "que el mayor tiempo estoy parade y me duelen las piernas se me inchan los pies" (that most of the time I am continuously working and my legs and feet hurt).

The impact of the assembly line work, however, went beyond this physical pain for many of the women. They worried about being away from their families for so many hours each day. As mothers separated from their children, their hearts ached as they thought about the children fending for themselves after school. A common sentiment was expressed by some of the women: "que no le paguen bien, que no tengo tiene tiempe para su familia" (that they don't pay good, that I don't have time for my family). And another woman commented, "el dejar tanto tiempo ahi a veces me molesta por no tener tiempo de estar con mis hijas que aun son pequeñas" (having to be there so much bothers me sometimes because I don't have time with my daughters who are still small). Women reported that they were often punished for taking their children to the doctor. Many women experienced this firsthand; others had friends or family members who were fired for leaving work to take their sick children to the doctor. One mother stated from experience, "No le den permiso cuando alguno de sus hijos se enferma y como no tiene familia esta sola con mis hijos" (They didn't let me leave when my sons were sick and I have no family and am alone with my sons). Another told what happened to her friend: "una compañera porque su hijo se enfermo de pulmonia y ella tuvo que pedir permiso y la despidieron" (one of my coworkers was fired because her son had pneumonia and she wanted permission to leave). Given full responsibility for their children, many of these working women appeared emotionally distraught over the situation they found themselves in. They had to work but did not want to leave their children. One woman admitted she didn't like leaving her children: "el sueldo tan poquito y que tengo que dejar a mis hijos en manos de otra persona porque el sueldo de mi marido no nos alcanza" (the salary because it is little and I have to leave my children in the hands of other people because the salary of my husband doesn't support us). This emotional tug-of-war is so strong that some women choose to work four consecutive twelve-hour days because it means they can be home with their children three days a week.

Forcing women to make even greater sacrifices, several maquilas required their workers to perform overtime duties. This is in direct violation of Mexican law, which states overtime must be voluntary. As a consequence, women stayed at work longer and were at home less. Women articulated their dislike of being forced to work overtime repeatedly.

Comments such as "que nos obligan a trabajar tiempo extra" (they obligate you to work overtime) and "que los supervisors se creuenos de tu tiempo y obligan a trabajar tiempo extra" (the supervisors think they own your time and they make you work overtime) were common. Typically supervisors would attempt to instill fear in their workers, threatening to cancel their contracts or fire them. This method of coercion was the most common, as revealed in the following responses: "Nos obligan a trabajar tiempo extra diciendo que pueden cancelar el trato" (They make you work extra, telling you that if you don't they will cancel your contract); "No gusta obligan a trabjar tiempo extra con el retexto que te van a despedir" (They make you work extra time with the pretext that they will fire you).

Conclusion

Women continue to work in maquiladoras, as they did in the 1980s and 1990s. Previous research has documented the prevalence of women in the assembly line jobs in the maquilas. This is where agreement ends and the two opposing views on how the jobs affect women's lives begin. One group of scholars supports the integration thesis that these jobs liberated women from the patriarchal authority of their fathers and husbands. Scholars arguing the opposing view, the exploitation thesis, believe that the maquila jobs extended the oppression of women outside the home and into the workplace. My research lends more support for the exploitation thesis, although there are certainly situations in which some women felt more liberated than exploited.

All the women in my sample were thankful to have a job, a steady income, and a way to feed their children. Some women liked their jobs, felt productive learning and performing tasks, and gladly accepted the new responsibilities. Many women enjoyed their coworkers and the camaraderie and noted they had made new friends. It is difficult to conclude, however, that they felt liberated by their jobs. On the other hand, there is overriding evidence that the majority of women working in the maquilas along the Mexican border are exploited in the jobs U.S. companies have created. These new employment opportunities did not pay a sustainable wage or teach any new skills and have not liberated them from a life of poverty. The maquiladoras pulled them from their homes and turned their family structure on its head. Instead of working in the informal economy while raising their children and maintaining a household, the women worked in the formal economy and were separated from their children. The pressures of the assembly line jobs, moreover, made it almost impossible to care for their children. Long hours on their feet and performing repetitive tasks left them exhausted by the time they returned home. The patriarchal authority of their fathers and husbands was now extended to someone outside the family, the line supervisor. These strangers didn't care if they needed to sit down because of menstrual cramps, if they had to use the bathroom, or if they had a sick child to take to the doctor. The supervisors needed to meet the quotas set by their bosses, and if their current workers complained too much, there were hundreds more lined up to take their jobs.

The promised benefits of profit sharing, medical care, and paid vacation were more the exception than the rule. The hope of hiring, production, and attendance bonuses was replaced with fear of significant wage deductions for tardiness, absenteeism, and needed bathroom breaks. In addition to the broken promises and unreasonable fines, the women suffered at many levels in the hands of their employers. Sadly, many U.S. companies operating maquilas along the border of Mexico ignored almost all the basic labor rights of the Mexican women. These women were exploited. The women often worked without a contract. Consequently, many women did not know their wage, the length of their employment, or what benefits they would receive. Employers clearly had all the power, and without job security the workers had none at all. History has taught us that when there is such an imbalance of power, one group will suffer at the hands of the other. And the women did suffer. They earned wages (once food, transportation, and bonuses were removed) that were so low their families went without meat on a weekly basis. They lived in makeshift homes without running water or drainage. They worked nine, ten, even twelve hours each day under the pressure of arrogant supervisors and forced to meet unreasonable production quotas. They were not treated like human beings but instead like animals, forced to withstand the burden of hard labor.

CHAPTER 7

Fancy Factories and Dilapidated Dwellings

The daily lives of the Mexican women who work in the U.S. factories are at best grueling and at worst humiliating. The two radically different realities they face every day reflects the integration of the best and worst each country has to offer. The women work in fancy factories but live in dilapidated dwellings. Multinationals from the United States, the leader of the first world, were willing to move operations to Mexico, a country still mired in the third world. The factories and jobs created provided employment opportunities for Mexicans living in a poor country still dominated by agriculture. Unfortunately, the working conditions of these new jobs are oppressive. Mexico, on the other hand, offers a workforce of young, healthy, and hardworking individuals. These able-bodied men and women were eager to work for U.S. companies. Promises made by their government through NAFTA meant lax enforcement of labor and environmental laws, leaving workers and border towns to absorb the consequences.

Several hundred thousand Mexican women work in fancy factories owned by multinational corporations along the border. Multinationals, through foreign direct investment, create assembly line jobs in clean, well-lit buildings surrounded by beautiful landscaping. In these jobs, workers operate relatively newer technologies that have been imported into Mexico. In most cases workers do not need more than an eighth-grade education to be trained to perform the tasks in less than fifteen minutes. By repeating simple tasks, the Mexican workers are able to meet high production quotas. The companies have successfully moved operations to Mexico where labor is productive and cheap. Although some of these companies are from Germany, Korea, Japan, and Canada, the predominance of U.S. multinationals along the border is undeniable. Lear

Corporation, General Electric, Motorola, Mattel, and Whirlpool operate maquilas in the Export Processing Zone created by the Border Industrialization Program and extended by the North American Free Trade Agreement (Maquila Portal 2011). As neighbors, these American companies are able to increase profits by outsourcing assembly operations to Mexico. There are many advantages to American companies operating maquilas in Mexico. The Mexican government created tax holidays, which lowered costs. It promised compliant workers, which would increase productivity. Labor is cheap and tariffs are negligible. Transportation and distribution costs are low due to their close proximity, and administrative costs are minimized with the help of shelter companies. As costs fell, profits soared and stockholders enjoyed high returns on their investments. U.S. companies clearly benefited from NAFTA and moving operations to Mexico.

The Mexican workers hired by the U.S. companies also benefited, although not nearly as much. The growth of the maquila industry created manufacturing jobs that offered the unemployed wages. The maquila workers, primarily women, had a better chance of supporting their families with consistent income and access to health care. The Mexican women who work in these maquiladoras are hardworking, highly productive, and cooperative. They are thankful to have a job. But these benefits have required considerable sacrifices by the workers. The new jobs in the maquilas were assembly line jobs. The jobs involved repeating simple one-step tasks over and over. The monotony and repetition of this type of work leads to boredom and alienation. The high quotas, moreover, dictated a rapid pace and a high level of stress imposed on workers by the supervisor. The rules on the factory floor seem overly restrictive, leading workers to feel more like robots and less like human beings. The working conditions at times become unbearable, but the workers have no recourse. The unions in most maquilas were established by the employer and the government, giving the workers no voice. Unwilling to give in or give up, workers dedicate themselves to their job and their employers. By working for a U.S. company in manufacturing, maquila workers thought they had a better chance of surviving.

At the end of a long workday, maquila workers return to their homes in colonias. Unlike the factories, their homes are dilapidated dwellings scattered along dirt roads and among trash. The dwellings are made of cardboard pieces and wood or cinder blocks, often without doors or windows. Roofs are held down by boulders or cinder blocks, and there are no chimneys for the wood-burning stoves. Most homes have only one room and an outhouse nearby or attached to the back. Inside the dwelling, the family has electricity but no running water or drainage system. Despite working hard, families can barely survive. Although the minimum wage set by the government increased from $3.80 per day in 2000 to $4.50 in 2004 and $5.70 in 2010, families can barely afford to eat. Due to migration from the south, demand for food, water, and tortillas increased, causing prices to rise. As prices increase more than the nominal minimum wage, workers' purchasing power was cut in half.[1] Surprisingly, it is actually less expensive to cross the border and buy food in the United States. Instead of moving upward to join the working class, the maquila workers have become the working poor.

if you can get visa'd

No More NAFTA

The BIP created maquilas along the Export Processing Zone, improving the daily lives of many Mexican families who sought employment in the manufacturing sector. The factories employed mainly men and treated them reasonably. They typically worked a forty-eight-hour week and received two weeks' paid vacation as Mexican law dictated. Workers in this "old factory regime" were not exploited but instead earned above the minimum wage and received medical benefits, housing credits, and money for their children's education. NAFTA was designed to help Mexico industrialize by promoting the growth of the maquila industry. The incentives offered in NAFTA to multinational companies did dramatically increase the number of maquilas operating along the border. The maquila industry, moreover, provided jobs for millions of unskilled Mexicans. But Mexico has not industrialized and remains a poor country. The maquila workers did not improve their standard of living and continue to live without modern amenities. With the passage of NAFTA, the composition of the workforce and the working conditions changed dramatically. The maquilas hired women instead of men and treated them poorly. This explains why many maquila workers refer to NAFTA as *la gran mentira* (the Big Lie). The CFO in conjunction with the American Friends Service Committee concluded, "We do not support NAFTA because we do not receive any of its benefits. On the contrary, its effects are prejudicial to us" (Arriola 2000, 4). This sentiment was echoed in a report titled "Women in the Maquiladoras of Piedras Negras, Coahuila and Frontera Norte Sur." The report stated that instead of improving working conditions and living standards of Mexican workers, the maquila industry has led to "years of backbreaking work for paltry wages for Mexican women. Women work under the constant fear that any resistance to their unjust treatment will result in verbal harassment by their supervisors or worse yet, being fired" (Arriola 2000, 3–4).

Basic labor rights were not included in NAFTA. Instead they were marginalized in a separate agreement that few knew existed, the North American Agreement on Labor Cooperation. This labor agreement, although well intentioned, has been entirely ineffective. The NAALC failed to establish common minimum standards for labor in all three countries (United States, Mexico, and Canada), reducing its labor principles to mere guidelines. These guidelines were essentially ignored because the penalty for violating one of the labor principles was inconsequential. Unfortunately, the companies operating the maquilas took advantage of the lax regulations and put practices into place that increased production but overburdened workers. Maquila workers under this "new factory regime" worked more than eight hours a day, were forced to work overtime, had only four days off per year, and were required to take pregnancy tests as a condition of employment. Their families were no longer able to live in suitable housing and send their children to school because their wages, although above the minimum, were unsustainable (Cravey 1998). Mexican maquila workers were clearly the losers from this free trade agreement.

The unintended consequences of NAFTA for border town residents have been devastating. The maquilas brought jobs and the promise of a better life for poor Mexicans. Jobs in manufacturing, unlike agriculture, were thought to offer continuous regular employment and high wages. With only a primary school diploma in hand, men and women left farms as far south as Vera Cruz to seek employment in the maquiladoras. As a consequence of this northward migration, the border towns of Tijuana, Nogales, Agua Prieta, Nuevo Laredo, Ciudad Juárez, and Reynosa saw soaring populations. In Nogales, the population grew from 30,000 in 1994 to 300,000 in 2004. This is not an unusual phenomenon; the industrial centers of developing countries typically expand as the agricultural sector shrinks. The problem created by NAFTA, however, was the lack of infrastructure growth for the local economy of the border towns. Ordinarily, factories pay taxes that are used to build and maintain roads, bridges, schools, hospitals, and other public projects. If the factories locate in very poor areas, the tax revenue will also be used for bringing potable water, sanitation, and electricity to the residents who live and work there. Theoretically, workers' wages should be sufficient to stimulate lo-

[margin handwritten notes: "issues with public goods provision b/c of NAFTA's tax holidays"]

cal businesses as well as imports. Unfortunately, the tax holidays granted by NAFTA and the nature of foreign direct investment prevented this economic growth and modernization from occurring. Despite investing in the Mexican economy by building plants or leasing space, U.S. companies do not reinvest the profits made from these operations in the community. Consequently, few improvements are made to the factory and no new local businesses are created. Better technology is not used, more skilled workers are not hired, higher incomes are not created; industrialization does not proceed. The reality of border towns is overpopulation, congestion, and a severe housing shortage. Schools and hospitals are overcrowded and lack sufficient resources to offer satisfactory services. Necessary public services that promote a safe and healthy environment, such as police, fire, and waste management, rarely exist. The booming populations of the border towns are hurt rather than enhanced by NAFTA.

Residents of Nogales can see and feel the changes in their tranquil border town as a result of NAFTA. Several residents who were interviewed bemoaned the problems caused by overpopulation. When asked about what changes he had witnessed since NAFTA was passed, an employee of BorderLinks in Mexico commented on the overpopulation in the schools (seventy students to one teacher in a classroom) and the growing need for social programs to help the women who work in the maquilas (day care, school lunches, and health clinics). He also noticed more crime and more trash outside the city in many colonias. He believed that the trash was symptomatic of the clashes in culture between longtime residents and newly arrived migrants. "People don't have an attachment to Nogales," he said, "so they litter, and children grow up with the same attitudes and litter in the schools."[2] Jeannette Pazos, director of Hogar de Esperanza y Paz, worried more about NAFTA's impact on families and children. She remarked that children now walk to school without their parents since their parents are working in the maquilas and that parents don't spend much time with their children since the mothers, who run the households, are now working in the maquilas.[3] Chester, a longtime resident of Nogales, was also concerned about the impact the maquilas had on families. She worried that kids were home alone more since both parents worked in many families. And even when parents did return home, some women who worked all week were very tired. Chester remarked that many women who work on Saturday and Sunday don't have time for church.[4] Cecilia believed the increases in premature pregnancy, abortion, drug addiction, and suicide are to be blamed on the growing maquila industry in Nogales. She summed up the situation by saying, "No hay justicia para el pobre" (There is no justice for the poor).[5] The overwhelming sentiment of people who lived and worked along the border was that NAFTA created more problems than it solved.

American Sweatshops in Mexico

U.S. multinational companies became plunderers of border towns in Mexico—taking what they needed to have a profitable business (land, labor, water) and giving very little in return (low wages, tired workers, polluted water). Instead of maintaining the same standards they have in the United States for workers in terms of safety, health, and respect, multinationals abandoned their morals in pursuit of profit maximization. As a result, many of the maquilas owned and operated by multinationals have become sweatshops across the Mexican border. The factories are sweatshops because their operations violate provisions established by NAFTA and the NAALC, as well as several Mexican laws. The maquilas have violated Principles 1, 2, 6, and 7 of the North American Labor Agreement (see table 5.1) and have broken at least three Mexican labor laws.

The experiences of the working women surveyed in this research demonstrate the blatant violations by the multinationals of NAFTA and the NAALC. Women were fired if they joined an independent union (such as AFO or CFO) that represented their interests. In some cases, they were fired if they had talked to a representative of either of these unions. This is clearly in violation of Principles 1 and 2, which give workers the right to unionize and bargain collectively. The statistical results and personal statements of the women provide irrefutable evidence that many employers did not have minimum employment standards (Principle 6). Although women did receive more than the minimum wage and health coverage, they did not get paid for overtime or vacation and had extremely short bathroom and lunch breaks. And finally, as the next section highlights, employers continued to discriminate against women by infringing on their reproductive rights (Principle 7).

The illegal behavior of many U.S. companies extends beyond international trade agreements that were signed by their government. Most of the companies violated at least three of the laws established by the Mexican government designed to protect their workers. The majority of women surveyed, 85 percent, worked nine or more hours per day when the legal limit set by Mexican law is eight. Most women were required to work overtime, which is illegal if not compensated 200 percent of their current wage for every hour over eight hours. Surprisingly, the women were never paid at all for overtime hours. Most of the mandatory employee benefits required by Mexican law were not given to the women. None of the women surveyed received a percentage of the firm's pretax profits or the nine paid legal holidays required by Mexican law. Less than one-third of the women, 30 percent, received two weeks' paid vacation—also Mexican law. Instead, firms grant only one week of unpaid vacation. More recently, companies have adopted the practice of telling women when to take vacation. Consequently, some families can no longer celebrate the holy weeks of Easter and Christmas together (Pascua y Navidad). Mexican law clearly states that all workers must have seven legal paid holidays per year, which includes January 1, February 5, March 21, September 16, November 20, and December 25. Mexican law also states that most business offices, banks, and large stores must observe the religious holidays (Thursday and Friday before Easter, November 1 and 2, and December 12). The Mexican women did not complain about these unfair and illegal practices because they learned that questioning the jefe could result in losing their job. Thus, although it may seem that staying in these jobs is irrational, they have no choice but to work in a place that does not treat them well because it is a matter of family survival.

The most shocking finding of this research is the violation of the women's reproductive rights. Not many Americans are aware of this issue, and not many Mexicans talk about it. Previous scholarly research rarely mentions it. Newspapers in the United States and Mexico are silent on the topic. The few human rights and labor rights activists who uncovered this practice in 1996 thought the illegal practices had been stopped. But, sadly, the discrimination continues into the twenty-first century. Some multinational corporations operating maquiladoras in Mexico discriminate against women in three serious ways. The first violation occurs in the hiring procedures: the maquilas require women to reveal their pregnancy status as a condition of employment. If a woman is pregnant she is not hired. The second violation takes place while the women are working: the maquilas require women to take contraceptives as a condition of continued employment.[6] If they refuse to take contraception, their contract is not renewed. The third violation occurs at termination: the maquilas fire women who become pregnant while working. When a company discovers a woman is pregnant she is terminated. Many of the women interviewed for this research experienced at least one of these illegal practices while working in the maquilas.

These practices are hard to document because companies are secretive and women are embarrassed to share their personal experiences. Field studies on women working in the maquilas by Cravey (1998), Kopinak (1996), Ruiz (1991), Tiano (1994), and Wilson (1992) make no mention of these illegal activities by employers. At the time the report by Human Rights Watch was published in 1996, there was only one reference in the existing literature on the maquiladoras. In the Spanish literature, Norma Iglesias Prietos mentions pregnancy testing in her book, *Beautiful Flowers of the Maquiladoras* (1997). One of the fifty women she interviewed describes the various procedures used to determine if a woman is pregnant. The woman was applying for work in a maquiladora in Ciudad Juárez and discovered a medical exam was part of the application process. The doctor asked a number of questions about her sex life, whether she was a *señorita* (virgin), how often she had sex, and the date of her last menstrual period. Unlike an American woman who would be outraged at such invasive and inappropriate questions, she cooperated and even offered a rationale for such questions:

> In their job interviews these firms seek those characteristics that best fill their needs. For the owners it is very important that the applicants not be pregnant, which explains the medical exam and all the questions related to one's sex life. . . . The business is interested in two fundamental issues: productivity and quality. A pregnant woman is not going to produce at the same level as a woman who is not pregnant. Pregnancy entails an extra expenditure because the firm is required to compensate the woman for a three-month maternity leave. For the firm—which subscribes to the motto "Time is money"—maternity leave constitutes a lapse during which the laborer is unproductive. (40)

More recently this type of discriminatory treatment has been mentioned in several scholarly works, although none includes a full investigation of the problem in Mexican maquiladoras. Leslie Salzinger (2003) mentions pregnancy testing in a footnote when describing how a teenager first discovered she was pregnant. The footnote reads, "Maquilas routinely and openly test women for pregnancy prior to hiring. The practice violates Mexican law and has been hard fought by local and international labor organizations" (2003, 188). Not surprisingly, the practice of sex discrimination has become global as outsourcing moves from one developing country to another. In search of the lowest wages, multinational corporations move operations to Central America and Asia. These factories employ predominantly women and preventing pregnancy continues to be a priority. Jennifer Swedish's (2005) work on maquilas in Honduras offers an excellent analysis of the legal and ethical implications of sex discrimination in maquiladoras. Her research reveals that these practices persist in factories located in free trade zones, in this case a textile factory manufacturing clothes for U.S. companies and universities in Choloma, Honduras. Data collected by the National Labor Committee in 2003 and 2005 document pregnancy testing and other serious abuses in the Honduran maquiladora industry (Swedish 2005, 2). Honduran women in the industry were subjected to "mandatory sterilization as a condition of hiring, injections of the contraceptive Depo Provera disguised as tetanus shots, the dispensing of oral contraceptive pills disguised as malaria medication, and injections given to pregnant women to cause abortions (2). Wright (2006) uncovers the use of pregnancy testing in discussions with the general manager of a Chinese facility owned by a U.S.-based corporation. Although the information is outdated since it is based on interviews in 1993, her research reveals that management had established policies that prevent the employment of pregnant women. Women's reproductive cycles were monitored and controlled through periodic pregnancy testing, regular physical checkups, and close monitoring by supervisors (39–40). This type of gender discrimination is not only illegal; it is unethical. The fact that the management of U.S. factories in Mexico, Honduras, and China systematically practiced discrimination against women workers should have caused public outrage.

This important scholarship on the violation of women's reproductive rights in developing countries, however, has not been read by the general public. One news article that did draw some attention to the issue in Mexico was written by Phoebe McKinney and Leslie Gates in *Z Magazine* in July 1994, "Zenith Electronics's Mexican Maquiladora Factories." The article explores the injustices experienced by the workforce in a Zenith plant in Reynosa: "Many of the women working for Zenith are from rural areas, where strict concepts of traditional feminine docility or timidity are stressed. This past spring, all of the women workers in Zenith's plant #12 in Reynosa were given pregnancy exams and several workers were fired as a result. Women waiting to apply for work at Zenith are frequently told, 'Only single women need apply,' and part of the job application includes a pregnancy test. If a woman tests positive, she is not hired" (McKinney and Gates 1994, 2).

Two years later, Human Rights Watch investigated the situation after discovering that the practices were considered normal operating procedure in the maquilas along the border. Outraged by this blatant disregard for the regulations in NAFTA and Mexican labor law, the Human Rights Watch Women's Rights Project wrote a report in 1999 titled "No Guarantees: Sex Discrimination in Mexico's Maquiladora Sector." They interviewed fifty-three women who sought work or were working at fifty different maquiladoras. Their research documented that women applying for work as assemblers were required to reveal their pregnancy status as a condition of employment. They found that major U.S.-based corporations "routinely subject prospective female employees to mandatory urine testing, invasive questions about their contraceptive use, menses schedule or sexual habits in order to screen out pregnant women and deny them jobs" (Human Rights Watch 1996a). The Support Committee for Maquiladora Workers concurred with their findings and argued that the experiences of the fifty women sampled were widespread. These practices were "an industry standard in Tijuana" (Cross-Border CONNECTION 1996).

The practices uncovered in the Human Rights Watch Report are not only illegal but also unethical. The humiliation the women experience is unfathomable. The procedures are described in their report:

> Pregnancy testing is conducted in several ways, most commonly through urine samples—often obtained in the course of legal pre-hire medical exams given to job applicants. Maquiladora personnel also request information from women applicants about their menses schedule, sexual activity and use of contraceptives. Pregnant applicants are not hired. In some cases, recently hired women workers are again required to provide proof of pregnancy status by submitting to additional pregnancy tests, often in the form of urine samples or medical exams. Those found to be pregnant are routinely forced to resign. We also found evidence of a particularly disturbing practice, notably some companies used mandatory sanitary napkin checks to verify their employees' non-pregnant status. (Human Rights Watch 1998, 1)

This report made the discrimination public knowledge and begged for a swift response from the Mexican government. Unfortunately the government did not remedy these blatant violations of Mexico's labor law or uphold its international human rights obligations. Frustrated with the government's response, Human Rights Watch, the International Labor Rights Fund, and the National Association of Democratic Lawyers (Asociación Nacional de Abogados Democráticos) submitted a petition against Mexico to the U.S. National Administrative Office (U.S. NAO 9701) that charged sex discrimination. In January 1998 the U.S. NAO found that Mexico's constitution and labor code did prohibit discrimination based on sex and that preemployment pregnancy testing did occur in Mexico. In an unbelievable finding, the U.S. NAO decided not to fine the maquilas guilty of this practice; instead they claimed that Mexico's labor law was unclear on whether this practice was actually illegal. They found, however, that on-the-job pregnancy tests were clearly illegal under Mexican labor law but suggested no remedy or penalty for the violators. The decision by the NAO concluded with one rather innocuous suggestion—"that greater efforts needed to be made toward awareness programs for women workers" (U.S. Department of Labor 1997, 6).

Despite the inaction of the Mexican government and the U.S. NAO, Mexican labor rights advocates believed these illegal practices had been severely curtailed. A report by the Comité Fronterizo de Obreras in October 1999, "Six Years of NAFTA: A View from Inside the Maquiladoras," claimed there was considerably less sex discrimination. The Executive Summary highlighted the progress:

> The report does note one key victory for workers and their allies on both sides of the border: the suspension by several major border employers of the illegal but widespread practice of compulsory pregnancy testing as a condition of employment. This practice violates both Mexican law and international human rights norms, attracted broad condemnation in both Mexico and the United States after it was documented in a 1996 report issued by Human Rights Watch and developed with help from the CFO and other Mexican organizations. Now reports the CFO, after years of sustained pressure, several of the largest maquiladora firms, including Delphi, Alcoa, General Electric, and Lucent Technologies, have backed away from pregnancy testing. (CFO 1999, 2)

One would hope a decade later that these illegal practices have completely disappeared in the maquilas. Pressure from local media and international human rights groups would force multinationals to assure that Mexican women's reproductive rights were no longer being violated.

Unfortunately, evidence gathered in this research has found these illegal and unethical practices continue to this day. The persistence of pregnancy tests in the maquilas also came up in several of the presentations to BorderLink's semester students. Juana, the only full-time employee of AFO in Nogales, gave an in-home presentation in February 2004. She informed the students that pregnant women had certain rights according to Mexican labor law. They have the right to three months off from work (maternity leave); to return to the same job with seniority; and to one hour every day to nurse the baby. After talking with many women, she concluded that the maquilas respect only one of these rights, the three-month maternity leave. She said that women's jobs were not protected and that many women were fired if they got pregnant. She said she had spoken with a number of women who were required to take a pregnancy test before the maquila would hire them. Juana was hoping to educate more women about their rights so that these illegal practices would stop. Juana was not the only person who worried about the violation of women's rights.[7] Similar concerns were voiced by Tracy Carroll, a physical therapist, during an interview. I asked her, "Can you give me an example of one of the worst cases of a health-related problem due to working in a maquila?" Without hesitating she replied, "My biggest concern is the treatment of women in the maquilas. For example, in the garment industry women are kept from getting pregnant with birth control. Also, a lot of time women are not removed from dangerous situations once they become pregnant. This is sexual discrimination against the women in the maquilas."[8]

These are not just a few carefully selected cases to exaggerate discrimination against women working in the maquilas. Complete disregard for the reproductive rights of Mexican women by the maquilas is still prevalent and pervasive. The survey used in this research contained two questions (#12 and #13) related to reproductive rights. In response to Question 12, "Are you required to take contraceptives to work?" 25 percent of the 538 women reported having to take contraceptives as a requirement for employment. The women's responses indicate varying degrees of pressure to take birth control. Some maquilas required women to use some form of contraception, while others strongly encouraged it. Many women reported that maquilas offered workshops on how to use contraceptives. The women who did not feel they had a choice and understood they must take the pills to keep their job, responded simply in the affirmative, "Sí" (Yes). There were only a few cases where women elaborated on this response by saying, "Sí obligatoriamente" (Yes, it is required);

"Sí nos dan inyecciones cada meses" (Yes, they give us injections every month); and "Sí ponen dispositivo en el brazo" (Yes, they put a birth control implant in my arm). It is clear from the following responses that even the women who responded negatively to this question, knew the maquilas actively supported contraception:

> "No pero si quieres te dan inyeccion o te dan las pastillas." (No, but if you want they give you a shot or they give you the pill.)
> "No pero hay mucha publicidad para evitar embarazarse." (No, but there's a lot of advertisements about how to avoid getting pregnant.)
> "Nos sugieren casi todo el tiempo." (They suggest it to us all of the time.)
> "No pero nos revisan cada cierto tiempo para saber si estamos embarazadas." (No, but they check us regularly to see if we are pregnant.)
> "No pero nos hacen campanas para regalarnos y nos ponen el dispositivo gratis si queremos." (No, but they do campaigns to give stuff away and they will give us the birth control implant for free if we want.)

If a woman did get pregnant while working on the assembly line the consequences in some maquilas were quite severe. Twenty-eight percent of the 592 women who responded to Question 13, "What do your supervisors do if you get pregnant?" reported that they were fired. Many of the women responded "te corre" or "estaba correr" to this question. In Nogales, the expression means "they fire you." Other common responses were "presonan para que renuncien" (they pressure you to resign) and "te cambian de puesto te hostigan para que renuncies" (they change you from position to position and harass you so you'll quit).

The majority of maquilas, however, did not discriminate against pregnant women. Often the maquilas went beyond what is required by law and helped women who became pregnant while working for them. Women indicated there was a distinction made between those who had contracts and those who did not. It was clear from the responses that women with contracts who had worked at the maquila for three months were not fired: "apoyan si tiene uno mas de 3 meses trabajando si no las corren" (they help you out if you've been working there for more than three months, if not they fire you); "si tengo poco tiempo me despiden" (if I have little time they would fire me); and "si hay contracto no me hacen nada" (if you have a contract they can't do anything). The remaining women responded positively and indicated their supervisor moved them to lighter work and that the maquila *apoya* (helped) them.

Several common responses revealed employers respected Mexican law and women's rights: "nos pone a hacer trabajos mas faciles," (they give us easy work to do); "toman precauciones de que no trabaje en algo pesado o en sustancias quimicas que afecten el embarazo" (they take precautions and make sure you aren't working in something too hard or with chemicals that effect the pregnancy); "apoyan con medicos, permisos, trabajo livianito incapacidades" (they help with doctors, leave, lighter work, and workers compensation). Only a handful of women received benefits based on Mexican law, which states, "las incapacitan por medio de seguro. 48 dias antes de nacio. 48 dias despues de nacio" (disability and medical assistance; 48 days (off) before birth and 48 days after birth). It is heartening to discover that most of the maquilas were respectful of pregnant women. The fact that 166 women knew they would be fired is distressing.

The existence of pregnancy testing as a condition of employment was documented by many of the women. When I developed and administered the survey, I focused more on other forms of sex discrimination, including control of women's reproductive rights. Consequently, I did not ask the women specifically about employers requiring women applying for a job to submit to a pregnancy test. Despite this oversight on my part, many women volunteered this information in their responses to Question 12. Although I am unable to conclude how widespread this illegal practice is among the maquilas, I am able to document that the practice exists. One-sixth of the sample volunteered information on whether or not a pregnancy test was required before they were hired. Eighty-five percent of these 111 women said they had to take a pregnancy test (*prueba de embarazo*) at their current workplace before they were hired. Their responses were clear and unequivocal. As one woman said, "Antes de entrar te hacen un examen medico analisis para que no entre embarazada" (Before you start they make you have a medical exam to make sure you are not pregnant when you start working). Several others remarked when answering Question 12: "no pero la prueba de embarazo es obligatoria" (no pills but pregnancy test is obligatory); "no, pero si nos hacen periodicamente preuba de embarazo" (no, but they periodically do a pregnancy test); and "se me hizo la preuba de embarazo me checaron el estomago" (they gave me a pregnancy test and they checked my stomach). These findings, however, cannot be used to generalize and only offer a glimpse into an invasive and often humiliating experience for the Mexican women. In summary, this evidence documents that many of the Mexican women working in the maquilas in Nogales are forced to reveal whether or not they are pregnant. They are encouraged to take birth control to prevent any future pregnancies and are fired if they do become pregnant. The fact that this practice is still so prevalent within the maquiladora industry, ten years after it was discovered and documented, is unbelievable.

Who Should be Held Accountable?

Under NAFTA, any country has the power to bring a case against another country in the event of known violations. The violations must be submitted to and accepted by the NAO of Mexico, the United States, or Canada. A complaint may be filed by individuals, organizations, corporations, and governments charging violation(s) of the NAALC. As table 7.1 illustrates, since the passage of NAFTA in 1994, there have been more cases filed with the U.S. NAO than the Mexico NAO and Canada NAO combined. The majority of cases are brought forth on company violations of workers' rights to organize unions that represent their interests. Although most were accepted as legitimate cases by the NAO, the outcomes are inconsequential. The first two hearings conducted by the U.S. NAO involved submission by the Teamsters Union against Honeywell and the United Electrical Workers Union against General Electric. Despite stating in their case reports in 1994 that they found "a number of relevant issues regarding the enforcement of labor law in Mexico, particularly in the maquiladora sector," the NAO did not recommend ministerial consultations (the stiffest penalty established in the trade agreement). Critics argued that "the commission seemed to show a remarkable lack of interest in carrying out its task" (CJM 1994, 9). Such criticism seemed to change their thoughtless response to proven injustices such that subsequent complaints did recommend ministerial consultations. The effectiveness of these actions, however, and their associated "follow-up activities" are questionable. For example, the conclusion to U.S. NAO Submission No. 2003-1 stated, "The U.S. NAO recommends ministerial consultations with the Government of Mexico on the issues of freedom of association, minimum employment standards and occupational safety and health" (U.S. Department of Labor 2004b, 88). If the recommendation of the NAO on behalf of the workers at the factories of Matamoros Garment and Tarrant de Ajalpan in Puebla is any indication of their strongest "penalty," then worker exploitation is likely to go unchecked. The follow-up activities, which involve "seminars" or "public outreach sessions" to government labor boards, moreover, are unlikely to change the behavior of many multinational corporations.

The remaining cases are brought forth on company violations of minimum employment standards, occupational health and safety in the workplace, and sex discrimination. Many of these cases reveal violations by multinationals of Mexican labor law documented in this book. Evidence of nine- to twelve-hour workdays, forced and unpaid overtime, and short bathroom breaks in other companies in Mexico show that the findings of this research are representative of the treatment workers endure by foreign companies. The most disturbing evidence discovered in this research regarding the violation of women's reproductive rights is not unique to Nogales, Sonora. Other foreign companies, some American, located in Mexico are continuing to perform illegal practices on women workers. Mandatory pregnancy testing, "optional" contraceptive use, and firing pregnant women is more prevalent than anyone imagined. The submissions to the United States (U.S. NAO 9701, 9804) and Mexico (Mexico NAO 9801, 9802 and 9803, 2003–2003-1) for employment discrimination most likely represent only a small percentage of the violations that exist.

The concerted and sustained efforts of many unions, lawyers, national and international labor rights groups, and American university students have not been sufficient to improve Mexican workers' rights. The scrutiny of concerned representatives from each country are successful in evaluating the evidence of NAALC violations but ineffective in giving workers a voice against powerful multinationals. Very few Mexican organizations, including the powerful union of the CTM, have filed complaints against the operators of the maquilas. The only complaint submitted by the CTM (Mexico NAO 9803) focuses mainly on migrant workers, not maquila workers. The CTM instead appears to be trying to cover up any problems by silencing the working women. At the Congreso Anual Sector Femenil that I attended on March 28, 2004, in Nogales, women who complained about working conditions in the maquilas were cut short and escorted off the stage. One woman stood at the podium facing the audience of female workers and CTM union members stating that managers do not respect women's rights and that as working mothers it was hard to see their children because they worked from early in the morning until late in the evening. As she was whisked off the stage another woman took her place and demanded more day care facilities and clinics. She said there were not enough day care centers for the number of children whose mothers must work and the ones

Table 7.1. Selected NAO Cases, 1994–2004

Recipient NAO and Case Number	Submitter(s)	Issue/Principle	Outcome
U.S. NAO 940001	Teamsters	Freedom of association/Right to organize	Accepted, no ministerial consultation
U.S. NAO 940002	United Electrical Radio and Machine Workers of America (UERMW)	Freedom of association/Right to organize	Accepted, no consultation
U.S. NAO 940003	ILRF, AFSC, ANAD	Freedom of association/Right to organize	Accepted, consultation
U.S. NAO 940004	United Electrical, Radio and Machine Workers of America	Freedom of association/Right to organize	Accepted, submission withdrawn
Mexico NAO 9501	Sindicato de Telefonistas	Freedom of association/Right to organize	Accepted, consultation agreement on implementation
U.S. NAO 9601	ILRF, Human Rights Watch, ANAD	Freedom of association/Right to organize	Accepted, consultation
U.S. NAO 9602	Comm. Workers of America	Freedom of association/Right to organize	Accepted, withdrawn
U.S. NAO 9701	ILRF, Human Rights Watch, ANAD	Employment discrimination	Accepted, consultation
U.S. NAO 9702	ANAD, ILRF, Support Committee for Maquila Workers, Sindicato de la Industria del Metal, Acero, Hierro, etc.	Freedom of association/Right to organize	Accepted, consultation

Case	Organizations	Issues	Outcome
U.S. NAO 9703	United Steelworkers, AFL-CIO, UERMW, Teamsters	Freedom of association/Right to organize, occupational injuries	Accepted, consultation
Mexico NAO 9801	Oil, Chemical & Atomic Workers, Local 1-675; Sindicato de Trabajadores Industria y Comercio; Unión de Defensa Laboral Comunitaria	Freedom of association/Right to organize, minimum employment standards, occupational injuries, employment discrimination	Accepted, consultation
Mexico NAO 9802	Frente Auténtico del Trabajo, Union Nacional de Trabajadores, Sindicato de Trabajo Industria del Metal	Freedom of association/Right to organize, employment standards, protection of migrant workers, employment discrimination, occupational injuries	Accepted, consultation
Mexico NAO 9803	CTM	Migrant workers, employment standards, discrimination, occupational injuries	Accepted, consultations led to joint declaration
Mexico NAO 9804	Yale University School of Law, ACLU	Migrant workers, employment standards	Accepted, consultation
U.S. NAO 2001–2001	AFL-CIO, Allied-Industrial Chemical and Energy Workers International Union	Freedom of association/Right to organize	Not accepted
U.S. NAO 2003–2001	USAS, Centro de Apoyo al Trabajador	Freedom of association/Right to organize, employment standards, occupational injuries	Accepted, consultation

Source: U.S. Department of Labor 2004; U.S. National Administrative Office, Bureau of International Labor Affairs. Abbreviations: ACLU, American Civil Liberties Union; AFSC, American Friends Service Committee; ANAD, Asociación Nacional de Abogados Democráticos; CTM, Confederación de Trabajadores de México; ILRF, International Labor Rights Fund; UERMW, United Electrical, Radio and Machine Workers; USAS, United Students Against Sweatshops.

that do exist are too expensive, costing 260 pesos per child per week. She also complained that families living in the colonias do not have access to clinics and the sick do not get benefits. As she demanded access to clinics and day care in the next two years she was escorted off the stage by a union official. The last woman allowed to address the group focused her remarks on education. She wanted education for women like herself who had only a basic education but worked in the maquilas. She shared her hope for a preparatory school in Nogales. Although this is just an example of the position of the CTM on work in the maquiladoras, it is revealing.

Can the U.S. government or the American consumer do anything to improve the plight of the Mexican maquila worker? Obviously the U.S. government has no jurisdiction in Mexico to enforce their labor laws and levy sanctions when there are violations. Similarly, the American consumer cannot ask the Mexican government to enforce its laws. Instead, consumers around the world could have an impact on the profits of multinational corporations that break the laws in Mexico. Because consumers are sovereign and essentially "vote" with their dollars, pounds, yen, and so on, a boycott of goods made by these maquilas could impact the bottom line of the multinationals. Although consumer boycotts have been fairly successful in the past (the Nike and Wal-Mart campaigns), they affect the profitability of companies only if hundreds of thousands of consumers change their buying habits. Media pressure and exposure that uses "name and shame" tactics can also be effective in reducing consumer purchases of certain products. These responses require knowledge of the illegal behavior. This book provides direct verifiable evidence of the illegal and inhumane activities of the maquilas along the border. The website www.maquilaportal.com or a quick trip across the border through the well-marked industrial parks will result in a current list of the U.S. companies producing "offshore" in Mexico. Once exposed, however, the result is often worse for the workers because companies shut down operations and move to another developing country where they can exploit a new group of workers. This "race to the bottom" will move the sweatshops to countries in Central America and Asia where the plight of workers remains deplorable.

Mexican Workers Fight Back

Despite formidable obstacles, these exploited workers are fighting for their rights, just as workers did in Great Britain in the nineteenth century and in the United States in the twentieth century. Recent feminist literature has explored several strategies that maquiladora women have adopted to assert themselves in both their living and working environments. Irasema Coronado's (2006) research makes a significant contribution to the literature on social activism among women along the border. She categorizes women's activism into three types: political system activism; creation of Asociaciones Civiles (AC); and independent activism (150–155). I would add a fourth type to this list, participation in nongovernmental organizations. There is a dearth of literature of women working within the system and forming groups that take demands to city officials. As Coronado points out, the women living in *colonias populares* "have little energy or time left over in the day to meet and strategize or to organize politically" (150). The formation of women-headed ACs along the border is more pronounced. Coronado lists eight ACs that have been established in various border cities to work on women's issues of health, education, and employment (152). The only one she mentions that deals with labor issues is located in Ciudad Juárez, the Centro de Investigación y Solidaridad Obrera. In Nogales, the Centro de Apoyo Contra Violencia offers counseling for women victimized by violence. ACs have been successful in publicizing violations of women's rights by forming alliances with international organizations. In one case in Chihuahua, ACs have become so effective that state officials have initiated an investigation into their funding sources (153).

Although it is more difficult, women do work alone to further themselves and their communities both inside and outside the maquilas. For some women in Ciudad Juárez, working in maquiladoras empowers them to improve their own position (Bergareche 2006). By participating in the formal labor market, women leave the isolation and dependence associated with the home and join other women in similar predicaments. According to Bergareche, the solidarity gained from their work community helps some women to become active agents in their lives instead of victims (95–96). The women in her study were effective in securing essential services for colonias and protection of physically and sexually abused women. Evidence exists that some women are making their way up the corporate ladder in maquiladoras. Instead of trying to change the corporate structure, these women are fighting individual battles within the system. Wright (1997, 2006) has contributed to this discussion by sharing the professional and personal factors that lead women to embracing power and successfully becoming managers in a plant. The women who effectively moved up the ranks were able to assimilate American customs and culture into their Mexican personae. Outside the plant, there are women working independently as volunteers in the community. Coronado (2006, 153–155) mentions a few independent activists who volunteered at migrant shelters and community centers. There are many others diligently working in orphans' centers, battered women's shelters, children's lunch programs, and women's cooperatives.

Women's creation of and participation in NGOs is currently the most prevalent form of activism among maquila workers. Women have joined organizations of human rights activists, labor rights activists, and church members to secure better working and living conditions. Some of the organizations have an international base (Fair Labor Association and Workers' Rights Consortium), while others arise from local support (Fronteras Unidas Pro Salud in Tijuana and Centro de Apoyo para Mujeres in Ensenada). Silvia Estrada (2006) specifically examines NGOs advocating for women along the border in Tijuana, Mexicali, Ensenada, and Tecate. Her research uncovers fourteen different NGOs fighting for women's reproductive, sexual, and labor rights (166–167). An NGO aimed at protecting women's labor and reproductive rights, Casa de la Mujer Factor X, was founded in Tijuana in 1989. Despite the challenges they face securing funding and reliable volunteers, Estrada argues that NGOs "are contributing to civil society by promoting a gender dimension to public policies, institutions, and local governments and by offering vision and alternative strategies regarding gender equity" (177). Swedish (2005) also believes NGOs can be successful in protecting women's rights. In Honduras three NGOs have evolved into effective educational organizations.[9] El Centro de Derechos de Mujeres is particularly targeted at improving working conditions by educating women on labor law (9). Other NGOs have taken a more confrontational approach by challenging government officials to enforce Mexican labor law and penalize violations. Typically, these groups attempt to establish unions independent of the government sanctioned unions.

In Mexico, there are three independent unions that have been fighting for decades to protect women's rights in the maquiladoras. The Coalición por Justicia en las Maquiladoras, a trinational coalition, has worked to pressure U.S. transnational corporations to adopt socially responsible practices in the maquiladoras by supporting worker and community struggles. Efforts to educate the women workers of their rights under Mexican law at the local level by the CFO and the AFO have helped women confront injustices imposed by their employers. Unfortunately, their collective efforts have not changed the overall culture of labor violations in the maquila industry. Their efforts have been successful, however, in assisting plant-specific and worker-specific complaints.

The CJM has been fighting the injustices inflicted on Mexican workers by the maquiladoras locally and nationally since 1994. This proworker advocacy group based in San Antonio, Texas, has tenacious volunteers with limited financial resources to pressure specific companies to respect workers' rights. Their continuous involvement with workers in maquilas across Mexico reveals the long history and prevalence of labor rights violations by multinationals. In 1994 CJM supported the workers at Sony's Magnéticos de México plants in Nuevo Laredo, Tamaulipas. They tried to form an independent union and in 1995 assisted with filing a complaint with the U.S. NAO, stating that the company violated the workers right to freedom of association and union organization (CJM 1994, 10–11). Similarly, in 1997 they helped the workers at the Custom Trim/Breed Mexicana and Autotrim plant in Valle Hermoso and Matamoros (owned by Breed Technologies in Florida) file a complaint with the Secretariat of Labor and Social Welfare (STPS) and later with the U.S. NAO for unsafe working conditions. The CJM also supported the twelve hundred workers at Duro Bag Company (which makes bags for Hallmark) in Río Bravo, Tamaulipas, to establish an independent union in June 2000. After continued support and donations for CJM's three years of legal fees, the workers fired for striking were paid full severance and back wages by Duro (CJM 2001a, 2003). More recent CJM-led campaigns on behalf of maquila workers took place in Reynosa against Delphi (2004–2005) and TRW (GM, Ford, and Chrysler) (2008–2010).

Similar attempts to organize small plant-specific independent unions by CFO and AFO have been met with serious resistance from workers and management alike. Workers are afraid of the consequences of organizing, and management is ruthless in its treatment of protesters and union members. Juan Pablo Hernández, a CFO organizer in Piedras Negras, Coahuila, revealed his frustration in organizing workers at the Dimmit plant:

> Many workers are afraid. They worry that if the plant closes, that they would prefer to receive meager severance payment than to demand what is fair according to the Labor Law. They fear that if they stand up for their rights that they won't get anything. This is what makes it so difficult to organize workers, and it's a sad reality. (Hernández 2001)

This sentiment is shared by Elisa and Pola, who were volunteers for CFO in Agua Prieta. Pola stated that CFO had been unable to organize an independent union in Agua Prieta because workers are afraid they will be fired or blacklisted by the maquilas. She said they have been working as volunteers since January 2004 because funding ran out. Elisa said all the remaining money was placed in AFO in Nogales because there are more maquilas there. She told me there were more responses from workers to organize in Nogales, and she was hopeful that Juana would be success-ful.[10] In March 2005 AFO was very close to establishing an indepen-dent union in a plant in Nogales when they had secured twenty-one sig-natures on a petition. Both leaders of AFO, Juana and Polita, were very excited and anxious to register the petition in Hermosillo. As we inter-viewed women on March 16, 2005, in the colonia Las Torres, we dis-covered that five people from the list had been fired the day before, four of them members of the same family. We found out that someone had gotten a copy of the list and had showed it to the manager of the plant. The family that lost their employment was angry and devastated. Unfor-tunately, the only comfort Juana and Polita could offer them was help finding a new job. After word spread through the colonias about this in-cident, it was much harder to convince maquila workers to take action against the companies and sign the petitions. In the fifteen years since the inception of AFO, despite considerable effort and financial support, no independent union has been formed in Nogales.

The CFO has been more successful in other parts of Mexico. In 2004 they assisted workers in the Macoelmex (Alcoa) factory in Piedras Ne-gras with filing a complaint with the ILO against Mexico for violation of workers' rights. Workers had tried to form an independent union and organized a walkout and protest at the Piedras Negras plant. The ILO subsequently submitted the case to the Mexican government.[11] The CFO has also supported workers' struggles against violations of the law in 2005 at the Arneses y Accesorios (Alcoa) plant in Ciudad Acuña, Coahuila, and at the Delphi Automotive and Maytag plants in Reynosa, Tamaulipas. They were instrumental in organizing a strike of 150 work-ers at a Dimmit plant in Piedras Negras in 2000 that eventually led to a walkout of all 1,620 workers from Dimmit's six plants (Arriola 2000, 5). Dimmit factories make pants for Levis, Liz, Polo, and Calvin Klein. The plant suspended eight employees who complained (on separate oc-casions) about treatment by supervisors and pay. Eventually a charge was made against the company and the CTM to the Conciliación de Arbi-traje, which settles disputes under Mexican labor laws. At the time of publication no decision had been made public.

Endeavors to improve working conditions on a more local level have faced an uphill battle as well. Efforts to educate the women workers about their rights under Mexican law by CFO and AFO have helped a few women confront the injustices of their employers. Armed with knowledge about Mexican laws and pamphlets describing them, members of these *sindicatos independientes* (independent unions) go door-to-door and have one-on-one conversations with workers about their rights in the maquilas. In other instances, they meet with groups of workers weekly or biweekly in someone's home. The foot soldiers of these independent unions believe "these house meetings are the seeds for future labor and political movements" (AFO 2004b). Juana and Polita, with whom I worked during the field study period of my research, shared materials with me that stated that AFO seeks to organize maquiladora workers in Sonora and to assist workers in gaining legal skills, building solidarity networks, and improving their working conditions and living standards. According to the pamphlet, the AFO aims to "empower workers through education to protect their health and well-being and to ensure a safe workplace, free from environmental contamination and occupational risk" (AFO 2004a, 1). They list among their successes the many fired or laid-off workers who received severance packages; injured workers who received reimbursement for medical care and disability pay; female workers who stopped sexual harassment; and frustrated workers who received their protected bonuses instead of having them taken away (AFO 2004b). Knowing many of the workers personally and having spent considerable time with their families, these union organizers view the struggle as one victory at a time.

Most labor rights groups and union organizers believe that Mexican labor laws are the fairest and most comprehensive in the world. The problem lies in their execution and enforcement. Despite this, the existence of such legislation gives hope to local and national labor organizers. Judith Rosenberg said:

> The Mexican Federal Labor Law (LFT), with which I for one have become enamored, is truly a unique document on this earth, a legacy of the Mexican revolution and its aim to distribute wealth and resources more equitably. Though Mexico has not yet been able to fulfill the potential of its Constitution and of the LFT, those monuments enliven labor struggles and give workers tools and strategies through which they forge collective movements. In this, they do not depend ultimately on lawyers but rather on themselves. Sometime they win a victory in court but sometime not; rather on the street or on the factory floor. (2004)

Labor activists and independent unions in Mexico are committed to continuing the fight for workers' rights established in the LFT. The CJM has promised to move forward and shared their current goals in a letter to members. A letter dated November 16, 2007, committed the organization to put time, energy, and money toward establishing a "work strategy for maquila workers and their communities—to prioritize workers' empowerment through training and exchanges of experiences in different areas, prioritizing the mapping process of production as well as organizational mapping with a gender focus in the four regions." They promised to stay "committed to expose the internationalization of the maquilas, the precarious labor and the exploitation that they create and the need to exchange and articulate the experiences, struggles and resistance of workers at the global level" and in particular "to present the collective complaint before the ILO regarding violations of the freedom of association of maquila workers since the passage of NAFTA" (CJM 2007). Similarly, the CFO is concentrating on the injustices wrought by NAFTA. Their two-pronged approach continues to engage workers locally and attempts to impact policy makers globally. The CFO has established goals in response to free trade agreements that hurt workers. The CFO "intends to: 1) educate and organize more maquiladora workers; 2) renegotiate NAFTA so that workers have a voice in its development; 3) defend the historic gains of workers that are codified in Mexico's Federal Labor Law; 4) work for the implementation of the conventions of the International Labor Organization and; 5) support the formation of a WTO working group to explore the relationship between trade agreements and labor rights" (CFO 1999, 8–10). In conjunction with the American Friends Service Committee (AFSC), the CFO concluded, "NAFTA should be renegotiated to promote fair trade relations among Mexico, the United States, and Canada. A new treaty should assure just treatment for workers and full enforcement of the labor laws of each country" (2–3). Not willing to give up the fight for workers rights, the CJM and CFO are hopeful for a fair and just future for the maquila workers. To date, however, the results have not been impressive.

The Mexicans working in the U.S.-owned factories are ordinary people, most of whom have families. They are striving to make a sustainable living and improve their lives. This research has given them a voice. This book has told their story. They do not want the companies to leave. They desperately need the jobs they provide. But they deserve decent working conditions, better wages, and the right to organize. Is this too much to ask?

Maquilas in Nogales, Sonora, 2004

Company	Number of Employees	Product	Affiliate Company
Acco Development	1,500–1,620	carpets	Acco Brands, AZ
Accucad de México	1–15	precision machines	CAD Enterprises, AZ
Acrylic Idea Factory	150–200	acrylic plaques	Acrylic Idea Factory, AZ
Agro Industrias Intl.	1–30	oil of jojoba	Snoi International, AZ
Alcatel de Nogales	750–900	computer circuit boards	Alcatel Network System, AZ
Amphenol Optimize	1,400–1,500	computer cables	Amphenol Optimize, AZ
Anchor Tool & Plastic	50–100	plastic components	Anchor Tool & Plastic, MN
Avent	1,150–1,250	disposable medical products	Avent, Inc., AZ
Badger Meter México	175–225	gas & water meters	Badger Meter, AZ
Barton Nelson	175–350	almanacs & notebooks	Barton Nelson, MO
B&D Medical Systems	650–750	catheters for hospital	Becton Dickinson, UT
Bergman Precision	1–50	remote controls	Bergman Precision, AZ
Camex	400–450	magnetic components	Javid Industries, AZ
C&D Die Casting	75–125	lawnmowers	C&D Die Casting, CA
C&D Technologies	800–900	circuit boards	C&D Technologies, AZ
Covexmex	100–150	back braces	Coventry Mfg., AZ
Crescent/Mexico	225–275	cardboard cartons	Crescent Cardboard, IL
Curtis de Mexico	100–150	radio filters	Curtis Industries, WI
Charles Gillman	125–175	cables, harnesses	Charles Gillman, AZ
Denticon	100–150	metal fillings	Denticon Intl., AZ
Electro Canada	100–150	cables, harnesses	

(continued)

Company	Number of Employees	Product	Affiliate Company
Electronic Products	1–50	tables & magnetics	EPI, AZ
Electromec	1–50	traffic light switches	
Enelme	1–25	electronics	Pre Inc., AZ
Ensambladora Intl.	620–650	cables, connectors tables, harnesses	International Assemblers, AZ
Ensambles Hyson	1–50	irrigation valves	Rainbird, CA
Grupo Chamberlain	4,000–4,500	garage door openers	Chamberlain Group, AZ
Grupo Mourve	1–50	electric coils	
Grupo Sigmex	50–110	machinery	
Hasta Mex	475–500	control boxes	United Technologies, AZ
ICT México	225–275	fluorescent lamps	CTM-Mexico, AZ
Industrias Tectrol de México	150–175	electric coils	Tectrol, Inc., Canada
Industrias Tres Estados	550–620	window blinds	Palco, Inc., AZ
ITT Cannon de México	620–650	computer cables	ITT Cannon, CA
Jeld Wen de México	50–100	windows, glass doors	Summit, AZ
Jerrik	100–125	Connectors	Jerrik, AZ
Laidlaw	125–150	clothes hooks	Laidlaw Corp., AZ
Leech Industries	125–175	computer cables	Leech Industries, PA
Legacy de México	100–125	print cartridges	Legacy Mfg., CO
Magnetics Electronica	50–100	engine testing machines	Hytronics West Corp., FL
Magnetics Metals	160–210	switches	Magnetic Metals Corp., NJ
Chambers de México	200–225	leather belts	Chambers Belt Co., AZ
Master Lock	850–900	door locks	Master Lock, WI
Megas	150–200	cotton balls, swabs	Megas Beautycare, OH
Mexicap	275–325	disposable paper caps	Cellucap, PA
Midcom	1,100–1,200	communication-transformers	Idcom, Inc., SD
Miden Industrial	75–110	electric coils	MDN Coil International, GA
Milacron Resin Abrasives	1–50	foundation for esmeril	Resin Abrasives, PA
Milotec	100–150	car harnesses	Atronic, Inc., AZ
Moen Sonora	125–175	toilet parts	Moen, Inc., OH
Molex	700–800	cables & harnesses	Molex Corp., AZ
Motorola de Nogales	5,000–5,500	cablevision parts	Motorola Broad One Communication Center, PA

Company	Number of Employees	Product	Affiliate Company
MSS de México	250–300	sprinklers, lamp wires	M.S. Services, AZ
Nogales Plastic Molding	1–50	plastic molding	Nogales Plastic Molding, AZ
Osborn International	1–50	industrial brushes	Osborn Manufacturing, OH
OSDP	200–250	data processors for disks and videos	Offshore Data Processing Inc., AZ
Parque Industrial De Nogales	1–15	rental office	Parque Industrial, AZ
Pfaltzgraff Nogales	300–350	ceramic dishes	Pfaltzgraff Co., PA
Power Systems Inc.	50–100	electronics	Power Systems, AZ
Prestolite Wire	250–300	cables & harnesses	Prestolite Wire Corp., MI
Productos de Control	450–500	electric cable wires	GE, AZ
Productos para el Cuidado de la Salud	1,200–1,300	medical products	C. R. Bard Inc., AZ
Ryobi Outdoor Products	650–750	na	Ryobi Outdoor Products, AZ
Samco Cientific	1–60	transfer pipes	Samco Cientific, CA
Samson	1,200–1,300	suitcases & briefcases	Samsonite Corp., AZ
Sistemas Coraza			
Sistemas Textiles	100–150	computer covers	Textile Mfg., AZ
Sistemas y Conexiones Integradas	620–650	harnesses for Ford & Whirlpool	Noma, AZ
	450–500	na	na
Sonitronies	100–150	industrial lodging	Collectron of Arizona, AZ
Steward	300–350	electromagnetics	Steward, Inc., TN
Stewart Connectors Systems de México	800–850	cables, connectors, harnesses	Stewart Connectors, PA
Subcontractors de México	1–75	na	na
Sumex	300–350	printer & fax cartridges	Xerox Corp., AZ
Sunbelt	1–75	cardboard boxes	Sunbelt Packaging, AZ
Tecnología Mexicana	1,200–1,300	high voltage capacitors	Tusonix, Inc., AZ
Thermax Wire	400–450	wire insulation	Thermax Wire, AZ
VZ Industrial Solutions	1–50	decorative figures	
Waber de México	200–250	simple and multiple electric plugs	S. L. Waber, Inc., AZ

(continued)

Company	Number of Employees	Product	Affiliate Company
Walbro de México	1,450–1,550	boat & lawnmower carburetors	Walbro Corp., AZ
Waterloo de Nogales		toolboxes	Waterloo Industries, Inc., DE
Weiser Lock	750–850	locks	Weiser Lock, AZ
West Mex Assembly	1–25	clothing	Western World, AZ
Winchester Electronics	450–500	electronics for computers	Winchester Electronics, CT
Wire Pro Viking Division	450–500	electronic components	Viking Electronics, CA
W. L. Gore	1–5	cables	W. L. Gore, AZ

Source: BorderLinks (2004); List of Maquilas in Nogales, Sonora, Chamber of Commerce.

Survey of Maquila Workers

For the Workers
Para los Obreros

Questions about your family history . . .
Preguntas sobre la historia de su familia . . .

How old are you?
¿Cuántos años tiene Ud.?
Did you go to school? If so, for how many years?
¿Fue a la escuela? ¿por cuántos años?
Where were you born?
¿Dónde nació Ud.?
How many people are in your family? How many people are under the age of 16?
¿Cuántas personas hay en su familia? ¿Cuántas personas son menores de 16 años?
How many people do you support on your salary?
¿A cuántas personas mantiene Ud. con su salario?

Questions about your work . . .
Preguntas sobre su trabajo . . .

How long have you worked in the maquiladora?
¿Por cuánto tiempo ha trabajado Ud. en esta maquiladora?
Where did you work before working in this maquiladora?
¿Dónde trabajaba Ud. antes esta aqui? (¿en otra maquiladora? ¿servicio domés-tico? ¿en la casa?)
How many hours do you work in a day? in a week?
¿Cuántas horas trabaja Ud. al día? ¿a la semana?
How much do you get paid? Is it more than you earned in your last job?
¿Cuánto les paga esta maquila a sus obreros? ¿Es más de lo que Ud. ganaba?
What benefits do you receive? Can you give some examples?

¿Qué tipo de beneficios recibe Ud.? ¿Puede darme ejemplos? (días de vacaciones, el cuidado médico, la comida)

What do you make at the factory where you work? What company labels do the products have?

¿Cuáles productos fabrica Ud. en la maquila? ¿Cuáles son las marcas de los productos que Ud. fabrica? ¿ejemplos?

Are you required to take contraceptives to work?

¿Se le pide a Ud. que tome pastillas anticonceptivas en esta planta maquiladora?

What do your supervisors do if you get pregnant?

¿Qué hace su jefe o los supervisores si Ud. queda embarazada?

What do you like about your job? What don't you like about your job?

¿Qué es lo que le gusta de su trabajo? ¿Qué es lo que no le gusta de su trabajo en la maquila?

Describe your home—the number of rooms, if there is electricity, running water, and indoor plumbing.

Describa su casa, el número de cuartos, electricidad, tiene tuberías interiores, piso está asfaltado, o de madera, o saltillo, cuáles pertenencias tiene, etc.

Notes

Chapter 1

1. Since the removal of barriers to trade (tariffs, duties, and quotas) were purposefully phased in over five years, the full impact of the agreement could not be measured sooner.

2. Stage 2, or the second-generation maquilas, never arrived in Nogales. This stage went beyond the assembly line technique to flexible production with sophisticated machinery and work groups. The labor force would have been older, married males who were hired through advertisements (Kopinak 1996, 9).

3. Elizabeth Fussell (2000) and Susan Tiano (1994) studied female maquila workers in Tijuana; Patricia Fernandez-Kelly's (1983) and Melissa Wright's (2006) research focused on female maquila workers in Ciudad Juárez.

4. Over four hundred young Mexican women have been murdered in Ciudad Juárez over the past fifteen years. Many of the women were maquila workers who were abducted while they were going home after their shifts. Some believe many of these murders are linked. To date, no one has been charged.

5. The semester program began with a one-week orientation tour of Nogales and the border area and was then followed by a month of formal classes in Tucson. Students returned to Nogales to take classes and work on individual projects while living in the community with local families in a working-class colonia. Activities centered on BorderLinks' Casa de la Misericordia (now called Hogar de Esperanza y Paz [HEPAC]) in the colonia of Bella Vista. The semester concluded with a longer traveling seminar tour of the Southwest border area (Agua Prieta, Ciudad Juárez, and Mata Ortiz) and ended with two more weeks in Tucson of capstone reflection and analysis. BorderLinks no longer has a semester program but instead sends delegations to the border for an immersion experience with our southern neighbors for varying lengths of time.

Chapter 2

1. Anderson and Gerber (2007) provide a thorough economic analysis of the differences and similarities between the border cities over the past fifty years.

2. Twelve hundred miles of the border span the Rio Grande over which no fence or wall has been built.

3. At present the wall closest to the port of entry in Nogales is being replaced with large cylindrical bars.

4. The Border Patrol was created to prevent Chinese immigration through Mexico into the United States.

5. Heyman calls this a controlled border "because of the combination of legally restricted immigration, contract labor, and physically constrained border crossing" (1991, 10).

6. Ejidal lands are small communal plots used for farming. Farmers did not own this land until the Mexican Constitution gave them ownership in 1916.

7. A shelter plan is a form of subcontracting whereby the foreign (i.e., U.S.) firm supplies material and components while the shelter company contracts with a Mexican company to provide a plant, labor, and administrative services (Kopinak 1996, 38).

8. This corridor connects the Canadian provinces of British Columbia and Alberta and Washington, Oregon, Nevada, Idaho, Montana, Wyoming, Utah, and Arizona with Mexico City, running through Sonora and Guadalajara.

9. For a thorough analysis of the development of colonias on the U.S. side of the border, see Chapa and Eaton 1997; Esparza and Donelson 2008; Pagán 2004; Ward 1999.

10. The nominal wage is higher than the income they earned on the farm or in a cottage industry, but they have not realized that the cost of living is higher along the border and that this higher nominal wage is a lower real wage.

11. The supervisors, who are mostly Mexican, are paid in dollars.

12. The minimum wage set by the government is considered the nominal minimum wage (measured in current pesos or dollars), while the purchasing power of the minimum wage is called the real minimum wage (measured in constant pesos or dollars). The real minimum wage is the nominal minimum wage divided by the price level.

13. The increase in the real minimum wage from 2004 to 2005 is misleading and occurs for statistical reasons. The base year was changed in 2005, which set the Consumer Price Index at 100. The recalculations, therefore, do not represent an increase in purchasing power for the workers.

14. The Mexican government lowered the minimum wage after NAFTA as a strategy to attract more foreign direct investment. Free trade meant that Mexico had to compete with China for production facilities of multinationals.

15. The exchange rate changes frequently. It was eleven pesos for every U.S. dollar at the time this research was completed.

16. Recently there has been an attempt by workers' rights groups to define a wage that if earned in a full-time job would raise people above the poverty level. Typically the "living wage" is greater than the minimum wage and includes some savings, which could be used for higher education (Workers Rights Consortium n.d.).

17. In a traditional machismo world, men rule in both the private and public domains. Women are supposed to be obedient and take care of the family and derive satisfaction and complete fulfillment from their home duties.

18. Personal interview, Jeannette Pazos, April 25, 2004.

19. Maria Murillo (2001) and Dale Hathaway (2002) have conducted research on the influence of the PRI on unions in Mexico.

20. Personal interview, Jeannette Pazos, April 25, 2004.

Chapter 3

1. This contract was created based on the suggestion of two BorderLinks staff members who had considerable experience hiring local men and women as language tutors.

2. Melissa Wright was successful in gaining access to managers and their factories. Her book, *Disposable Women and Other Myths of Global Capitalism* (2006), provides this extremely valuable perspective on women working in maquiladoras.

Chapter 4

1. They were called "twin plants" because originally the idea was that two new plants would be built, a capital-intensive one on the U.S. side and a labor-intensive one on the Mexican side of the border. This promised to create new jobs for both Americans and Mexicans.

2. The Bracero Program (1942–1964) officially assigned Mexican migrants to agricultural and railroad construction jobs in the United States while many American men were off fighting in the war.

3. Most analysts agree that the U.S. recession in 2000 and the Great Recession in 2008 caused the closure of a number of maquilas from 2000 to 2004 and from 2008 up to the present.

4. In the Keynesian model a dollar increase in investment (I) creates a much larger increase in total output (GDP) because it increases income, which increases consumption, which further increases income.

5. A. Guthrie, Dow Jones Newswire, (5255) 5080-3453, October 10, 2003.

6. The importance of sociopolitical factors when entering an emerging market cannot be overstated. Both cultural barriers and local business practices must be taken into account if the multinational company plans to be successful in the new market (Luo 2002, 189).

7. Organized Labor n.d. Retrieved May 23, 2005, from www.countrystudies .us/mexico/87.

8. Ibid.

9. Ibid.

10. Ibid.

11. Initially, in the early 1990s, the CJM led an environmental campaign in Matamoros against Stephan Chemical. Since 1994 with the passage of NAFTA the CJM has focused all its efforts on labor issues.

12. In the fifteen years since the inception of AFO, despite considerable effort and financial support, no independent union has been formed in Nogales or Agua Prieta.

Chapter 5

1. Draper (1994) and Hufbauer and Schott (1993, 2005) were outspoken proponents of NAFTA who emphasized the benefits to Mexico.

2. The negative consequences of NAFTA are developed by Brown 2006; Comité Fronterizo de Obreras 2005; Dillon 2001; Oxfam 2004; and Valadez and Cota 1996.

3. Current updates on the existence of sweatshops and campaigns for workers' rights connected to American companies can be found at the following websites: www.educatingforjustice.org, www.globalexchange.org, and www.global laborrights.org.

4. The U.S. negotiators also demanded improvements in Mexico's system of copyright protection and intellectual property rights.

5. Canada reluctantly joined the negotiations on NAFTA because it had already signed a free trade agreement with the United States in 1987.

6. Although labor activists and organizations such as United Students Against Sweatshops continue to target campaigns at certain companies operating sweatshops in many developing countries.

7. This specific information was obtained during the question-and-answer periods of the tours.

8. Jennifer Swedish (2005), a lawyer, has written on the labor and human rights violations in a Honduran maquila.

9. According to the AFO representatives in Nogales, weekly wages of maquila workers were derived by multiplying the daily wage by seven days, not six. This practice was confirmed by others working closely with workers. When maquilas run at full capacity the workweek is six days, and some overtime hours are put in on Sunday to avoid overtime wages.

10. Because all the women in the sample were currently working, they did not know whether they would receive the pension that employers were supposed to be contributing to on a weekly basis.

11. There were a few other "extra" benefits mentioned by the women. Nine percent of the women reported receiving loan services, and one percent reported having access to on-site day care. At the time, of the eighty-five maquilas in Nogales, three provided day care services for their workers (Chamberlain, Weiser Lock, and Otis).

12. Personal interview, Elisa Ortega, April 26, 2004.

13. Personal interview, Elisa Ortega and Pola Pontoja, April 26, 2004.

14. Personal interview, Juana Jiménez Sánchez, April 1, 2004.

15. Personal interview, Polita Acuña Valenzuela, April 3, 2004.

Chapter 6

1. Wright (2005, 94) adopts the phrase "maquiladora mestiza" for self-identified *mexicanas* who have made gains in the maquiladoras. They have defied traditional roles and become managers.

2. Rather than buy and store goods hoping to sell them, retailers track sales

with bar codes and can reorder the correct amount of products to restock their shelves. The advantage is that it "maximizes their retail sales per square meter of shop space, and shifts order risk back onto suppliers and producers" (Oxfam 2004, 36).

3. Fifty-nine percent of the electronic assemblers and 33 percent of the apparel assemblers completed between 7 and 11 years of school (Fernandez-Kelly 1983, 52–53).

4. There were a number of reasons husbands were absent from the family. Many of the women's husbands had died or had become very ill or incapacitated. A few women said that their husbands were in jail. For others, it was part of the family's plan for husbands to cross the U.S.-Mexico border and secure higher-paid work as an undocumented worker. For others it meant heartache as well as financial instability because of separation, divorce, and no alimony or child support.

5. Women in all stages of life may find themselves needing money and working for a short period of time—single women before they marry, newly married women before children are born, and middle-aged and older women who have lost the main breadwinner through death or desertion.

6. Ana Bergareche (2006, 96) reported similar comments from the women she interviewed in Ciudad Juárez. She argued that these social contacts could lead to gender solidarity and support for individual or collective resistance.

7. This number represents the sum of the percent of women who liked the environment (20 percent), who liked everything (16 percent), and who liked the type of work (12 percent).

8. Women earning less than the average would need to earn a higher wage in order to reach a sustainable standard of living, and those earning more would not need as much.

9. Women could, and often did, have more than one response to this question.

10. For research on job satisfaction, see Bender, Donohue, and Heywood 2005; Green and Heywood 2008; and Mohr and Zoghi 2008.

11. The residents of Nogales usually referred to nonpotable water as contaminated water. They explained that it was dirty and contained chemicals, including petroleum, and animal and human waste.

12. In the maquiladoras in Mexico the concept of a bonus is very different from that in the United States. A woman's standard pay includes a bonus for perfect attendance and another for meeting the production quota. If she did not receive one or more of her bonuses, her total pay for the week actually decreased.

Chapter 7

1. The real minimum wage decreased by 50 percent from 1990 to 2004.
2. Personal interview, former employee of BorderLinks, March 3, 2004.
3. Personal interview, Jeannette Pazos, March 3, 2004.
4. Personal interview, Chester Torres, April 14, 2004.

5. Personal interview, Cecilia Guzmán, April 21, 2004.

6. The two types of contraception most commonly found in maquiladoras were oral contraceptives (birth control pills) and injections (Depo Provera).

7. Personal interview, Juana Sanchez, February 22, 2004.

8. Personal interview, Tracy Carroll, March 3, 2004.

9. The three NGOs are Colectiva de Mujeres Hondureñas, Asociación Andar, and Centro de Derechos de Mujeres.

10. Personal interview, Elisa Ortega and Pola Pontoja, April 26, 2004.

11. Complaint of the Sindicato de Trabajadores de la Empresa Manufacturera de Componentes Eléctricos de México S.A. de C.V. for violating the right of workers to freely associate, organize, and bargain collectively.

Glossary

bonus   two additional weekly payments to maquiladora workers for perfect attendance and meeting production quotas.

colonia   a neighborhood located on the border that lacks basic infrastructure (access to potable water, sewer, electricity, and paved streets) and offers inadequate social services (health care, fire and police services, waste management) to its residents.

fordism   method of production wherein processes are divided into simple one-step tasks and workers become expert at the task they are assigned.

jefe   boss.

Keynesian multiplier   the degree to which an initial change in a component of aggregate demand causes a much greater change in total output because of household behavior to spend a large portion of additional income.

law of comparative advantage   two countries can gain from trade if they have different relative costs or efficiencies for producing the same good (or service). A country is said to have the comparative advantage in producing a good (or providing a service) if relative to another country it has the least cost method of production.

foreign direct investment   investment in the physical capital (machinery, buildings, technology) of a country by a foreign company.

gross domestic product   the total market value of all final goods and services produced in a country for a specific year.

maquila, maquiladora   a foreign-owned assembly plant that imports intermediate goods and exports the finished product.

maquiladora mestiza   self-identified *mexicanas* who advance within maquiladoras and become managers.

protectionism   the use of quotas, tariffs, and customs duties on imports to protect domestic industry.

recession   a period in which the economy experiences negative growth and is plagued with unemployment.

sindicatos   labor unions.

sweatshop   a workplace that violates more than one domestic labor law (e.g., minimum wage, maximum hours, child labor, or the right to collective bargaining).

tortuosidad   work slowdown.

zonas libres   free trade zones.

Bibliography

Alfred [Samuel Kydd]. 1857. *The History of the Factory Movement*. London: Simpkin, Marshall, and Co.

Alianza Fronteriza de Obreros (AFO). 2004a. Information pamphlet. AFO, Nogales, Mexico.

———. 2004b. Handout. AFO, Nogales, Mexico.

Allen, R. 2009. *The British Industrial Revolution in Global Perspective*. Cambridge: Cambridge University Press.

Anderson, J., and J. Gerber. 2007. *Fifty Years of Change on the U.S. Mexican Border: Growth, Development, and Quality of Life*. Austin: University of Texas Press.

Anderson, S., and J. Cavanagh, with T. Lee. 2005. *Field Guide to the Global Economy*. New York: New Press.

Arriola, E. R. 2000. "Becoming Leaders: The Women in the Maquiladoras of Piedras Negras, Coahuila." Retrieved May 25, 2004, from www.womenon theborder.org/Articles/becoming_leaders.htm. (Reprinted from Frontera Norte-Sur, October 2000.)

Ashenfelter, O., and S. Jurajda. 2001. *Cross-Country Comparisons of Wage Rates: The Big Mac Index*. Working Paper, Princeton University, October.

Ashton, T. S. 1964. *The Industrial Revolution, 1760–1830*. New York: Oxford University Press.

Barclay, E. 2005. "Analysis: Border Walls Block Coordination." United Press International, Mexico City, March 22.

Barnett, A. S. n.d. *The Industrialization of Nogales, Sonora*. Retrieved June 18, 2010, from www.municiodenogales.org.

Barry, J. 2000. "U.S.-Mexican Border: Can Good Fences Make Bad Neighbors?" Retrieved June 8, 2005, from www.speakout.com/activism/issue _briefs/1370b-1.htm.

Beard, R. 1999. "Maquiladora Workers Demonstrate Solidarity at Gap Protest, Talk Solidarity at Church Forum." Retrieved June 25, 2004, from www .cfomaquiladoras.org. (Reprinted from *Working Stiff Journal* 2, no. 8 [October]: 1999).

Bender, K., S. Donohue, and J. Heywood. 2005. "Job Satisfaction and Gender Segregation." *Oxford Economic Papers* 57 (3): 479–496.

Bensusan, G. 2004. "Labor Regulations and Trade Union Convergence in North America." In S. Weintraub, ed., *NAFTA's Impact on North America: The First Decade* (pp. 123–155). Washington, DC: CSIS Press.

Berg, M., and P. Hudson. 1992. "Rehabilitating the Industrial Revolution." *Economic History Review*, 2nd ser., 45: 25–50.

Bergareche, A. 2006. "The Roots of Autonomy through Work Participation in the Northern Mexico Border Region." In D. Mattingly and E. Hansen, eds., *Women and Change at the U.S.-Mexico Border: Mobility, Labor, and Activism* (pp. 91–102). Tucson: University of Arizona Press.

Bhagwati, J. 2004. *In Defense of Globalization*. New York: Oxford University Press.

Blinder, A. 2006. "Offshoring: The Next Industrial Revolution?" *Foreign Affairs*, March–April, Council on Foreign Relations.

Bloom, G. 2001. "Agua Prieta's Comité Fronterizo de Obreras. *La Prensa* (San Diego), December 21.

Bluestone, B., and B. Harrison. 1982. *The Deindustrialization of America: Plant Closings, Community Abandonment, and the Dismantling of Basic Industry*. New York: Basic Books.

Borderlines. 2001). "Border Briefs: Study Finds Maquila Wages Insufficient." 9, no. 8 (September).

BorderLinks. 2004. *List of Maquilas in Nogales*. Nogales, Sonora: Chamber of Commerce.

———. 2005. *Semester on the Border*. BorderLinks brochure. Tucson: Border-Links Organization.

Boserup, E. 1970. *Woman's Role in Economic Development*. New York: St. Martin's.

Brown, S. 2006. *Why American Trade Policy Has Failed: Myths of Free Trade*. New York: New Press.

Bustamante, J. 1983. "Maquiladoras: A New Face of International Capitalism on Mexico's Northern Frontier." In J. Nash and M. P. Fernandez-Kelly, eds., *Women, Men, and the International Division of Labor* (pp. 224–256). Albany: SUNY Press.

Cameron, M., and B. Tomlin. 2000. *The Making of NAFTA: How the Deal Was Done*. Ithaca, NY: Cornell University Press.

Carrillo, J., and R. Gomis. 2003. "Challenge for Maquiladoras Given the Loss of Competitiveness." *ComercioExterior* 53, no. 4 (April). Retrieved June 15, 2010, from www.revistas.bancomext.gob.mx/rce/en/articleReader.jsp?id=2&idRevista=8.

Carrillo, J., and A. Hernández. 1985. *Mujeres fronterizas en la industria maquiladora*. Mexico, DF: SEP Cultura.

Carrillo, J., and A. Huadle. 1996. "Third Generation Maquiladoras: The Case of Delphi-General Motors." *Journal of Borderland Studies* 13: 79–97.

Chapa, J., and D. Eaton. 1997. *Colonia Housing and Infrastructure*. Austin: LBJ School of Public Affairs, University of Texas.

Christman, J. H. 2004. "Mexico's Maquiladora Industry Outlook: 2004–2009 and Its Future Impact on the Border Economy." IHS Global Insight, Inc., presentation to the Federal Reserve Bank of Dallas-El Paso and San Antonio Branches: Framing the Future: Tomorrow's Border Economy, El Paso, TX, December 3.

Christman, J. H. 2003. "Prospects for Recovery of the Maquiladora Industry." IHS Global Insight, Inc., presentation to the Federal Reserve Bank of Dallas–El Paso and San Antonio Branches: Conference on Mexico's Maquiladora Industry, San Padre Island, TX, November 21.

Center for Reflection, Education, and Action (CREA). 2001. "Mexico Purchasing Power Index Study 2000—Making the Invisible Visible." June. Retrieved April 14, 2010, from www.crea-inc.org/pdf_files/ppi_reports /mexico%20PPI%202000–English.pdf.

Coalición por Justicia en las Maquiladoras (CJM). 2003a. *Annual Report*. San Antonio, TX: CJM.

———. 2003b. *Manual de la Ley Federal del Trabajo*. San Antonio, TX: CJM.

———. 1994. *Annual Report and Newsletter* 5, no. 1 (Spring). San Antonio, TX: CJM.

———. 1999a. *Annual Report and Newsletter* 9, no. 1 (Spring). San Antonio, TX: CJM.

———. 1999b. *¿Cuales son mis derechos en el trabajo? Guía sobre la Ley Federal del Trabajo, parte 1*. San Antonio, TX: CJM.

———. 2000. *Conozco mis derechos en el trabajo, pero ¿Cuales son mis obligaciones? Guía sobre la Ley Federal del Trabajo, parte 2*. San Antonio, TX: CJM.

———. 2001a. *Annual Report*. San Antonio, TX: CJM.

———. 2001b. "Border Briefs: Study Finds Maquila Wages Insufficient." *borderlines* 9 (8): 1.

———. 2001c. "New Study: Mexicans Unable to Live on Sweatshop Wages." June 28. Retrieved August 25, 2008, from www.corpwatch.org/article/phn?id =426.

———. 2007. New CJM Statement, Letter to Members. November 16. San Antonio, TX: CJM.

Collectron. n.d. "Maquiladora Program." Retrieved June 2, 2005, from www .collectron.com.

Columbia Encyclopedia. 2001. "Sonora." New York: Columbia University Press.

Comisión Nacional de los Salarios Mínimos. 2003. "Salarios mínimos por area geográfica." Retrieved June 15, 2010, from www.conasmi.gob.mx/clasif _muni_area_geografica.html.

Comité Fronterizo de Obreras (CFO). 1999. "Six Years of NAFTA: A View from Inside the Maquiladoras." October. Retrieved June 5, 2005, from www .cfomaquiladoras.org/seistlc.english.html.

———. 2000. "The CTM and the 'Gringo Conspiracy' in the Maquiladoras." Retrieved June 5, 2005, from www.cfomaquiladoras.org. (Reprinted from *Masiosare, La Jornada*, October 1, 2000.)

———. n.d.a. "Cost of Living." Retrieved April 20, 2011, from www.cfo maquiladoras.org/english%20site/cuanto_cuesta_vivir.en.html. (Based on the study of the Center for Reflection, Education and Action, June 2001.)

———. n.d.b. "Towards Independent Unionization." Retrieved June 5, 2005, from www.cfomaquiladoras.org/english%20site/haciasindicalizacion .en.htm.

———. 2005. "2005: New Assault on Workers Rights." Retrieved June 5, 2005, from www.cfomaquiladoras.org/english%20site/nuevoasalto.en.htm.

———. 2009. "Workers and Free Trade: Mexican Workers Say NAFTA Was a Swindle." March. Retrieved April 14, 2011, from www.cfomaquiladoras .org/librecomercio_y_trabajador.e n.html.

Coronado, I. 2006. "Styles, Strategies, and Issues of Women Leaders at the Border." In D. Mattingly and E. Hansen, eds., *Women and Change at the U.S.-Mexico Border: Mobility, Labor and Activism* (pp. 142–158). Tucson: University of Arizona Press.

CorpWatch. 1999. "Maquiladoras at a Glance." June 10. CorpWatch Issue Library: U.S.-Mexico Border. Retrieved June 30, 1999, from www.CorpWatch .org.

Crafts, N. F. R. 1977. "Industrial Revolution in England and France: Some Thoughts on the Question Why Was England First?" *Economic History Review* 30 (3): 421–441.

Cravey, A. 1998. *Women and Work in Mexico's Maquiladoras.* Lanham, MD: Rowman & Littlefield.

Cross-Border CONNECTION. 1996. "October 1996 Newsletter—Report Draws Attention to Women's Rights Violations." Retrieved June 25, 2010, from www.enchantedwebsites.com/maquiladora/newsltr1.html.

Dana. 2007. *Hershey's Moves to Mexico, Part 2* [Web log post], August 22. Retrieved November 20, 2008, from www.blisstree.com/eat/hersheys-moves -to-mexico-part-2/owned by b5 Media, Inc.

Davidson, M. 2000. *Lives on the Line: Dispatches from the U.S.-Mexican Border.* Tucson: University of Arizona Press.

De Castro, R. F. 2004. "The Functioning of NAFTA and Its Impact on Mexico-U.S. Relations." In S. Weintraub, ed., *NAFTA's Impact on North America: The First Decade* (pp. 159–185). Washington, DC: CSIS Press.

Denman, C. 2008. *Mujeres, maquila, y embarazo: Prácticas de atención de madres-trabajadoras en Nogales, Sonora, México.* Hermosillo, México: El Colegio de Sonora.

Dillon, S. 2001. "Profits Raise Pressure on U.S.–Owned Factories in Mexican Border Zone." *New York Times*, February 15.

Draper, R. 1994. "A Marriage of Convenience." *New Leader*, July, 13–15.

Dreier, P., and R. Appelbaum. 2006. "Campus Breakthrough on Sweatshop Labor." *The Nation*, June 1. Retrieved June 3, 2009, from www.thenation .com/doc/20060619/dreier.

Economic Development Council for Sonora. n.d. "Workforce." Retrieved June 23, 2010, from www.copreson.sonora.org.mx.

Ehrenreich, B., and A. Fuentes. 1981. "Life on the Global Assembly Line." *Ms Magazine*, January, 53–71.

Elliott, K., and R. Freeman, eds. 2003. *Can Labor Standards Improve under Globalization?* Washington, DC: Institute for International Economics.

Elson, D., and R. Pearson. 1989. *Women's Employment and Multinationals in Europe.* London: Macmillan.

Esparza, A., and A. Donelson. 2008. *Colonias in Arizona and New Mexico: Border Poverty and Community Development Solutions.* Tucson: University of Arizona Press.

Estrada, S. 2006. "Border Women's NGOs and Political Participation in Baja California." In D. Mattingly and E. Hansen, eds., *Women and Change at the U.S.-Mexico Border: Mobility, Labor and Activism* (pp. 159–177). Tucson: University of Arizona Press.

Fatemi, K., ed. 1990. *The Maquiladora Industry: Economic Solution or Problem?* New York: Praeger.

Federal Reserve Bank of Dallas. 2002. "Maquiladora Industry: Past, Present and Future." (El Paso) *Business Frontier* 2.

Fernández, J. A. 2002. "Redesigning the Strategy of the Frente Auténtico del Trabajo in the Maquiladoras." Trans. A. Fink. *Labor History* 43 (4): 461–463.

Fernandez-Kelly, M. P. 1983a. *For We Are Sold, I and My People: Women and Industry in Mexico's Frontier*. Albany: SUNY Press.

———. 1983b. "Mexican Border Industrialization, Female Labor Force Participation, and Migration." In J. Nash and M. P. Fernandez-Kelly, eds., *Women, Men, and the International Division of Labor* (pp. 205–223). Albany: SUNY Press.

Frontera Norte-Sur (FNS) News. 2007. "President Felipe Calderón: Year One." Retrieved December 3, 2007, from fnsnews@nmsu.edu. (Reprinted from *El Universal*, November 28, 29; December 1, 2007.)

———. 2008. "Felipe Calderón and the Super-Maquiladoras." Retrieved July 26, 2008, from fnsnews@nmsu.edu. (Reprinted from *Ciudad Juarez News*, July 23, 2008.)

Fuentes, A., and B. Ehrenreich. 1983. *Women in the Global Factory*. New York: South End.

Fussell, E. 2000. "Making Labor Flexible: The Recomposition of Tijuana's Maquiladora Female Labor Force." *Feminist Economics* 6 (3): 59–79.

Ganster, P., and D. Lorey. 2008. *The U.S.-Mexican Border into the Twenty-First Century*. 2nd ed. New York: Rowman & Littlefield.

Garcia, M., et al. 2005. "While West Looks East, East Looks to the Border." June 14. Retrieved June 15, 2005 from fnsnews@nmsu.edu (Reprinted from *Baja California News—Norte* [Agencia Reforma, June 13, 2004.)

Gerber, J., and J. Carrillo. 2007. "The Future of the Maquiladora: Between Industrial Upgrade and Competitive Decline." In V. Miller, ed., *NAFTA and the Maquiladora Program: Rules, Routines, and Institutional Legitimacy* (pp. 43–60). El Paso: Texas Western Press.

George. 2007. *Hershey's Moves to Mexico, Part 2* [Web log post], November 15. Retrieved November 20, 2008, from www.blisstree.com/eat/hersheys-moves-to-mexico-part-2/. owned by b5 Media, Inc.

Gill, J. H. 2004. *Borderlinks II: Still on the Road*. Tucson: BorderLinks Organization.

Global Exchange. 2000. "Tear Down the Wall—Global Exchange Statement on U.S.-Mexico Border Migration Programs in the Americas." August 8. Retrieved June 8, 2005, from www.globalexchange.org/countries/americas/unitedstate/california/immigration.html.

Goldin, C., and K. Sokoloff. 1982. "Women, Children and Industrialization in the Early Republic: Evidence from the Manufacturing Censuses." *Journal of Economic History* 42(4): 741–774.

González, P. 2004. "Conflict and Accommodation in the Arizona- Sonora Region." In V. Pavlakovich-Kochi, B. Morehouse, and D. Wastl-Walter, eds., *Challenged Borderlands: Transcending Political and Cultural Boundaries* (pp. 121–151). Burlington, VT: Ashgate.

Gordon, D. 2002. *Site Visit: Borderlinks-Tucson, Arizona & Nogales, Sonora, Mexico, November 13–16, 2002*. Report of the Director of International Programs. Santa Clara, CA: Santa Clara University.

Green, C., and J. Heywood. 2008. "Does Performance Pay Increase Job Satisfaction?" *Economica* 75 (300): 710–728.

Greenhouse, S. 2010. "In Indiana, Centerpiece for a City Closes Shop." *New York Times*, January 19. Retrieved July 23, 2010, from www.nytimes.com/2010/06/20/us/20whirlpool.html.

Hathaway, D. 2002. "Mexico's Frente Auténtico del Trabajo and the Problem of Unionizing *Maquiladoras*." *Labor History* 43 (4): 427–438.

Heather. 2007. *Hershey's Moves to Mexico, Part 2* [Web log post], July 23. Retrieved November 20, 2008, from www.blisstree.com/eat/hersheys-moves-to-mexico-part-2/ owned by b5 Media, Inc.

Hernandez, A., and L. A. Tirana. 2005, June 4). "Labor Protests Break Out in Maquiladoras." *Prensa de Reynosa*, June 4. (Reprinted from Frontera Norte-Sur, June 6, 2005.)

Hernández, J. P. 2001. "Organizing for Justice in the Maquiladoras," August. American Friend Service Committee—Texas, Arkansas, Oklahoma. Retrieved May 19, 2009, from www.cfomaquiladoras.org/organizingforjustice.english.htm.

Hernandez, R. 2004. "Cfomaquiladoras: Lo nuevo en el sitio/Updater." October. American Friends Service Committee. Retrieved October 28, 2004, from RHernand@afsc.org.

Heyman, J. 1991. *Life and Labor on the Border: Working People of Northeastern Sonora, Mexico, 1886–1986*. Tucson: University of Arizona Press.

Hill, S. 2003. "Metaphoric Enrichment and Material Poverty: The Making of 'Colonias.'" In P. Vila, ed., *Ethnography at the Border* (pp. 141–165). Minneapolis: University of Minnesota Press.

Hindman, H. 2002. *Child Labor: An American History*. New York: M. E. Sharpe.

Horrell, S., and J. Humphries. 1992. "Old Questions, New Data, and Alternative Perspectives: Family Living Standards in the Industrial Revolution." *Journal of Economic History* 52 (4): 849–880.

———. 1995. "Women's Labor Force Participation and the Transition to the Male Breadwinner Family, 1790–1865." *Economic History Review* 47 (1): 89–117.

Hufbauer, G., and B. Goodrich. 2004. "Lessons from NAFTA." In J. Schott, ed., *Free Trade Agreements: U.S. Strategies and Priorities* (pp. 37–50). Washington, DC: Institute for International Economics.

Hufbauer, G. C., and J. Schott. 1993. *NAFTA: An Assessment*. London: Longman Group.

———. 2005. *NAFTA Revisited: Achievements and Challenges*. Washington, DC: Institute for International Economics.

Human Rights Watch 1996a. "Mexico's Maquiladoras: Abuses Against Women Workers." August 16. Retrieved June 25, 2010, from www.hrw.org.en/news /1996/08/16/mexicos-maquiladoras-abuses-against-women-workers.

———. 1996b. "No Guarantees: Sex Discrimination in Mexico's Maquiladora Sector." August 1. Retrieved August 24, 2008, from www.hrw.org/en /reports/ 1996/08/01/no_guarantees.

———. 1998. "Mexico—A Job or Your Rights: Continued Sex Discrimination in Mexico's Maquiladora Sector." Retrieved April 4, 2011, from www.hrw .org/legacy/reports98/women2. (Reprinted from Human Rights 1998 Report, 10(1B), December 1998.)

Humphrey, B. 2000. "The Post-Nafta Mexican Peso Crisis: Bailout or Aid? Isolationism or Globalization?" *Hinckley Journal of Politics* 2, no. 1 (Spring): 33–40.

Ibarra, I. 2000. "Border Workers Struggle to Survive." Retrieved May 19, 2009, from www.cfomaquiladoras.org. (Reprinted from *Arizona Daily Star*, July 23, 2000.)

Instituto Nacional de Estadísta y Geografía (INEGI). 1988–2000. "Sistema de cuentas nacionales de México: La producción, salaries, empleo y productividad de la industria maquiladora de exportacíon" (No. Ficha 10852) [Data]. Retrieved July 23, 2010, from www.inegi.gob.mx.

———. 1998–2004. "Sistema de cuentas nacionales de México: La producción, salarios, empleo y productividad de la industria maquiladora de exportacíon" (No. Ficha 10466) [Data]. Retrieved July 23, 2010, from www.inegi .gob.mx.

———. 2009. "Estadística de la industria maquiladora de exportación." Retrieved July 23, 2010, from www.inegi.gob.mx.

Ita, de A. 2008. *Fourteen Years of NAFTA and the Tortilla Crisis.* Trans. A. Ramos and M. Roof. Americas Policy Program Special Report, January 10. Washington, DC: Center for International Policy.

Jansen, H., et al. 2007. *The Impact of the Central American Free Trade Agreement on the Central American Textile Maquila Industry.* International Food Policy Research Institute Discussion Paper 00720, September.

Kamel, R. 1990. *The Global Factory.* Philadelphia: American Friends Service Committee.

Kamel, R., and A. Hoffman. 1999. *The Maquiladora Reader: Cross Border Organizing since NAFTA.* Philadelphia: American Friends Service Committee.

Katz, D. 1994. *Just Do It: The Nike Spirit in the Corporate World.* Holbrook, MA: Adams Media Corporation.

Klein, N. 2002. *No Logo.* New York: Picador USA.

Kopinak, K. 1996. *Desert Capitalism: Maquiladoras in North America's Western Industrial Corridor.* Tucson: University of Arizona Press.

La Botz, D. 1999. "Girl's Murder Sad Symbol of Corporate Power, Child Labor, Female Exploitation on the Border." *Mexican Labor News and Analysis,* March 2, www.CorpWatch.org. Issue Library: U.S.-Mexican Border.

Landau, S. 2002. "The End of the Maquila Era." *The Progressive,* September, 24–26.

Landes, D. 1969. *The Unbound Prometheus*. Cambridge: Cambridge University Press.

Lim, L. 1983. "Capitalism, Imperialism, and Patriarchy: The Dilemma of Third World Women Workers in Multinational Factories." In J. Nash and M. P. Fernandez-Kelly, eds., *Women, Men, and the International Division of Labor* (pp. 70–91). Albany: SUNY Press.

Luo, Y. 2002. *Multinational Enterprises in Emerging Markets*. Denmark: Copenhagen Business School Press.

Made in Mexico. n.d. "Discover the Cost-Saving Benefits of Mexico Manufacturing with Maquildoras." Retrieved November 20, 2008, from www.madeinmexicoinc.com/?source=GoogleAd_manufacturing.html.

———. n.d. "What Are Maquiladoras? The Maquiladora Industry." Retrieved November 20, 2008, from www.madeinmexicoinc.com/maquiladoras_industry.html.

Manjarrez, A., and N. Corral. 2004. "Average Mexican Worker's Income Varies by State along the Northern Border." Retrieved April 14, 2004, from fns news@nmsu.edu. (Reprinted from *El Imparcial*, April 13, 2004.)

Manor, R. 2005. "Bowling Ball Plant Moving to Mexico." *Chicago Tribune*, June 17, sec. 3, p. 1.

Manufacturing in Sonora, Mexico [Advertisement]. 2010. *MexicoNow* 44 (January-February): inside cover.

Mattingly, D., and E. Hansen, eds. 2006. *Women and Change at the U.S.-Mexico Border: Mobility, Labor and Activism*. Tucson: University of Arizona Press.

Maquila Portal. 2004. "100 Top Maquilas." Retrieved February 20, 2005, from www.maquilaportal.com/cgi-bin/top100/top100.pl.

———. 2011. "100 Top Maquilas." Retrieved June 13, 2011, from www.maquilaportal.com/cgi-bin/top100/top100.pl.

———. n.d. "Mexico Will Assemble 3 Million Cars." Retrieved November 20, 2008, from www.maquilaportal.com/cgi-bin/public/board.pl?klie=2. (Reprinted from *El Norte*, November 19, 2008).

McKinney, P., and L. Gates. 1994. "Zenith Electronics' Mexican Maquiladora Factories." *Z Magazine*, July. Retrieved May 25, 2004, from www.cfomaquiladoras.org/english%20site/zenith_electronics.en.html.

McPhail, B. 2000. "Pregnancy-Free Work: 28 Percent Savings in Labor Costs." *San Diego NewsNotes*. Retrieved June 25, 2010, from www.sdnewsnotes.com/ed/articles/1999/0499bm.

Mexconnect. n.d.a. "Mexico's Labor Market and Laws." Retrieved June 8, 2009, from www.mexconnect.com/articles/196–mexico-s-labor-market-and-laws.

———. n.d.b. "Unions." Retrieved June 8, 2009, from www.mexconnect.com/articles/196–mexico-s-labor-market-and-laws.

MexicoNow. 2005a. Maquila Portal edition, 16, May-June. Servicio Internacional de Información S.A. de C.V., Chihuahua, Mexico.

———. 2005b. Staff Report. State of Sonora, May-June.

———. 2006a. Maquila Portal edition, 24, September-October. Servicio Internacional de Información S.A. de C.V., Chihuahua, Mexico.

———. 2006b. Maquila Portal edition, 25, November-December. Servicio Internacional de Información S.A. de C.V., Chihuahua, Mexico.

———. 2010. Maquila Portal edition, 44, January-February. Servicio Internacional de Información S.A. de C.V., Chihuahua, Mexico.

———. 2011. Maquila Portal edition, 53, July-August. Servicio Internacional de Información S.A. de C.V., Chihuahua, Mexico.

Mexico's Bimonthly Economic News. 2000. "The Maquiladora Industry." Ministry of Finance and Public Credit of Mexico. Retrieved May 25, 2005, from www.shcp.gob.mx. (Reprinted from no. 21, October 2000.)

Mill, J. S. 1848. *Principles of Political Economy.* London: Longmans, Green and Co.

Mohr, R., and C. Zoghi 2008. "High-Involvement Work Design and Job Satisfaction." *Industrial and Labor Relations Review* 61 (3): 275–296.

Mokyr, J. 2004. *The Gifts of Athena: Historical Origins of the Knowledge Economy.* Princeton, NJ: Princeton University Press.

———. 2010. *The Enlightened Economy: An Economic History of Britain, 1700–1850.* New Haven, CT: Yale University Press.

Murillo, M. 2001. *Labor Unions, Partisan Coalitions, and Market Reforms in Latin America.* Cambridge: Cambridge University Press.

NACLA. 1975. "U.S. Runaway Shops on the Mexican Border." *North American Congress for Latin America and Empire Report* 9, no. 7 (July): 1–22.

NAFTA Office of Mexico in Canada. n.d.. "Mexican Labor Laws." Retrieved June 8, 2005, from www.nafta-mexico.org/sphp_pages/canada/invierte/doing_business/labor_law.html.

Nash, J., and M. P. Fernandez-Kelly, eds. 1983. *Women, Men, and the International Division of Labor.* New York: SUNY Press.

National Labor Committee. n.d. "Children Found Sewing Clothing for Wal-Mart, Hanes & Other U.S. & European Companies." Retrieved April 22, 2011, from www.law.harvard.edu/programs/lwp/NLC_childlabor.html.

National Commission of Minimum Wages. 2004. "Minimum Wages 2004." Retrieved January 14, 2004, from www.mexicanlaws.com/minwages2004.html.

Núñez, H. J. 2002. "Maquila Workers in Mexico: The Prospects for Organization and International Solidarity" Trans. C. Boyer. *Labor History* 43 (4): 439–450.

OECD Factbook. 2005. *Economic, Environmental and Social Statistics.* n.p.: OECD Publishing.

Ojeda, M., and R. Hennessy, eds. 2006. *NAFTA from Below: Maquiladora Workers, Farmers, and Indigenous Communities Speak Out on the Impact of Free Trade in Mexico.* San Antonio, TX: Coalition for Justice in the Maquiladoras.

Oneal, M. 2008. "The Big 3 and Two Hard Choices." *Chicago Tribune,* November 18, sec. 1, pp. 1, 4.

Orme, W. A. 1996. *Understanding NAFTA: Mexico, Free Trade, and the New North America.* Austin: University of Texas Press.

Ornelas, S. 2006b. "Maquiladora Industry: Ideas for Innovation." *MexicoNow* 24, September-October.

Ornelas, S. 2006a. "Mexico 2007–2012 in a Nutshell: A Toddler Democracy in an Open Market Economy." *MexicoNow,* 25, November-December.

Ornelas, S. 2010. "Mexico's Industrial Real Estate Market 2010 Outlook." *MexicoNow*, 44, January–February.

O'Rourke, K., and J. Williamson. 2000. *Globalization and History: The Evolution of a Nineteenth-Century Atlantic Economy.* Cambridge, MA: MIT Press.

Oxfam. 2004. *Trading Away Our Rights: Women Working in Global Supply Chains.* Oxford: Oxfam International.

Pagán, J. 2004. *Worker Displacement in the U.S.-Mexico Border Region.* Northhampton, MA: Edward Elgar.

Pavlakovich-Kochi, V. 1995. "Regional Inequalities, Infrastructure, and Economic Integration: Policy Implications for the Arizona-Sonora Region." *Estudios Sociales, Revista de Investigación del Noroeste* 5 (10): 139–169.

Pavlakovich-Kochi, V., B. Morehouse, and D. Wastl-Walter, eds. 2004. *Challenged Borderlands: Transcending Political and Cultural Boundaries.* Aldershot: Ashgate.

Peña, D. 1987. "*Tortuosidad*: Shop Floor Struggles of Female Maquiladora Workers." In V. Ruiz and S. Tiano, eds., *Women on the U.S.-Mexico Border: Responses to Change* (pp. 129–54). Boston: Allen and Unwin.

Pinchbeck, I., and M. Hewitt. 1973. *Children in English Society.* 2 vols. London: Routledge and Kegan Paul.

Prieto, N. Iglesias. 1997. *Beautiful Flowers of the Maquiladora.* Trans. M. Stone and G. Winkler. Austin: University of Texas Press.

Public Citizen. 2004. "The Ten-Year Track Record of the North American Free Trade Agreement—The Mexican Economy, Agriculture, and Environment." NAFTA at Ten Series. Retrieved December 2, 2008, from www.tradewatch.org.

Quinones, S. 2003. "In Living Color." *Latin Trade*, January, 50–52.

Rhodes, K. 2004. "Global Gain Local Pain." *Region Focus*, Winter, 12–18.

Ricardo, D. 1817. *On the Principles of Political Economy and Taxation.* London: John Murray.

Richardson, C. 1996. "Building Strength from Within: Colonias of the Rio Grande Valley." *Journal of Borderlands Studies* 11: 51–68.

Rosenberg, J. 2004. *Boiling under the Surface.* Retrieved December 28, 2005, from www.cfomaquiladoras.org/cfomedicos. (Reprinted from American Friends Service Committee, News from the Austin Area Office, December 2004).

Ruiz, V., and S. Tiano, eds. 1991. *Women on the U.S.-Mexican Border: Response to Change.* Boulder, CO: Westview Press.

Sachs, J. 2006. *The End of Poverty: Economic Possibilities for Our Time.* New York: Penguin Group.

———. 2008. *Common Wealth: Economics for a Crowded Planet.* New York: Penguin Press.

Safa, H. 1983. "Women, Production, and Reproduction in Industrial Capitalism: A Comparison of Brazilian and U.S. Factory Workers." In J. Nash and M. P. Fernandez-Kelly, eds., *Women, Men, and the International Division of Labor* (pp. 95–116). Albany: SUNY Press.

Salzinger, L. 2003. *Genders in Production: Making Workers in Mexico's Global Factories.* Berkeley: University of California Press.

Secretariat of the Commission for Labor Cooperation. n.d.a. *Appendix B: Status of Submissions Under the North American Agreement on Labor Cooperation.* Retrieved June 19, 2009, from www.new.naalc.org/index.cfm?page=252.

———. n.d.b. "Public Communications Submitted to the United States National Administrative Office." Retrieved June 19, 2009, from www.new.naalc.org/indexcfm?page=229.

———. n.d.c. "Summary of Public Communications." Retrieved June 19, 2009, from www.new.naalc.org/public_communications/summary_of_activity.htm.

Smith, G. 2002. "The Decline of the Maquiladora." *Business Week,* April 29.

———. 2004. "Made in the Maquilas Again." *Business Week,* August 16.

Stiglitz, J. 2006. *Making Globalization Work.* New York: Norton.

———. 2007. *Fair Trade for All: How Trade Can Promote Development.* Oxford: Oxford University Press.

Stoddard, E. 1987. *Maquila: Assembly Plants in Northern Mexico.* El Paso: Texas Western Press.

Swanger, J. 2002. "Laboring in a 'Borderless' World: The Threat of Globalization." *Qualitative Studies in Education* 15 (1): 11–32.

Sweatshop Watch. 2001. "The Garment Industry" [Supplemental material]. Retrieved June 3, 2009, from www.sweatshopwatch.org [now defunct].

Swedish, J. 2005. "The SETISA Factory: Mandatory Pregnancy Testing Violates the Human Rights of Honduran Maquila Workers." *Journal of International Human Rights* 4, www.law.northwestern.edu/journals/jihr/v4/n2/4.

Thottam, J. 2004. "Is Your Job Going Abroad?" *Time,* March 1, 26–36.

Tiano, S. 1991. "Maquiladoras in Mexicali: Integration or Exploitation?" In V. Ruíz and S. Tiano, eds., *Women on the U.S.-Mexican Border: Response to Change* (pp. 77–101). Boulder, CO: Westview.

———. 1994. *Patriarchy on the Line: Labor, Gender, and Ideology in the Mexican Maquila Industry.* Philadelphia: Temple University Press.

———. 2006. "The Changing Gender Composition of the Maquiladora Workforce along the U.S.-Mexican Border." In D. Mattingly and E. Hansen, eds., *Women and Change at the U.S.-Mexico Border: Mobility, Labor and Activism* (pp. 73–90). Tucson: University of Arizona Press.

Tuttle, C. 1999. *Hard at Work in Factories and Mines: The Economics of Child Labor during the British Industrial Revolution.* Boulder, CO: Westview Press.

Ufford-Chase, R. 1999. "Glimpsing the Future." In R. Kamel and A. Hoffman, eds., *Maquiladora Reader: Cross-Border Organizing since NAFTA* (pp. 14–17). Philadelphia: American Friends Service Committee.

U.S. Central Intelligence Agency. 2009. *CIA World Fact Book—Mexico.* Retrieved June 9, 2009, from www.cia.gov/.

U.S. Department of Labor. 1993. *The North American Agreement on Labor Cooperation.* September 13. Retrieved May 27, 2005, from www.dol.gov.

———. 1994. *North American Free Trade Agreement, Annex 302.2.* Retrieved May 27, 2005, from www.dol.gov.

———. 1997. *U.S. NAO Public Submission 9701: Submission Concerning Pregnancy-Based Sex Discrimination in Mexico's Maquiladora Sector.* May 15.

Retrieved June 19, 2009, from www.dol.gov/ilab/media/reports/nao/sub
missions/Sub9701.html.

———. 2004a. *Public Hearing on U.S. National Administrative Office Submission 2003–1 (Puebla)*, April 1. Retrieved June 1, 2005, from www.dol.gov
/ilab/media/reports/nao/submissions/2003–1Transcript.htm.

———. 2004b. *Report of Review of U.S. NAO Submission No. 2003–1*, August 3. U.S. National Administrative Office, Bureau of International Labor
Affairs. Retrieved August 2004 from www.dol.gov/ilab/media/reports
/nao/ pubrep2003–1.htm.

———. 2004c. *Report of Review of U.S. NAO Submissions (as of March 2004)*.
U.S. Administrative Office, Bureau of International Labor Affairs. Retrieved
April 14, 2004, from www.dol.gov/ilab/media/reports/nao/submissions
.htm

U.S. Trade Representative. n.d. "Trade Agreements." Retrieved February 10,
2011, from www.ustr.gov.html.

Valadez, C., and J. Cota. 1996. "Perspective from Mexico, Race, Poverty & the
Environment," September 1. Retrieved May 19, 2003, from www.corpwatch
.org/issues/PID.jsp?articleid=643.

Vila, P., ed. 2003. *Ethnography at the Border*. Minneapolis: University of Minnesota Press.

Ward, P. 1999. *Colonias and Public Policy in Texas and Mexico: Urbanization by
Stealth*. Austin: University of Texas Press.

Warnock, J. 1995. *The Other Mexico: The North American Triangle Completed*.
Montreal: Black Rose Books.

Wear, A. 2002. "Class and Poverty in the Maquila Zone." *International Socialist Review*, May–June. Retrieved December 4, 2008, from www.thirdworld
traveler.com/Mexico?Class_Poverty_MaquilaZone.html.

Wilson, P. 1992. *Exports and Local Development: Mexico's New Maquiladoras*.
Austin: University of Texas Press.

Wilson, T. 2002. "The Masculinization of the Mexican Maquiladoras." *Review
of Radical Political Economics* 34 (1): 3–17.

Wolf, M. 2004. *Why Globalization Works*. New Haven, CT: Yale University
Press.

Workers Rights Consortium. n.d. "The Importance of a Living Wage. Designated Suppliers Program." Retrieved April 15, 2010, from www.workers
rights.org/verification/Living%20Wage.asp.

World Bank. 2002. *Globalization, Growth, and Poverty: Building an Inclusive
World Economy*. Policy Research Report. New York: Oxford University Press.

World Development Report. 2009. *Reshaping Economic Geography*. Washington,
DC: World Bank.

Wright, M. 1997. "Crossing the Factory Frontier: Gender, Place, and Power in
a Mexican Maquiladora." *Antipode: A Journal of Radical Geography* 29 (3):
278–302.

———. 2006. *Disposable Women and Other Myths of Global Capitalism*. New
York: Routledge.

Young, G. 1991. "Gender Identification and Working-Class Solidarity among
Maquila Workers in Ciudad Juárez." In V. Ruiz and S. Tiano, eds., *Women*

on the U.S.-Mexico Border: Responses to Change (pp. 105–28). Boston: Allen and Unwin.

Interviews

Tracy Carroll, physical therapist and instructor for BorderLinks in Tucson, Arizona, on March 3, 2004.

Cecilia Guzmán, staff member of BorderLinks at Hogar de Esperanza y Paz in Nogales, Mexico, on April 21, 2004.

Elisa Ortega, Alianza Fronteriza de Obreros (AFO), in Agua Prieta, Mexico, on April 26, 2004.

Jeannette Pazos, former director of Hogar de Esperanza y Paz, Nogales, Mexico, in BorderLinks van in Agua Prieta, Mexico, on March 3, 2004, and April 25, 2004.

Pola Pontoja, AFO, in Agua Prieta, Mexico, on April 26, 2004.

Juana Jiménez Sánchez, AFO, in Nogales, Mexico, on April 1, 2004.

Chester Torres, longtime resident of Nogales, host of my home stay in January 2004 and volunteer at the Hogar de Esperanza y Paz in Nogales, Mexico, on April 14, 2004.

Hipolita (Polita) Acuña Valenzuela, AFO, in Nogales, Mexico, on April 4, 2004.

Former employees of BorderLinks, on March 3, 2004.

Index

CPSIA information can be obtained at www.ICGtesting.com
Printed in the USA
LVOW11s1607090115

422058LV00003B/194/P